Autodesk 3ds Max 2021

Modeling Essentials

3rd, Edition

Pradeep Mamgain

Autodesk 3ds Max 2021: Modeling Essentials, 3rd Edition

NOTICE TO THE READER

Examination Copies

Electronic Files

Disclaimer

Book Code: PDX018P

*For information about the books, eBooks, and video courses published by PADEXI ACADEMY, visit our website: **www.padexi.academy***

Contents

Acknowledgments

I would like to express my gratitude to the many people who saw me through this book; to all those who provided support, offered comments, and assisted in editing, proofreading, and design.

Thanks to:

Parents, family, and friends.

Teachers and mentors: Thank you for your wisdom and whip-cracking—they have helped me immensely.

I am grateful to my many students at the organizations where I've taught. Many of them taught me things I did not know about computer graphics.

Everyone at Autodesk [www.autodesk.com].

Finally, thank you for picking up the book.

About the Author

I'll keep this short, I am a digital artist, coder, teacher, open-source advocate, and founder of Padexi Academy [**www.padexi.academy**]. I am self-taught in computer graphics, The Internet has been the best source of training for me [thanks to those amazing artists, who share the knowledge for free on YouTube]. I have worked with several companies dealing with animation and VFX. I love helping young aspiring 3D artists to become professional 3D artists. I helped my students to achieve rewarding careers in 3D animation and visual effects industry.

I have more than ten years of experience in CGI. I am passionate about computer graphics that helped me building skills in particles, fluids, cloth, RBD, pyrotechnics simulations, and post-production techniques. The core software applications that I use are Maya, 3ds Max, CINEMA 4D, Photoshop, Nuke, After Effects, and Fusion. In addition to computer graphics, I have a keen interest in web design/development, digital marketing, and search engine optimization. You can contact me by sending an e-mail to **pradeepmamgain@gmail.com.**

This page is intentionally left blank

Introduction

The **Autodesk 3ds Max 2021: Modeling Essentials, 3rd Edition** textbook walks you through every step of creating 3D models with 3ds Max 2021. This guide is perfect for both novices and those moving from other software to 3ds Max. This book will help you to get started with modeling in 3ds Max, you will learn important concepts and techniques about 3D modeling which you can utilize to create hard-surfaced objects for your projects. You will also learn about managing external design data in 3ds Max 2021.

Using a structured and pragmatic approach, this guide begins with the basics of modeling, then builds on this knowledge using practical examples to enhance your modeling skills. Each unit builds on the knowledge gained in the previous unit, showing you all the essentials of modeling with 3ds Max 2021. As you go from hands-on exercise to hands-on exercise, you'll develop a strong arsenal of skills that combined will form a complete end to end process to create high-quality models using 3ds Max 2021.

This book shares tips, tricks, notes, and cautions throughout, which will help you become a better 3ds Max artist and you will be able to speed up your workflow. This book is aimed to be a solid teaching resource for learning 3ds Max. It avoids any jargon and explains concepts and techniques in an easy-to-understand manner. The first page of every unit summarizes the topics that will be covered in the unit. Hands-on exercises in this book instruct users how things can be done in 3ds Max step-by-step.

Practicing is one of the best ways to improve skills. This book contains practice activities which you are highly encouraged to complete and gain confidence for real-world projects. By completing these activities, you will be able to master the powerful capabilities of 3ds Max. By the time you're done, you'll be ready to model any scene in 3ds Max.

If you buy this book, you'll also get access to all 3ds Max files, texture files, and any other resource used in the book. You are free to use these resources in your own projects personal or commercial. These working files allow you to follow along with the author throughout the units.

What are the key features of the book?
- Covers 3ds Max's user interface, navigation, tools, functions, and commands.
- Explains the polygon, subdivision, and spline modeling techniques.
- Covers all modifiers.
- Explains how to manage external design data.
- Detailed coverage of tools and features.
- Features **34** hands-on exercises – complete with before and after files.
- Features **40+** practice activities to test the knowledge gained.
- Additional guidance is provided in the form of tips, notes, and cautions.
- Important terms are in boldface so that you never miss them.
- The content under **"What just happened?"** heading explains the working of the instructions.
- The content under **"What next?"** heading tells you about the procedure you will follow after completing a step(s).
- Tech support from the author.
- Access to each exercise's initial and final states along with the resources used in hands-on exercises.
- Quiz to assess knowledge.
- Bonus hands-on exercises.
- Includes a PDF file that contains the color images of the screenshots/illustrations used in the textbook. These color images will help you in the learning process. This PDF file is included with the resources.

Who this book is for?
- Beginners and intermediate users of 3ds Max
- Digital artists
- Motion graphics artists
- Indie game developers
- And anyone who wants to learn 3ds Max

What are the prerequisites?
- Decent familiarity with computers
- Before you start this book, you should have 3ds Max 2021 installed on your system
- You should have the desire to learn
- Willingness to be awesome

What you will learn?
- Polygon, subdivision, and spline modeling techniques
- Edit geometry using modifiers
- Handle external design data
- Speed up your workflow
- Create cool looking models

How this book is structured?

This book is divided into the following units:

Unit 1: Introduction to 3ds Max -I, introduces the 3ds Max interface as well as the tools that allow you to transform objects in the viewport.

Unit 2: Introduction to 3ds Max -II, covers the tools and procedures that will help you immensely during the modeling process. You will know about various explorers as well as various precision tools that 3ds Max offers.

Unit 3: Geometric Primitives and Architectural Objects, explains the **Standard** and **Extended** primitives and how you can use them to create some basic models. This unit also covers AEC objects.

Unit 4: Polygon Modeling, introduces you to the polygon modeling tools, concepts, and techniques. This chapter talks about polygons components, selection tools, polygons structure tools, and modeling objects.

Unit 5: Graphite Modeling Tools, describes the tools available in the **Ribbon** interface and how you can use them to improve your modeling workflow.

Unit 6: Spline Modeling, introduces you to the spline modeling tools, concepts, and techniques.

Unit 7: Modifiers, walks you through the various modifiers available in 3ds Max that you can use to sculpt or edit the objects without changing its base structure.

Unit 8: External Design Data, explains in ways that you can use the external data with 3ds Max in your design and visualization workflow.

Unit 9: Bonus Hands-on Exercises, contains bonus hands-on exercises.

Icon	Description
	Tip: A tip tells you about an alternate method for a procedure. It also shows a shortcut, a workaround, or some other kind of helpful information.
	Note: This icon draws your attention to a specific point(s) that you may want to commit to the memory.
	Caution: Pay particular attention when you see the caution icon in the book. It tells you about possible side-effects you might encounter when following a particular procedure.
	What just happened?: This icon draws your attention to the working of instructions in a hands-on exercise.
	What next?: This icon tells you about the procedure you will follow after completing a step(s).
NEW	This icon indicates the new command or tool introduced in the book.
UPDATED	This icon indicates that an existing command or tool has been enhanced in the book.

Given below are some examples with these icons:

Note: The editable poly objects vs editable mesh objects
The editable poly object is similar to the edit mesh object with the only difference is that the edit mesh object comprises of triangular faces whereas the editable poly object comprises polygons with any number of vertices.

Tip: Dragging a modifier to an object
*To drag a modifier form one object to another object in the scene, select an object that already has a modifier. To copy a modifier without instancing it, drag the modifier name from the stack display to the target object in the scene. If you want to create an instance, **Ctrl**-drag the modifier's name.*

Caution: Preserving the parametric nature of a primitive
*When you convert an object to an editable poly object, you lose all of its creation parameters. If you want to retain the creation parameters, use the **Edit Poly** modifier.*

What next?
Now, you will create a sphere and then conform the splines to the sphere.

What just happened?
Here, you have made a connection between the drawing file and 3ds Max. If you now make changes in the drawing, the changes will automatically affect the 3D models in the scene.

Important Words

Important words such as menu name, tools' name, name of the dialogs/windows, button names, and so on are in boldface. For example:

In the **Create** panel, click **Geometry**, and then choose **Standard Primitives** from the drop-down list located below **Geometry**. In the **Object Type** rollout, click **Tube**. Create a tube in the **Top** viewport. Place the tube at the origin. Switch to the **Modify** panel and then in the **Parameters** rollout, change **Radius 1** to **30**, **Radius 2** to **50**, **Height** to **15**, **Height Segments** to **1**, **Cap Segments to 2**, and **Sides** to **24**.

Figure Numbers

In theory, figure numbers are in the following sequence **Fig. 1**, **Fig. 2**, and so on. In exercises, the sequence is as follows: **Fig. E1**, **Fig. E2**, and so on. In exercises, the sequence restarts from number **E1** for each hands-on exercise. In the practice activities section, the sequence is as follows: **Fig. A1**, **Fig. A2**, and so on.

Naming Terminology

LMB, MMB, and RMB
These acronyms stand for the left, middle, and right mouse buttons, respectively.

Tool

If you click an item in a palette, toolbar, manager, or window and a command is invoked to create/edit an object or perform some action then that item is termed as tool. For example: **Align** tool, **Mirror** tool, **Select and Move** tool.

Quad Menus

The right-click menus or quad menus [see Fig. 1] are the contextual menus in 3ds Max that provide quick access to the commands/functions/tools related to the currently selected entities.

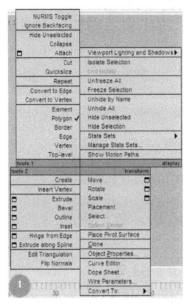

Checkbox

A small box [labeled as 1 in Fig. 2] that, when selected by the user, shows that a particular feature has been enabled or a particular option chosen.

Button

The term button [sometimes known as a command button or push button] refers to any graphical control element [labeled as 2 in Fig. 2] that provides the user a simple way to trigger an event, like searching for a query, or to interact with dialog boxes, like confirming an action.

Dialog Box or Dialog

An area on the screen in which the user is prompted to provide information or select commands. Fig. 2 shows the **Array** dialog box.

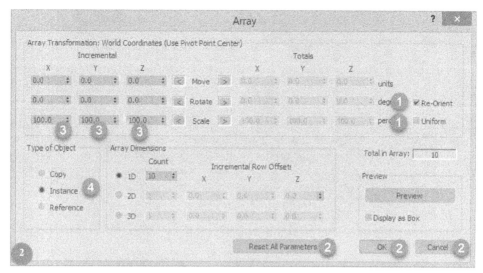

Spinner
Spinners [labeled as 3 in Fig. 2] are controllers that you will touch on the regular basis. They allow you to quickly amend numerical values with ease. To change the value in a spinner, click the up or down arrow on the right of the spinner. To change values quickly, click and drag the arrows. You can also type a value directly in the spinner's field.

Radio Button
A radio button [labeled as 4 in Fig. 2] is the one in which a set of options, only one of which can be selected at any time.

Drop-down
A drop-down [abbreviated drop-down list; also known as a drop-down menu, drop menu, pull-down list, picklist] is a graphical control element, similar to a list box, that allows the user to choose one value from a list. Fig. 3 shows the **Workspaces** drop-down list.

Window
A window is a separate viewing area on a computer display screen in a system that allows multiple viewing areas as part of a graphical user interface (GUI). Fig. 4 shows the **Reaction Manager** window.

Trademarks
Windows is the registered trademarks of **Microsoft Inc**. **3ds Max** is the registered trademarks of **Autodesk Inc**.

Access to Electronic Files

This book is sold via multiple sales channels. If you don't have access to the resources used in this book, you can place a request for the resources by visiting the following link: *http://www.padexi.academy/contact*. Fill the form under the **Book Resources [Electronic Files]** section and submit your request.

Tech Support

At **PADEXI Academy**, our technical team is always ready to take care of your technical queries. If you are facing any problem with the technical aspect of the textbook, please send an email to the author at the following address:
pradeepmamgain@gmail.com

Errata

We have made every effort to ensure the accuracy of this book and its companion content. If you find any error, please report it to us so that we can improve the quality of the book. If you find any errata, please report them by visiting the following link: *http://www.padexi. academy/errata*.

This will help other readers from frustration. Once your errata is verified, it will appear in the errata section of the book's online page.

- Understanding workspaces
- Navigating the workspace
- Customizing the interface
- Understanding various UI components
- Working with the file management commands
- Setting preferences for 3ds Max
- Working with viewports
- Setting preferences for the viewports
- Creating objects in the scene
- Selecting objects
- Using the navigational gizmos
- Moving, rotating, and scaling objects
- Getting help
- Per-view Preferences, Asset Library, and Game Exporter

Unit 1: Introduction to 3ds Max - I

Welcome to the latest version [2021] of **3ds Max**. In any 3D computer graphics application, the first thing you see is the interface. The interface is where you view and work with your scene. 3ds Max's interface is intuitive and highly customizable. You can make changes to the interface and then save multiple 3ds Max User Interface [UI] settings using the **Workspaces** feature. You can create multiple workspaces and switch between them easily.

 Note: Interface Customization
By default, 3ds Max starts with a dark theme [white text on the dark gray background]. This is good for those digital artists who spend hours working with 3ds Max, however, the default theme is not good for printing. I have customized the theme so that the captures appear fine when the book is printed. You can easily switch between the custom color themes from the **Choose initial settings for tool options and UI layout** *dialog box. To open this dialog box, choose* **Custom UI and Default Switcher** *from the* **Customize** *menu.*

When you first time open 3ds Max, you will see the **Welcome Screen**. This screen hosts a slide show designed to inspire as well as provide new users with some basic information to get them started.

Close **Welcome Screen** to view the default UI of 3ds Max [refer Fig. 1]. Notice, I have marked different components of the UI with letters to make the learning process easier. In 3ds Max, commands and tools are arranged in groups so that you can find them easily. For example, all viewport navigation tools are grouped in the bottom-right corner of the interface [marked as I in Fig. 1].

The 3ds Max interface can be divided into 11 sections. I have marked those sections in Fig. 1. Table 1 summarizes the letters and the sections of the UI they represent.

Table 1: 3ds Max interface overview		
	Item	**Description**
A	Menubar	The menubar provides access to command and tools.
B	Main toolbar	This toolbar consists of many commonly used tools.
C	Ribbon	**Ribbon** contains many tools for modeling and painting in the scene. Also, here you will find tools for adding people to populate a scene.

D	Scene Explorer	The **Scene Explorer** lets you view, sort, filter, and select objects in a scene. You can also use it to rename, delete, hide, and freeze objects. It is also used to create and amend object hierarchies.
E	Status Bar	The **Status Bar** contains the prompt and status information about the scene. The **Coordinate Transform Type-In** boxes in the **Status Bar** let you transform the objects manually.
F	Viewport Label Menus	These menus let you change the shading style for the viewport. They also contain other viewport related commands and features.
G	Time Slider	Allows you to navigate along the timeline.
H	Create and Play Back Animation	These controls affect the animation. This area also contains buttons to playback animation in the viewports.
I	Viewport Navigation	These buttons allow you to navigate your scene [Active Viewport].
J	Viewports	Viewports let you view your scene from multiple angles. They also allow you to preview lighting, shading, shadows, and other effects.
K	Command panel	The **Command** panel is the nerve center of 3ds Max. It contains six panels that you can use to create and modify objects in 3ds Max.

There are some other elements of the interface that are not visible in the default UI. These elements appear when you run a command from the **Main** toolbar or menu, or choose an option from the **RMB** click menu. Here's is the quick rundown to those elements:

■ **Toolbars**: There are quite a few toolbars available in 3ds Max. To access these toolbars, **RMB** click on an empty gray area on the **Main** toolbar to open a context menu [see Fig. 2] containing the options for invoking the toolbars. When I chose **MassFx Toolbar** from the context menu, the **Mass FX Toolbar** appeared [see Fig. 3].

■ **Quad Menus**: Whenever you **RMB** click in an active viewport [except on a viewport label], 3ds Max opens a **Quad** menu at the location of the mouse pointer. The **Quad** menu can display up to four quadrants [see Fig. 4] with various commands and allows you to work efficiently because the commands in the menu are context-sensitive. The **Quad** menu is the quickest way to find commands. Fig. 4 shows a **Quad** menu that appeared when I **RMB** clicked on an **Editable Poly** object in the viewport.

■ **Caddy Controls**: A caddy control in 3ds Max can be described as **"in canvas"** interface that comprises a dynamic label and an array of buttons superimposed over a viewport. You can use the standard mouse operations such as clicking and dragging to change the values in the spinners. The changes you made are immediately updated in the viewport. The **Chamfer** caddy control that is shown in Fig. 5 appeared when I selected edges of a box and then clicked **Chamfer**'s settings button in the **Command** panel.

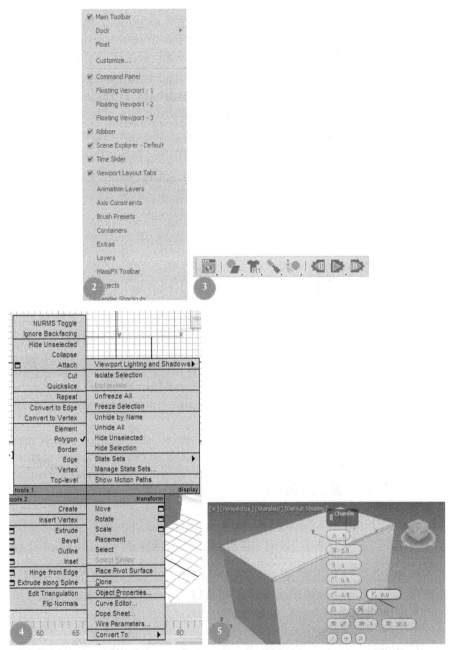

■ Dialogs, Windows, and Editors: Some of the commands in 3ds Max open dialog boxes, editors, and windows. Some of these elements have menu bars and toolbars. Fig. 6 shows the **Slate Material Editor**. You can use the **M** hotkey to open this editor.

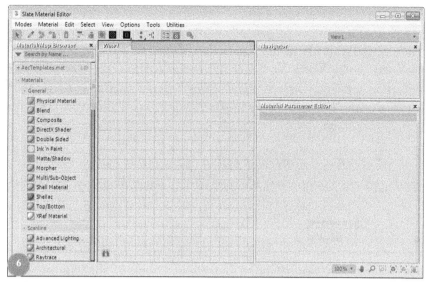

Note: Spinners

Spinners *are found everywhere in 3ds Max [I have marked* **U** *and* **V** *spinners with a black rectangle in Fig. 7]. Spinners are controllers that you will touch on a regular basis. They allow you to quickly amend numerical values with ease. To change the value in a spinner, click the up or down arrow on the right of the spinner. To change values quickly, click and drag the arrows. You can also type a value directly in the spinner's field.*

Tip: Fast and slow scroll rate in a spinner

Press and hold **Alt** *and then click-drag the spinner's up or down arrow for a slower numerical scroll rate. Hold* **Ctrl** *for the faster scroll rate.* **RMB** *click on a spinner to set it to its default value.*

Note: Numerical Expression Evaluator

If the type cursor is located inside a spinner and you press **Ctrl+N**, *the* **Numerical Expression Evaluator** *appears [see Fig. 8]. This evaluator lets you calculate the value for the spinner using an expression. For example, if you type* **30+50** *in this evaluator's field and click* **Paste**, *80 appears in the associated spinner.*

Note: Modeless dialogs, controls, windows, and editors
*Quite a few dialog boxes in 3ds Max are modeless meaning the dialog box doesn't need to be closed in order to work on other elements of the interface. A good example of a modeless dialog box is the **Slate Material Editor**. You can minimize the editor and continue working on the scene. Other modeless dialog boxes that you would frequently use are **Transform Type-In** dialog boxes, **Caddy** controls, **Render Scene** dialog box, and so on.*

Tip: Toggling the visibility of all open dialog boxes
*You can toggle the visibility of all open dialog boxes by using the **Ctrl+~** hotkeys.*

UI Components `UPDATED`

You can easily customize the workspace by floating and docking the window, panels, toolbars, and so on. You can dock any element of the interface that has a handle. A handle can be at the left or top of the element [see Fig. 9]. To float an element, click-drag the handle. As you move the handle around, target dock locations will be highlighted in blue. Drop the element on the blue highlight if you want to dock element in the interface.

 Caution: Toolbars
Toolbars can be docked only on the outer edge of the interface.

 Caution: Resize Elements
When you move around elements, some of the elements may not automatically resize. In such cases, you will have to resize elements manually.

 Note: Docking floating windows
*You can dock a floating window by **RMB** clicking on the title bar or handle of the window and then choosing **Dock** from the context menu. Now, you can select an available location from the menu displayed.*

NEW Once you are happy with the arrangement of the elements in the interface, you can save the arrangement using the **Workspaces** drop-down. The options in the **Workspaces** drop-down list allow you to switch quickly among different interface setups. This drop-down is available on the top-right corner of the interface.

A workspace is defined as the interface setup including any combination of toolbars, menus and quad menus, viewport layout presets, the ribbon, hotkeys, and the workspace **Scene Explorer**. You can define any number of workspaces as you want using the **Manage Workspaces** window. To open this window, select **Manage Workspaces** from the **Workspaces** drop-down. The **Reset To Default State** option in this drop-down is used to load the saved definition of the workspace based on the active workspace properties.

Here's the quick rundown to the available options:

- **Alt Menu and Toolbar:** It uses the alternate menu system. In this setup, the **Scene Explorer** is docked below the **Command** panel. The **Main** toolbar is modular and docked to the left.
- **Design Standard:** This setup in ideal for novice users. The commonly used features and learning resources are on the **Ribbon**.
- **Main Toolbar - modular:** In this setup, the viewport layout tab is removed and the **Main** toolbar is modular.
- **Modular - mini:** In this setup, the viewport layout tab is removed and the **Main** toolbar is modular with several groups of tools hidden.
- **Default:** The default layout on startup.

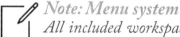 *Note: Menu system*
*All included workspaces in 3ds Max use the default menu system and horizontal ribbon except the **Alt Menu and Toolbar** which uses an alternate menu system and docks several toolbars to the left of the viewports.*

Different 3ds Max UI components are discussed next.

Caption Bar
The **Caption** bar is another name for the **Title** bar. It is the topmost element in the 3ds Max UI. The **Title** bar displays the name of the current 3ds Max file.

Menubar
The menubar is located below the **Caption** bar. The menus in the menubar gives you access to various commands and tools.

What is the function of the Reset command?

This command clears all data as well as resets 3ds Max settings such as viewport configuration, snap settings, Material Editor, background image, and so on. If you have done some customization during the current session of the 3ds Max, and you execute the **Reset** command, all startup defaults will be restored according to the setting stored in the **maxstrat.max** file. The **Reset** command is available in the **File** menu.

How can I use maxstart.max?

You can use this file to make the changes you would like to see at the startup. Start 3ds Max and make the adjustments. Then, save the file in the **scenes** folder with the name **maxstrat.max**.

Note: Templates

If you reset the scene, it will also affect the template that you had used to open the scene. The template will be reset back to its default settings.

How can I change the undo levels?

You can change it from the **Preferences** dialog box. By default, 3ds Max allows only **20** levels for the undo operations. To change it, choose **Preferences** from the **Customize** menu. In the **General** panel of the dialog box, you can set **Levels** from the **Scene Undo** group.

What is the use of the Preferences dialog box?

The **Preferences** dialog box contains options that 3ds Max offers for its operations. 3ds Max behaves according to the options you set in the **Preferences** dialog box. You have just seen an example of how you can change the undo levels. If you increase the number of levels, you force 3ds Max to obey that setting. The **Preferences** dialog box comprises many panels with many options that you can use.

Tip: Preferences dialog box

*You can also open the **Preferences** dialog box by selecting **Preferences** from the **File** menu.*

Can I undo all commands in 3ds Max?

No. You cannot undo some commands such as saving a file or using the **Collapse** utility. If you know an action cannot be undone, first hold your scene by choosing **Hold** from the **Edit** menu [Hotkeys: **Ctrl+H**]. When you want to recall, choose **Fetch** from the **Edit** menu [Hotkeys: **Alt+Ctrl+F**].

Why do I need a project folder?
When you work on a project, you have to deal with many scenes, texture files, third party data, rendering, material libraries, and so on. If you don't organize the data for the project, it would be very difficult for you to manage the assets for the project. The project folder allows you to organize all your files in a folder for a particular project. You can set a project by using the options available in the File > Project menu.

The menu system follows the standard **Windows** conventions. When you click on a menu item on the menu bar, a pulldown menu appears. You can also open a pulldown menu by pressing the associated menu hotkey with **Alt**. When you hold **Alt**, the hotkey is denoted by an underline in the name of the menu. For example, if you want to open the **Edit** menu, press **Alt+E**. Similarly, for the **Customize** menu, press **Alt+U**.

If a hotkey is available for a command, it will appear in the menu next to the command name. You can use these hotkeys to execute the command without invoking the menu. For example, to select all objects in a scene, you can press **Ctrl+A**. To execute this command from the menubar, you have to choose **Select All** from the **Edit** menu.

Not all the commands are available all the time, some commands are context-sensitive. If a black triangle appears [for example, the **Selection Region** command in the **Edit** menu] on the next to a menu command, it indicates that a sub-menu exists. Place the mouse pointer on the command to view the sub-menu.

Viewports | UPDATED

In 3ds Max, you will be doing most of the work in the viewports. Viewports are openings into 3D space you work. A viewport represents 3D space using the **Cartesian** coordinates system. The coordinates are expressed using three numbers such as **[10, 10, 20]**. These numbers represent points in 3D space. The origin is always at **[0, 0, 0]**.

By default, 3ds Max displays a four viewport arrangement: **Top**, **Front**, **Left**, and **Perspective**. The **Top**, **Front**, and **Left** are known as orthographic views. 3ds Max provides many options to change the viewport as well as the layout. Using multiple viewports can help you visualize the scene better.

What is an Orthographic View?
Most of the 3D designs created using the computer rely on the 2D representation of the designs. Some examples of the 2D representations are maps, elevations, and plans. Even to create a character model, you first design it on paper [front, side, and back views] [see Fig. 10] and then create a 3D model using these designs.

Note:
Blueprint Courtesy: *http://www.the-blueprints.com*

In layman's terms, you can think of the orthographic views as flat, or straight on. The orthographic views are two-dimensional views. Each dimension is defined by two world coordinate axes. The combination of these two axes produces three sets of orthographic views: **Top and Bottom**, **Front and Back**, and **Left and Right**. Fig. 11 shows a model in three orthographic views [**Top**, **Right**, and **Left**] and the **Perspective** view.

You can change a viewport to various orthographic views using the options available in the **Point-Of-View (POV)** viewport label menu. The **Perspective** view on the other hand closely resembles the human view. In 3ds Max, there are three ways to create a perspective view: **Perspective** view, camera view, and light view.

Can you tell me a little bit more about Viewport Label menus and how can I change a viewport to the orthographic views?
*Notice on the top-left corner of a viewport, there are four labels. Fig. 12 shows labels on the **Perspective** viewport. Each label is clickable [click or **RMB** click]. When you click on any of the labels, a popup menu appears.*

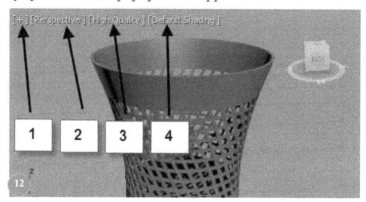

The leftmost menu is the **General Viewport** label menu [marked as 1], in the middle is the **Point-Of-View [POV]** viewport label menu [marked as 2], and on the right is **Lights and Shadows** viewport label menu [marked as 3]. The rightmost menu is the **Shading** viewport label menu [marked as 4]. The **General Viewport** label menu comprises of options for overall viewport display or activation. It also gives you access to the **Viewport Configuration** dialog box. The **POV Viewport** label menu provides options mainly for changing the viewports. To switch a viewport, for example, to change the **Top** viewport into the **Bottom** viewport, make sure the **Top** viewport is active and then click or **RMB** click on the **POV Viewport** label menu. Now, choose **Bottom** from the menu. You can also use the hotkey **B**. Table 2 summarizes the hotkeys that you can use to change the viewports.

View	Hotkey
Table 2: The hotkeys for switching the viewports	
View	**Hotkey**
Top	T
Bottom	B
Front	F
Left	L
Camera	C
Orthographic	U
Perspective	P

The **Shading Viewport** menu lets you control how objects are displayed in the viewport. I will discuss the options in this menu later in the unit. The **Lighting and Shadows** option lets you adjust the behavior of the lights and shadows in the viewport. You can also adjust quality settings from this menu.

(?) What is an active viewport?
*An active viewport is where all actions take place in 3ds Max. One viewport is always active in 3ds Max marked with a highlighted border. To switch the active viewport, you can use any of the three mouse buttons. It is recommended that you use the **MMB** for making a viewport active as **LMB** and **RMB** clicks are also associated with other commands in 3ds Max.*

When viewports are not maximized, you can press the **Windows** key and **Shift** on the keyboard to cycle the active viewport. When one of the views is maximized, pressing **Windows** key and **Shift** displays the available viewports [see Fig. 13] and then you can press **Shift** repeatedly with the **Windows** key held down to cycle among viewports. When you release the keys, the chosen viewport becomes the maximized viewport.

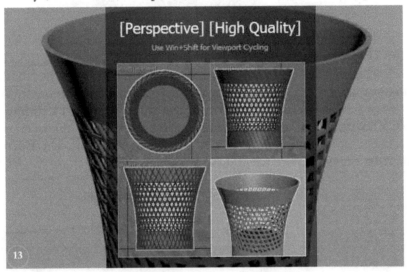

(?) How can I change the viewport configuration like the one shown in Fig. 11?
*The **Viewport Layouts** bar lets you quickly switch among different types of viewport layouts. This bar generally docked on the left of the viewports [see Fig. 14]. If it is not visible, **RMB** click on the empty area of the **Main** toolbar and then choose **Viewport Layout Tabs**. To change the layout, click on the arrow on the bar to open a flyout and then click on the desired layout to make it active.*

You can also change the layout using the **General Viewport** label menu. Click on the label and then choose **Configure Viewports**. The **Viewport Configuration** dialog box appears [refer to Fig. 15]. Select the **Layout** panel and then choose the desired layout. Now, click **OK** to accept the changes.

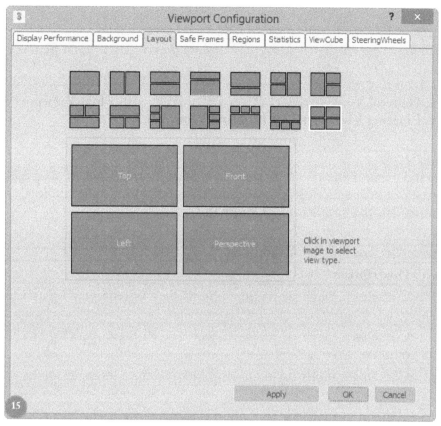

I can see a grid in each viewport, how can I use it?
The grid you see in each viewport is one of the three planes [along the **X**, **Y**, and **Z** axes] that intersects at the right angles to each other at a common point called origin [**X=0**, **Y=0**, and **Z=0**]. The three planes based on the world coordinate axes are called the home grid. To help you easily position objects on the grid, one plane of the home grid is visible in each viewport. The grid acts as a construction plane when you create objects on it.

Tip: Turning off the grid
You can turn off the grid in the active viewport by pressing the **G** hotkey.

Floating Viewports

3ds Max allows you to work in the floating viewport window. This floating window works just like the regular viewport and it is fully customizable. The floating viewport is not dockable, however, you can move it to another monitor if you have multiple monitors.

Caution: Floating viewport
If you are using the legacy Direct3D display driver, you can not float a viewport.

You can open up to three floating viewports. To open a floating viewport, click or **RMB** click on the **General Viewport** label menu and then choose **Float Viewport > Floating Viewport 1**, **Floating Viewport 2**, or **Floating Viewport 3**.

Command Panel

The **Command** panel is the nerve center of 3ds Max. It comprises of six panels that give you access to most of the modeling tools, animation features, display choices, and utilities. Table 3 summarizes the panels in the **Command** panel.

Panel	Description
Create	Contains options for creating objects such as geometry, lights, cameras, and so on.
Modify	Contains options for editing objects as well as for applying modifiers to the objects.
Hierarchy	Contains options for managing links in the hierarchy, joints, and inverse kinematics.
Motion	Contains options for animation controllers and trajectories.
Display	Contains options that let you hide/unhide objects. It also contains display options.
Utilities	Contains different utility programs.

Table 3: Different panels in the **Command** panel

Rollouts

Most of the parameters in the **Command** panel live inside rollouts. A rollout is a group of parameters, a section of the **Command** panel that shows parameters of the selected object. You can collapse the rollouts. When you collapse them, only the title bar of the rollout appears. Fig. 16 shows the **Parameters** rollout of the **Box** primitive in the **Modify** panel of the **Command** panel.

Once you create a box in the viewport, you can modify its parameters such as **Length** and **Width** using the **Parameters** rollout. Each rollout has a title bar that you can click to collapse or expand the rollout. You can also change the default position of the rollout by dragging the dots located on the right of the title and dropping on another place when a blue line appears [see Fig. 17].

By default, the rollout occupies a single column space in UI. However, you can increase the numbers of columns by dragging the leftmost edge of the **Command** panel. You can create as many columns as you want [see Fig. 17] as long as the screen real state is available. Multiple columns are helpful when you are working with an object with which many rollouts are associated.

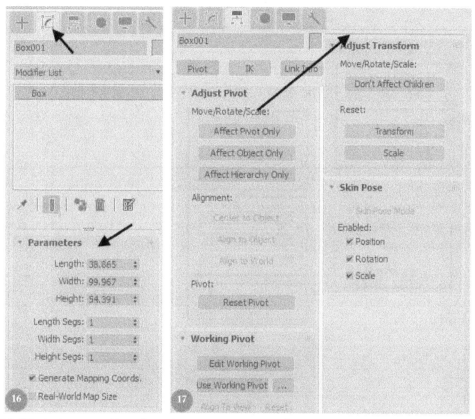

If you **RMB** click on a rollout [on the empty gray area], a context menu appears [see Fig. 18]. This menu allows you to open or close all rollouts at once, or close the rollout on which you **RMB** clicked. In the bottom section of the context menu, you will see a list of rollouts available for the selected object. No tick appears for the collapsed rollouts.

If you have changed the order of the rollouts, you can reset it by choosing **Reset Rollout Order** from the bottom of the menu [see Fig. 19]. If you have expanded the **Command** panel to more than one column and you **RMB** click on a rollout, only those rollouts appear on the context menu that are in the column.

Tip: The default value for the spinners
The nature of the spinners in 3ds Max is persistence meaning that value specified for the spinners remains set for the current spinners. For example, if you created a **Sphere** *primitive with* **64** *segments. When you create the next sphere, the value* **64** *will be the default for it. To reset spinners to their default values, choose* **Reset** *from the* **File** *menu.*

Main Toolbar | UPDATED

The **Main** toolbar comprises commonly used tools. Table 4 summarizes the tools available in the **Main** toolbar.

Table 4: The **Main** toolbar interface overview		
Item	**Icon**	**Description**
Undo/Redo	↶ ↷	**Undo** reverses the last command. **Redo** reverses the last undo command.
Select and Link	🔗	Defines the hierarchical relationship [links] between two objects.
Unlink Selection	🔗	Removes the hierarchical relationship between two objects.
Bind to Space Warp		Attaches the current selection to a space warp or vice versa.

Table 4: The **Main** toolbar interface overview

Item	Icon	Description
Selection Filter List		Limits the selection to specific types and combinations of objects.
Select Object		Selects objects and sub-objects. Hotkey: **Q.**
Select by Name		Allows you to select specific objects from a list of objects using the **Select From Scene** dialog box. Hotkey: **H.**
Selection Region Flyout		Allows you to select objects within a region using different methods. You can create different marquee shapes using the options available in this flyout.
Window/Crossing Selection Toggle		Switches between the window and crossing methods for selection. Hotkeys: **Shift+O.**
Select and Move		Selects and moves objects. Hotkey: **W.**
Select and Rotate		Selects and rotates objects. Hotkey: **E.**
Select and Scale		Selects and scales objects. Hotkey: **R** to cycle.

Table 4: The **Main** toolbar interface overview

Item	Icon	Description
Select and Place Flyout		Position an object accurately on the surface of another object.
Reference Coordinate System	Local ▾ / View / Screen / World / Parent / Local / Gimbal / Grid / Working / Local Aligned / Pick	Specifies the coordinate system used for a transformation (Move, Rotate, and Scale).
Use Center Flyout		Specifies geometric centers for the scale and rotate transformations.
Select and Manipulate		Selects objects and allows editing of the parameters for certain objects, modifiers, and controllers by dragging "manipulators" in the viewports.
Keyboard Shortcut Override Toggle		Allows you to toggle between using only the "Main User Interface" hotkeys or using both the main hotkeys and hotkeys for groups such as **Edit/Editable Mesh**, **Track View**, **NURBS**, and so on.
2D Snap, 2.5D Snap, 3D Snap		These options specify the snap types. Hotkey: **S** to cycle.

Table 4: The **Main** toolbar interface overview

Item	Icon	Description
Angle Snap Toggle		Enables angle increment snap for rotation. It allows you to snap rotations to certain angles. Hotkey: **A**.
Percent Snap Toggle		Toggles increment scaling of objects by the specified percentage. Hotkeys: **Shift+Ctrl+P**.
Spinner Snap Toggle		Sets the single-click increment or the decrement value for all of the spinners in 3ds Max.
Manage Selection Sets		Displays the **Named Selections Sets** dialog box, letting you manage named selection sets of sub-objects.
Named Selection Sets	Create Selection Se ▼	Allows you to name a selection set and recall the selection for later use.
Mirror		Enables you to move and clone selected objects while reflecting their orientation.
Align Flyout		Gives you access to six different tools for alignment. Hotkeys: **Align [Alt+A]** and **Normal Align [Alt+N]**.
Toggle Scene Explorer		Toggles the **Scene Explorer**.
Toggle Layer Explorer		Toggles the **Layer Explorer**.
Show Ribbon		Expands or collapses the **Ribbon**.
Curve Editor		Opens the **Track View - Curve Editor**.
Schematic View		Opens the **Schematic View** window.

Table 4: The **Main** toolbar interface overview

Item	Icon	Description
Material Editor flyout		Opens the material editor that provides functions to create and edit materials and maps. Hotkey: **M**
Render Setup		Opens the **Render Setup** window. Hotkey: **F10**.
Rendered Frame Window		Opens the **Rendered Frame Window** that displays the rendered output.
Render Production		Renders the scene using the current production render settings without opening the **Render Setup** window. Hotkeys: **Shift+Q, Shift+F9**
Render in the Cloud		Opens a dialog box for setting up cloud rendering with Autodesk A360.
Open Autodesk A360 Gallery		Opens the default browser that displays the home page of the Autodesk A360 image library.
Set Active Project		Opens the **Select Active Project** dialog box. It allows you to set a folder to be the root of the current project.
Create Empty Project		Opens the **Choose a folder** dialog box. It allows you to create a new project with no structure or hierarchy by selecting a single root directory.
Create Default Project		Creates a new project with the default folder structure using the **Choose a Folder** dialog box.
Crate from Current		Creates a new project based on the folder structure of the current project using the **Choose a Folder** dialog box.

Main Toolbar Flyouts

You might have noticed a small triangle on the lower-right corner of some icons on the **Main** toolbar. Click and hold on such icons to expand a flyout with additional icons. Fig. 20 shows the **Selection Region** flyout.

Ribbon

The **Ribbon** [see Fig. 21], is available below the **Main** toolbar. The **Ribbon** appears in the collapsed state by default. To expand it, double-click on it. You can toggle the display of the **Ribbon** by clicking **Show Ribbon** in the **Main** toolbar.

It contains many tabs. The content in these tabs is depended on the context. The items displayed may vary according to the selected sub-objects. I will cover the **Ribbon** in later units. Most of the tools are only visible in the **Ribbon** when you are editing a poly object.

Animation and Time Controls

The animation controls are found on the left of the **Viewport Navigation** controls [see Fig. 22]. Two other controls that are vital to animation are **Time Slider** and **Track Bar** [see Fig. 23]. These controls are available below the viewports. The **Time Slider** works with the **Track Bar** to allow you to view and edit animation. The sliders show the current frame and the total number of frames in the range. The **Track Bar** shows the frame numbers and allows you to move, copy, and delete keys.

Table 5 summarizes the animation controls.

Table 5: The animation controls		
Item	**Icon**	**Description**
Auto Key Set Key Set Keys		**Auto Key** toggles the automatic key mode. Hotkey: **N** **Set Keys** allows you to create keys for individual tracks of the selected object using a combination of the **Set Keys** button and **Key Filters**.
Selection List	Selected	Provides quick access to **Named Selection Sets** and track sets.
Default In/Out Tangents for New Keys		This flyout provides a quick way to set a default tangent type for new animation keys.
Key Filters	Key Filters...	Opens the **Set Key Filters** dialog box where you can specify the tracks on which keys are created.
Go To Start	|◄◄	Moves the time slider to the first frame of the active time segment. Hotkey: **Home**

Table 5: The animation controls

Item	Icon	Description
Previous Frame/Key		Moves the time slider back one frame. Hotkey: **,**
Play Animation Stop Animation		The **Play Animation** button plays the animation in the active viewport. You can stop the playback by clicking on the button again. Hotkey: **/**
Next Frame/Key		Moves the time slider ahead one frame. Hotkey: **.**
Go To End		Moves the time slider to the last frame of the active time segment. Hotkey: **End**
Current Frame (Go To Frame)	38	Displays the number or time of the current frame, indicating the position of the time slider.
Key Mode		Allows you to jump directly between keyframes in your animation.
Time Configuration		Opens the **Time Configuration** dialog box that allows you to specify the settings for the animation.

Viewport Navigational Controls

The **Viewport Navigation Controls** are located at the right end of the **Status Bar** [see Fig. 24]. The controls in the **Viewport Navigation Controls** depend on the type of viewport [**Perspective**, orthographic, camera, or light] active. Some of the buttons have a little black triangle at the right-bottom corner. The triangle indicates that there are some hidden buttons that exist. To view them, press and hold **LMB** on the button. When a button is active, it is highlighted. To deactivate it, press **ESC**, choose another tool, or **RMB** click in a viewport.

Table 6 shows the controls available for all viewports. Table 7 shows the controls available for the **Perspective** and orthographic views. Table 8 shows the controls available for the camera views. Table 9 shows the controls available for the light views.

Table 6: The viewport navigational controls available for all viewports

Item	Icon	Description
Zoom Extents All Zoom Extents All Selected		Allow you to zoom selected objects or all objects to their extent in the viewport.
Maximize Viewport Toggle		It switches any active viewport between its normal size and full-screen size. Hotkeys: **Alt+W**.

Table 7: The viewport navigational controls available for **Perspective** and orthographic views

Item	Icon	Description
Zoom		Allows you to change the magnification by dragging in a **Perspective** or orthographic viewport. Hotkeys: **Alt+Z**. You can also use the bracket keys, [and].
Zoom All		Allows you to adjust view magnification in all perspective and orthographic viewports at the same time.
Zoom Extents, Zoom Extents Selected		**Zoom Extents** centers all visible objects in an active perspective or orthographic viewport until it fills the viewport. Hotkeys: **Ctrl+Alt+Z**. **Zoom Extents Selected** centers a selected object or set of objects. Hotkey:**Z**.
Field-of-View		**Field-of-View** adjusts the area of the scene that is visible in a viewport. It's only available in the **Perspective** viewport. Hotkeys: **Ctrl+W**. **Zoom Region** magnifies a rectangular area you drag within a viewport.
Pan View		**Pan View** moves the view parallel to the current viewport plane. Hotkeys: **Ctrl+P**.
Walk Through		Allows you to move through a viewport by pressing arrow keys. Hotkey: **Up Arrow**.
2D Pan Zoom Mode		In this mode, you can pan or zoom a viewport without changing the rendering frame. It is especially useful when you are using a **Perspective** or **Camera** viewport in conjunction with **Perspective Match**.
Orbit, Orbit Selected, Orbit Sub-Object		**Orbit** rotates the viewport and uses the view center as the center of rotation. Hotkeys: **Ctrl+R**. **Orbit Selected** uses the center of the current selection as the center of rotation. **Orbit Sub-object** uses the center of the current sub-object selection as the center of rotation.

Table 8: The viewport navigational controls available for camera views

Item	Icon	Description
Dolly Camera, Target, or Both		This flyout replaces the **Zoom** button when the **Camera** viewport is active. Use these tools to move the camera and/or its target along the camera main axis.
Perspective		It performs a combination of FOV and dolly for target cameras and free cameras.

Table 8: The viewport navigational controls available for camera views

Item	Icon	Description
Roll Camera		Rotates a free camera around its local z-axis.
Field-of-View		Adjusts the amount of the scene that is visible in a viewport
Truck Camera		Moves the camera parallel to the view plane.
Walk Through		Allows you to move through a viewport by pressing a set of shortcut keys.
Orbit/Pan Camera		**Orbit Camera** rotates a camera about the target. **Pan Camera** rotates the target about the camera.

Table 9: The viewport navigational controls available for light views

Item	Icon	Description
Dolly Light, Target, or Both		Moves the light or its target or both along the light's main axis, toward, or away from what the light is pointing at.
Light Hotspot		Allows you to adjust the angle of a light's hotspot.
Roll Light		**Roll Light** rotates the light about its line of sight (the light's local Z-axis).
Light Falloff		Adjusts the angle of a light's falloff.
Truck Light		Moves a target light and its target parallel to the light view and moves a free light in its XY plane.
Orbit/Pan Light		Rotates a light about the target. **Pan Light** rotates the target about the light.

Interaction Mode Preferences

If you are an **Autodesk Maya** user then it's good news for you that you can change the interaction mode to **Maya**. The **Interaction Mode** panel of the **Preferences** dialog box [see Fig. 25] allows you to set the mouse and keyboard shortcuts according to **3ds Max** or **Maya**.

When you set **Interaction Mode** to **Maya**, most of the hotkeys and mouse operations behave as they do in **Autodesk Maya**. Here's the list:

- Pressing **Spacebar** maximizes the viewport that is beneath the mouse pointer.
- **Shift+Click** adds or removes from the selection. **Ctrl+Click** removes from the selection.

- The **Orbit** tools are not available in the orthographic views.
- **Alt+Home** switches to the default **Perspective** view.
- **Alt+LMB** drag rotates the view. **Alt+MMB** drag pans the view. **Alt+RMB** drag zooms in or out in the view.

Table 10 shows a comparison between the **3ds Max** and **Maya** hotkeys.

Table 10: The comparison between 3ds Max and Maya hotkeys		
Function	**3ds Max**	**Maya**
Maximize Viewport Toggle	Alt+W	Spacebar
Zoom Extents Selected	Z	F
Zoom Extents All	Shift+Ctrl+Z	A
Undo Viewport Operation	Shift+Z	Alt+Z
Redo Viewport Operation	Shift+Y	Alt+Y
Play Animation	/	Alt+V
Set Key	K	S
Group	None	Ctrl+G
Editable Poly > Repeat Last Operation	;	G

Getting Around in 3ds Max

In the previous section, you have seen various components of 3ds Max's UI. Don't get hung up on all the buttons, commands, menus, and options. It was a quick tour of the interface to get your feet wet. The more time you spent on **Unit 1** and **Unit 2**, the easier it will be for you to understand the rest of the units.

Creating Objects in the Scene

You can't do much with a blank scene. You need some objects in the scene in order to work on them. 3ds Max offers a wide range of standard objects. Let's start by creating some geometry in the scene.

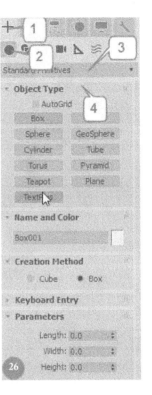

Start 3ds Max, if not already running. Choose **Reset** from the **File** menu to open the **3ds Max** message box. Click **Yes** to reset the scene. Notice there are several panels in the **Command** panel: **Create**, **Modify**, **Hierarchy**, **Motion**, **Display**, and **Utilities**. Position the mouse pointer on a panel's icon; a tooltip appears showing the name of the panel. The **Create** panel comprises of the following basic categories: **Geometry**, **Shapes**, **Lights**, **Cameras**, **Helpers**, **Space Warps**, and **Systems**. Each category is farther divided into sub-categories.

Notice in [see Fig. 26] the **Create** panel [marked as 1], the **Geometry** button [marked as 2] is active. Below that button, you will see a drop-down list [marked as 3] that contains the **Geometry** sub-categories 3ds Max offers. Notice the **Standard Primitives** is selected by default in the drop-down list.

Below the drop-down list, there is the **Object Type** rollout [marked as 4]. There are eleven buttons in this rollout. When you click on one of the buttons, the corresponding tool gets active and then you can create the corresponding object in the scene interactively using the mouse or by entering precise values using the keyboard.

Let's create an object from the **Standard Primitive** sub-category. Ensure you are in the **Command** panel > **Create** panel > **Geometry** category > **Standard Primitives**. Now, click on **Box** in the **Object Type** rollout. Notice four rollouts appears in the **Create** panel: **Name and Color**, **Creation Method**, **Keyboard Entry**, and **Parameters**.

The **Keyboard Entry** rollout is collapsed whereas the other three are in the expanded state. Expand the **Keyboard Entry** rollout by clicking on the title bar of the rollout. Change **Length** to **50**, **Width** to **50**, and **Height** to **10**. Click **Create**. You need to press **Enter** or **Tab** after typing the values. Congratulations, you have created your first object in 3ds Max [see Fig. 27].

You have not changed the values of the **X**, **Y**, and **Z** parameters in the **Keyboard Entry** rollout. As a result, the box is created at the origin of the home grid [0, 0, 0].

Also, notice the name of the object [**Box001**] in the **Name and Color** rollout. Every time you create an object, 3ds Max assigns it a default name. Collapse the **Keyboard Entry** rollout. In the **Parameters** rollout, change **Length** and **Width** to **100** each.

Notice the box in the viewports resizes as per the new dimensions you have set for the **Length** and **Width** parameters. The change occurs because still **Box001** is active in the **Object Type** rollout. If you select any other tool, then you would not be able to modify values from the **Create** panel.

Then, how to change the parameters? Well, once you select any other tool, you can change values for parameters from the **Modify** panel [panel available on the right of the **Create** panel]. Click the **Modify** panel [see Fig. 28] and notice the **Parameters** rollout appears there. Change **Height** to **20**.

Change **Length Segs**, **Width Segs**, and **Height Segs** to **2** each. Notice the change is reflected on the object in the viewport.

Notice the white brackets around the box in the **Perspective** viewport. These are selection brackets that show the bounding box of the object. I am not a big fan of the selection brackets and don't find them very useful. Press **Shift+J** to get rid of the selection brackets. To change values for parameters of an object from the **Parameters** rollout, the object must be selected in the viewport. I will cover selection methods later in the unit.

Click the **General Viewport** label in the **Perspective** viewport and choose **Configure Viewports** from the popup menu. In the **Viewport Configuration** dialog box that appears, choose the **Layout** tab and then click on the layout button highlighted with white borders in Fig. 29. Now, click **OK** to change the viewport layout [see Fig. 30].

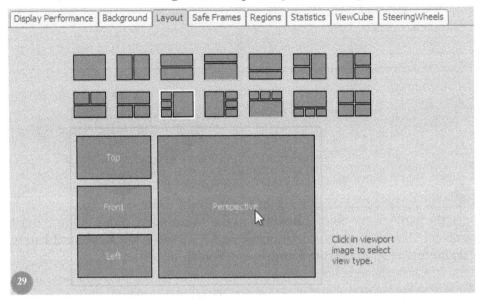

You have just changed the viewport layout. The **Top, Front**, and **Left** viewports are stacked over each other on the left whereas on the right you will see enlarged **Perspective** viewport.

Note: Viewport layout
I frequently change viewport layouts as per my needs. In hands-on exercises, if you find a different viewport layout in captures, this is the place from where you can change it. I have not written this process in hands-on exercises.

MMB click on the **Left** viewport to make it active. Press **T** to change it to the **Top** viewport. Press **L** to change it to the **Left** viewport. As discussed earlier, the options for changing the viewport are available in the **Point-Of-View [POV]** viewport label menu. Now onwards, I will refer **Point-Of-View [POV]** viewport label menu as the **POV** viewport label menu.

Tip: Viewports quad menu
*You can also change the viewports using the **Viewports** quad menu. To invoke this menu, press **V**. To change a viewport, select the desired option from the **Switch View** quadrant of the menu.*

Notice the text for the **Shading Viewport** label reads **Default Shading**. Click on the **Shading Viewport** label to display the **Shading Viewport** label menu. The options in this menu allow you to define the shading style for the viewport. Choose **Clay** from the menu to display the object in the **Clay** shading mode. The **Edged Faces** mode allows you to view object subdivisions in the viewports. **Hidden Line** hides the faces and vertices whose normals are pointing away from the viewport. Shadows are unavailable in this mode.

Wireframe Override displays objects in the wireframe mode. The hotkey for toggling the **Wireframe** mode is **F3**. **Bounding Box** displays the edges of the bounding box of the geometry. **Clay** displays geometry in a uniform terracotta color. Fig. 31 shows the teapot in the **Hidden Line**, **Wireframe**, **Bounding Box**, and **Clay** modes, respectively. My favorite shading mode for modeling is **Clay** with **Edged Faces** and I have extensively used it in this book. The shortcut to toggle the **Edged Faces** mode is **F4**.

Press **Ctrl+S** to open the **Save File As** dialog box and then type the name of the file in the **File name** text box and click **Save** to save the file. Now, if you want to open this file later, choose **Open** from the **File** menu or press **Ctrl+O** to open the **Open File** dialog box. Navigate to the file and then click **Open** to open the file. If you want to save an already saved file with a different name, choose **Save As** from the **File** menu.

You can also save a copy to the previous version of 3ds Max, choose **Save As** from the **File** menu to open the **Save File As** dialog box. In this dialog box, choose the appropriate option from the **Save as type** drop-down list [see Fig. 32]. Click **Save** to save the file.

Tip: Incremental Save
*When you are working on a file, I highly recommend that you save different versions of it. If the current version gets corrupt, you can always fall back to a previous version of the file. 3ds Max allows you to save the file incrementally. In the **Save File As** dialog box, click + at the left of the **Save** button to save the file with a name ending in a number greater than the current number displayed with the file name. For example, if the current name is **x1.max**, clicking + will save the file with the name **x02.max**.*

Selecting Objects

Selecting objects is an important process before you perform any action on an object or objects. Selection in 3ds Max works on the noun-verb terminology. You first select the object (**the noun**) and then execute a command (**the verb**). 3ds Max provides a wide variety of tools for selecting objects.

The **Selection** commands and functions are found in the following areas of the interface: **Main** toolbar, **Edit** menu, **Quad** menu, **Tools** menu, **Track View**, **Display** panel, **Modify** panel, **Ribbon**, **Schematic View**, and **Scene Explorer**.

Selecting Objects using Main Toolbar Selection Buttons

The buttons available on the **Main** toolbar provides a direct means of selection. These buttons are: **Select Object**, **Select by Name**, **Select and Move**, **Select and Rotate**, **Select and Scale**, **Select and Place**, and **Select and Manipulate**. To select an object, click on one of the selection buttons on the **Main** toolbar. Position the mouse pointer on the object that you want to select. The shape of the pointer changes to a small cross if the object is eligible for the selection. Click on the object to select it or de-select any selected object.

Note: Valid surface for selection
*The valid selection zone for the surface depends on the type of the object you are selecting and shading mode of the viewport in which you are selecting the object. In the **Shaded** mode, any visible area of the surface is a valid selection zone whereas in the **Wireframe** mode any edge or segment of the object is valid including the hidden lines.*

Adding and Removing Objects from the Current Selection

To extend a selection [adds objects to the existing selection], press and hold **Ctrl** while you make selections. For example, if you have selected two objects and you want to add the third object to the selection, press and hold **Ctrl** and click on the third object to add it to the selection. To remove an object from selection, press and hold **Alt** and click on the object that you want to remove from the selection.

Inverting Selection

To invert the selection, choose **Select Invert** from the **Edit** menu. The hotkeys for this operation are **Ctrl+I**. For example, if you have total of five objects in the scene and three of them are selected. Now, to select the remaining two objects and terminate the current selection, press **Ctrl+I**.

Selecting All Objects

To select all objects, choose **Select All** from the **Edit** menu or press **Ctrl+A**.

Locking the Selection

When the selection is locked, you can click-drag mouse anywhere in the viewport without losing the selection. To lock a selection, click **Selection Lock Toggle** [see Fig. 33] from the **Status Bar** or press **Shift+Ctrl+N**. Press **Shift+Ctrl+N** again to unlock the selection.

Deselecting an Object

To deselect an object, click on another object, or click on an empty area of the viewport. To deselect all objects in a scene, choose **Select None** from the **Edit** menu or press **Ctrl+D**.

Selecting by Region

The region selection tools in 3ds Max allow you to select one or more objects by defining a selection region using the mouse. By default, a rectangular region is created when you drag the mouse. You can change the region by picking a region type from the **Region** flyout [see Fig. 34] from the **Main** toolbar.

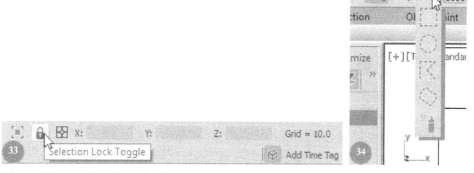

Note: Using Ctrl and Alt
*If you draw a selection region with the **Ctrl** held down, the affected objects are added to the selection. Conversely, if you hold down **Alt**, the affected objects are removed from the selection.*

Table 11 lists the types of region selection. Fig. 35 shows the rectangular, circular, fence, lasso, and paint marquee selections, respectively.

Table 11: The region selection types	
Type	**Description**
Rectangular	Allows you to select objects using the rectangular selection region.
Circular	Allows you to select objects using the circular selection region.
Fence	Allows you to draw an irregular selection region.
Lasso	Allows you to draw an irregular selection region with a single mouse operation.
Paint	Activates a brush. Paint on the objects to add them to the selection.

Note: Changing the Brush Size
*You can change the brush size from the **Preferences** dialog box. **RMB** on **Paint Selection Region** to open the dialog box. In the **General** panel > **Scene Selection** area, you can set the brush size by specifying a value for the **Paint Selection Brush Size** parameter. The default value for this parameter is **20**.*

Specifying Region Inclusion

The **Window/Crossing** button (Hotkey: **Shift+O**) on the right of the **Region Selection** flyout is a toggle button. It allows you to specify whether to include objects touched by the region border. This button affects all-region selection methods I have described above. The default state of the button is **Crossing**. It selects all objects that are within the region and crossing the boundary of the region [see Fig. 36]. The other state of the button is **Window**. It selects only those objects that are completely within the region [see Fig. 37].

Select By Name

On clicking the **Select By Name** button on the **Main** toolbar, the **Select From Scene** dialog box appears [see Fig. 38]. It allows you to select objects by their assigned names.

To select objects by name, click **Select By Name** on the **Main** toolbar or press **H** to open the **Select From Scene** dialog box. It lists all the objects in the scene. Click on the names of one or more objects to select them and then click **OK** to select the object(s), close the dialog box, and select the highlighted objects. Use **Ctrl**+click to highlight more than one entry in this dialog box.

Tip: Quickly selecting an object
To select a single object quickly, double-click on its name to select it and close the
Select By Scene *dialog box.*

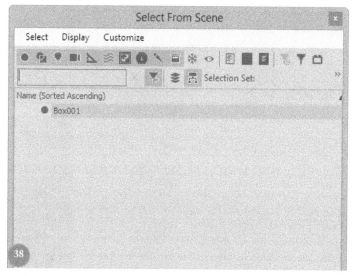

Named Selection Sets

You can name a selection in 3ds Max and then recall the selection by choosing their name from a list. To assign a name to the selection, select one or more objects or sub-objects in the scene. Click on the **Named Selection Sets** field [see Fig.39] on the **Main** toolbar to activate a text box and then type a name for your selection set. Press **Enter** to complete the operation.

Caution: Case sensitive names
The names you enter for the selection are case-sensitive.

To retrieve a named selection set, click the **Named Selection Sets** list's arrow. Choose the desired name from the list. The corresponding objects are selected in the viewport. You can also select the selection sets from the **Named Selection Sets** dialog box [see Fig. 40]. To open this dialog box, click **Edit Named Selection Sets** from the **Main** toolbar. Highlight the name of the set in this dialog box and then click **Select Objects in Set** {▪} from the **Named Selection Sets** dialog box's toolbar.

Using the Selection Filters

You can use the **Selection Filter** list [see Fig. 41] to deactivate the selection of all but a specific category by choosing a category from this list. For example, if you select **Lights** from this list, you would be only select the light objects in the scene. To remove filtering, select **All** from this list.

Using the Navigation Controls

3ds Max provides two controls to navigate a viewport: **ViewCube** and **SteeringWheels**. These semi-transparent controls appear on the upper right corner of a viewport and allow you to change the view without using any menu, command, or keyboard.

ViewCube

This gizmo [see Fig. 42] provides visual feedback to you about the orientation of the viewport. It also lets you quickly switch between the standard and orthographic views. The **ViewCube** does not appear in the camera, light, or shape viewport as well as in the special type of views such as **ActiveShade** or **Schematic**. When the **ViewCube** is inactive, the primary function of the **ViewCube** is to show the orientation of the model based on the north direction of the model. The inactive **ViewCube** remains in the semi-transparent state. When you position the mouse pointer on it, it becomes active.

If you hover the mouse pointer on top of the **ViewCube**, you will notice that faces, edges, and corners of the cube are highlighted. Click on the highlighted part of the cube; 3ds Max animates the viewport and orients it according to the clicked part of the cube. Click on the home icon on the **ViewCube** to switch to the default viewport orientation. You can also click and drag the ring to spin the model around its current orientation.

To change the **ViewCube's** settings, **RMB** click on the **ViewCube** and choose **Configure** from the context menu to open the **Viewport Configuration** dialog box with the **ViewCube** panel active. From this panel, you can change various settings of the **ViewCube**.

Table 12 lists the other option available in the context menu.

Table 12: The options available for **ViewCube** in the context menu	
Option	**Description**
Home	Restores the home view.
Orthographic	Changes the current orientation to the orthographic projection.
Perspective	Changes the current orientation to the perspective projection.
Set Current View as Home	Defines the home view based on the current orientation.
Set Current View as Front	Defines the front projection based on the current projection.
Reset Front	Resets the front projection to its default view.
Configure	Opens the **Viewport Configuration** dialog box.
Help	Launches the online help system and navigate to the **View-Cube's** documentation.

SteeringWheels

The **SteeringWheels** gizmo [see Fig. 43] allows you to access different 2D and 3D navigation tools from a single tool. When you first start 3ds max, the **SteeringWheels** gizmo is not available. To enable this gizmo press **Shift+W**. When the wheel is displayed, you can activate it by clicking on one of its wedges. If you click-drag a wedge, the current view changes. The navigation tools listed in Table 13 support click action.

Table 13: The navigation tools	
Tool	**Function**
Zoom	Adjusts the magnification of the view.
Center	Centers the view based on the position of the mouse pointer.
Rewind	Restores the previous view.
Forward	Increases the magnification of the view.

To close a wheel, you can use one of the following methods:

1. Press **Esc**.
2. Press **Shift+W** to toggle the wheel.
3. Click the small **x** button at the upper right area of the wheel.

 Tip: Changing wheel's settings
*You can change the **SteeringWheels'** settings from the **SteeringWheels** panel of the*
***Viewport Configuration** dialog box.*

There are other versions of the wheels available that you can activate from the **Wheel** menu. To open the menu, click on the down arrow on the bottom-right corner of the wheel. Table 14 lists those options.

Table 14: The options available in the **Wheel** menu.	
Option	**Function**
Mini View Object Wheel	Displays the mini version of the **View Object** wheel [see the first image in Fig. 44].
Mini Tour Building Wheel	Displays the mini version of the **Tour Building** wheel [see the second image in Fig. 44].
Mini Full Navigation Wheel	Displays the mini version of the **Full Navigation** wheel [see the third image in Fig. 44].

Table 14: The options available in the **Wheel** menu.

Option	Function
Full Navigation Wheel	Displays the big version of the **Full Navigation** wheel [see the fourth image in Fig. 44].
Basic Wheels	Displays the big versions of the **View Object** or **Tour Building** wheel [Fig. 45].
Go Home	Restores the **Home** view.
Restore Original Center	Pans the view to the origin.
Increase Walk Speed	Doubles the walking speed used by the **Walk** tool.
Decrease Walk Speed	Cuts the walking speed by half used by the **Walk** tool.
Help	Navigates you to the online documentation of the Steering Wheels.
Configure	Opens the **Viewport Configuration** dialog box that allows you to set preferences for the wheel.

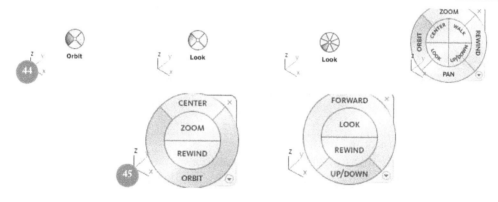

Zooming, Panning, and Orbiting Views using Mouse Scroll

To zoom in and out in the viewport, scroll the mouse wheel. It zooms in or out in steps and is equivalent to using bracket keys, [and]. If you want to gradually zoom, press and drag the wheel with the **Ctrl+Alt** held down. Press and hold **MMB** and then drag the mouse pointer to pan the view. You can pan the viewport in any direction. To rotate the viewport press and hold **Alt+MMB** and then drag the mouse pointer.

Moving, Rotating, and Scaling Objects

The transformation tools in 3ds Max allow you to move, rotate, and scale an object[s]. A transformation is the adjustment of position, orientation, and scale relative to the 3D space you are working in. 3ds Max provides four tools that allow you to transform the object: **Select and Move**, **Select and Rotate**, **Select and Scale**, and **Select and Place**. The **Select and Move**, **Select and Rotate**, and **Select and Scale** tools are generally referred to as **Move**, **Rotate**, and **Scale** tools. Now onward, I will use these names.

To transform an object, click the **Move**, **Rotate**, or **Scale** button from the **Main** toolbar. Position the mouse pointer on the object[s]. If the object[s] is already selected, the shape of the cursor changes to indicate transform. If object[s] is not selected, the shape of the mouse pointer changes to a crosshair. Now, drag the mouse pointer to apply the transform. You can restrict the motion to one or two axes by using the transform gizmos. The transform gizmos are the icons displayed in the viewport. Fig. 46 shows the **Move**, **Rotate**, and **Scale** gizmos, respectively.

 Tip: Changing the size of the gizmos
You can change the size of the gizmos by using the – and = keys on the main keyboard.

When no transform tool is active and you select objects, an axis tripod appears in the viewports [see Fig. 47]. Each axis tripod consists of three lines labeled as **X**, **Y**, and **Z**. The orientation of the tripod indicates the orientation of the current reference coordinate system.

The point where the three lines meet indicates the current transform center and the highlighted red axis lines show the current axis constraints. Each gizmo indicates axes by using three colors: **X** is red, **Y** is green, and **Z** is blue. You can use any of the axes handles to constrain transformation to that axis. The transform commands are also available from the **Quad** menu. To transform an object using the **Quad** menu, **RMB** click on the selected object[s], choose the transform command from the **transform** quadrant of the **Quad** menu and then drag the object to apply the transform.

Tip: Cancelling transform
*To cancel a transform, **RMB** click while dragging the mouse.*

Using the Transform Type-In dialog box
You can use the **Transform Type-In** dialog box to precisely enter the transformation values. To transform objects using this dialog box, make sure the **Move**, **Rotate**, or **Scale** tool is active, and then press **F12** to open the dialog box. You can also choose **Transform Type-In** from the **Edit** menu to open the associated **Transform Type-In** dialog box. Fig. 48 shows the **Move Transform Type-In**, **Rotate Transform Type-In**, and **Scale Transform Type-In**

dialog boxes, respectively. You can enter both the absolute and relative transformation values in this dialog box.

 Tip: Transform Type-In dialog box
*You can also open this dialog box by **RMB** clicking on the tool's button on the **Main** toolbar.*

The parameters in this dialog box are also replicated in the **Status Bar**. You can use these **Transform Type-In** boxes in the **Status Bar** to transform the object. To switch between the absolute and relative transform modes, click the **Relative/Absolute Transform Type-In** button in the **Status Bar** [see Fig. 49].

Getting Help

Autodesk provides rock-solid documentation for 3ds Max. There are several places in the UI from where you can access different forms of help. The help options are listed in the **Help** menu [see Fig. 50]. Click **Autodesk 3ds Max Help** from the **Help** menu to open the online documentation for 3ds Max. You can also download offline help from the Autodesk website and install it on your computer. If you have a slow internet connection, you can download the offline help and use it. To access offline help, download and install it on your system. Press **Alt+U+P** hotkeys to open the **Preferences** dialog box [refer Fig. 51].

To use offline help, choose the **Help** panel from the dialog box. Next, click on the **Download** button to open the **Download** and **Install 3ds Max Product Help** page in your browser. Download help files from this page and install it.

Now, in the **Preferences** dialog box > **Help** panel, select the **Local/Computer** radio box. Next, click **Browse** to open the **Choose Local Help Folder** dialog box. In this dialog box, navigate to the folder where you installed help and then click **Select Folder** to close the dialog box. Click **OK** from the **Preferences** dialog box to close it. Now, when you press **F1**, 3ds Max will navigate you to the offline help.

Search Command

This feature helps you in finding a specific command. For example, if you are looking for the **Sunlight** tool but not sure where it is on the interface. Press **X** to open the **Search Command** text box and then type **Sun**; **Sunlight System** appears in a list. Click on it, 3ds Max takes you to **Systems** category of the **Create** panel in the **Command** panel.

Explore More

Per-view Preferences and Presets

You can define display quality settings for each viewport. For example, you can specify the rendering level [**Basic**, **Advanced**, and **DX**], Lighting and Shadow settings, ambient occlusion settings, and so on. The Per-view Preferences and Presets can be accessed from the **Viewport Setting and Preference** dialog box [see Fig. 52]. To open this dialog box, choose **Per-View Presets** from the third viewport label menu or **Per-View Preference** from the fourth viewport label menu.

3ds Max Asset Library **|UPDATED|**

To open the library, choose **Launch 3ds Max Asset Library** from the **Content** menu; 3ds Max opens the **https://apps.autodesk.com/3DSMAX/en** page in the default browser. Click on the **Download** button and then accept term of use; the download will start. Save the file and then install it. After installing, a shortcut will appear on your desktop. Double-click on the icon to open the asset library [see Fig. 53].

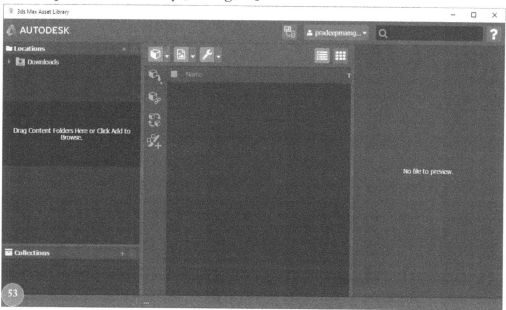

Game Exporter Utility

This utility [see Fig. 54] allows you to export the models and animations clips in **FBX** format to your game engine in a streamlined fashion.

This utility is specifically designed for game users to export game assets more efficiently. This utility uses a minimal amount of settings, as a result, you can easily export the model without changing too many settings. It also supports animation clips thus allows you to export multiple clips as a single FBX file or as multiple files.
You can open this utility from the **File** menu or **Utilities** panel:

- **Utilities** panel > **Utilities** rollout > **More** button > **Utilities** dialog box > **Game Exporter** option
- **File** menu > **Export** > **Game Exporter**

54

Default Hotkey Map [NEW]

You can use the default shortcut keys to quickly accomplish common tasks. Autodesk has modified some of the default shortcuts and also retired some of them. For example:

- The hotkey **J** was used to toggle selection brackets, now it is used to invoke **Windows Quad** [see Fig. 55].
- **Spacebar** now invokes the **Lock Quad** [see Fig. 56].
- You can press **V** to invoke the **Viewport Quad** [see Fig. 57].
- Pressing **F9** renders the view.
- The **0** key on the main keyboard is used to invoke **Texture Tools Quad** [see Fig. 58].

To know more about the modified and retired shortcuts, navigate to 3ds Max Documentation and search the following term: **Default Hotkey Maps**.

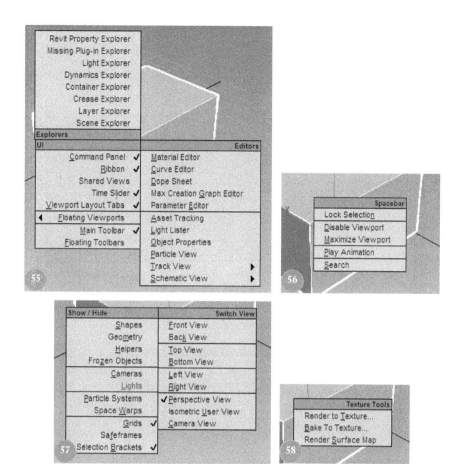

Hands-on Exercise

Before you start the exercise, let's first create a project folder for the hands-on exercise of this unit. You can proceed without creating a project folder but I highly recommend that you create one. The project folder allows you to keep your file organized.

Open **Windows Explorer** and create a new directory with the name **max2021projects** in the **C** drive of your system. Start 3ds Max. From the **File** menu, choose **Reset**. Click **Yes** from the dialog box that appears. From the **File** menu, choose **Project > Create Default** to open the **Choose a folder** dialog box.

In this dialog box, navigate to the **3dsmax2021projects** directory and then click **New Folder** and then rename the folder as **intro-1**. Select the folder and then click **Select Folder** to create the project folder. Now, if you navigate to the **\max2021projects\intro-1** directory, you will see several sub-directories [see Fig. E1].

archives autoback downloads export express

import materiallibraries previews proxies renderoutput

renderpresets sceneassets scenes vpost unit-mi1

What just happened?

Here, I have set a project folder for the hands-on exercise of this unit. When you set a project folder for a scene, 3ds Max creates a series of folders such as **scenes**, **sceneassets**, *and so on. These folders are default locations for certain types of operations in 3ds Max. For example, the* **scenes** *folder is used when 3ds Max opens or saves scene files.*

Tip: Resetting Scene

It is a good idea to reset the scene before you start new work because the **Open** *command defaults to the folder where the previous scene was saved. After the* **Reset** *operation, the* **Open** *command defaults to the* **scenes** *folder of the current project folder.*

Exercise 1: Creating a Simple Model of a House

OK, now it is time to work on the first exercise of the book. In this exercise, you will create a simple model of a house using **Standard Primitives** [see Fig. E2].

Table E1 summarizes the exercise:

Table E1	
Skill level	Beginner
Time to complete	20 Minutes
Resources folder	**intro-1**
Final file	**house-finish.max**

1. Start 3ds Max. Choose **Reset** from the **File** menu. Click **Yes** on the **3ds Max** message box to reset the settings. Choose **Units Setup** from the **Customize** menu to open the **Units Setup** dialog box. Ensure that **Generic Units** is selected in this dialog box and then click **OK** to close the dialog box.

2. Click **Box** in the **Object Type** rollout in the **Command** panel and then click-drag in the **Perspective** viewport to define the length and width of the box. Release the mouse button to define the length and width of the box. Release the **LMB** and then drag upward to define the height. Click to specify the height.

3. Press **Shift+J** to turn off the selection brackets and **F4** to turn on the **Edged Faces** mode. Now, click on the **Shading Viewport** label and choose **Clay** from the popup menu.

4. Press **G** to turn off the grid. Press **G** again to turn it on. Drag the mouse pointer with the **MMB+Alt** held down to rotate the view. Drag the mouse pointer with the **MMB** held down to pan the view. Drag the mouse pointer with the **Ctrl+Alt+MMB** held down to zoom in or out of the view. You need to place the mouse pointer on the area for which you want to change the magnification. Next, you will use the brackets keys to change the settings.

5. Place the mouse pointer on the area for which you want to change the magnification settings and then use the bracket keys [and] to change the level of magnification. **MMB** click on the **Perspective** viewport to make it active, if not already active. Press **Alt+W** to maximize the viewport. Click on the **Home** icon on the **ViewCube** to restore the home view. Alternatively, you can **RMB** click on the **ViewCube** and then choose **Home** from the **ViewCube's** menu.

6. Press **Alt+W** again to restore the four viewport arrangement. Click-drag the compass ring of the **ViewCube** to change the orientation of the viewport. Now, click-drag edges, corners, or faces of the **ViewCube** and experiment with various possibilities that **ViewCube** offers. When done, click on the **Home** icon to restore the view.

7. Press **Shift+Z** repeatedly to undo the scene view changes. Press **Shift+Y** to redo the scene view changes. Click on the **ViewCube's Home** icon to restore the home view.

8. Press **Ctrl+P** to activate the **Pan View** 🖐 tool and then drag in the viewport to pan the view. Now, press **Ctrl+R** to activate the **Orbit** tool 🪐 and drag in the viewport to rotate the view. Press **Q** to deactivate the **Orbit** tool and activate the **Select** tool. Press **Shift+W** to activate **StreeringWheels**. Click-drag the **ZOOM** wedge to change the magnification level. Similarly, experiment with other wedges of the wheel. Press **Esc** to deactivate **SteeringWheels**.

9. Make sure **Box001** is selected in the viewport and then **RMB** click on the **Move** ✛ tool to open the **Move Transform Type-In** dialog box. In the **Absolute: World** group of the dialog box, **RMB** click on the spinners' arrows to set them to their default values which is **0**. You will notice that the box is now placed at the origin in the viewports. The **Move Transform Type-In** dialog box is a modeless dialog box. You don't have to close it in order to work on the model you are creating in this exercise.

10. Choose the **Modify** panel 🗂 in the **Command** panel. In the **Parameters** rollout, change **Length**, **Width**, and **Height** to **80**, **50**, and **70**, respectively, to change the size of the box. Press **Ctr+Shift+Z** to zoom the box to its extents in all viewports [see Fig. E3]. If you press **Z** the box will be zoomed in the active viewport only.

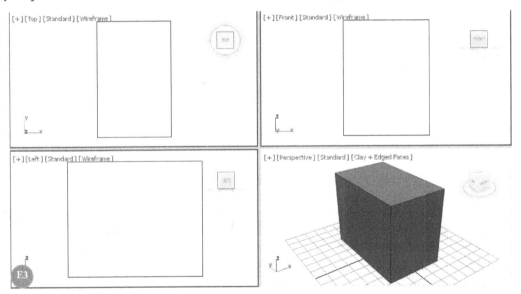

11. Now, let's create the door and windows of the house. Create another box in the **Perspective** viewport and then set its **Length**, **Width**, and **Height** to **23**, **6**, and **40**, respectively [see Fig. E4]. Ensure **Box002**, as well as the **Move** tool is selected and then enter **-25**, **-2.3**, and **-0.03** in the **Transform Type-In** boxes in the **Status Bar** [see Fig. E5].

12. Create two windows using the **Box** primitive. Use the values **23, 6**, and **18** for the **Length**, **Width**, and **Height** spinners, respectively. Now, align the boxes [see Fig. E6]. Ensure the **Box** tool is active and then select the **AutoGrid** checkbox from the **Object Type** rollout. Position the mouse pointer on the **Box001**, an axis tripod shows up [see Fig. E7]. Create a box on the **Box001**.

13. Ensure **Box005** is selected and then click **Align** in the **Main** toolbar. Now, click **Box001** in the **Perspective** viewport to open the **Align Selection** dialog box. In this dialog box, set the values as shown in Fig. E8 and click **OK** to align the boxes.

14. Ensure **Box005** is selected and then choose the **Modify** panel. In the **Parameters** rollout, change **Length, Width**, and **Height** to **91, 60**, and **2**, respectively [see Fig. E9]. Choose the **Create** panel and ensure **Auto Grid** is on.

15. Click **Pyramid** in the **Object Type** rollout and then create a pyramid on **Box005**. Align **Pyramid001** with **Box005** using the **Align** tool.

16. Ensure **Pyramid001** is selected and then in the **Modify** panel > **Parameters** rollout, set **Width, Depth**, and **Height** to **60, 90**, and **46**, respectively [see Fig. E10].

17. Now, let's create a chimney for the house. In the **Create** panel, choose **Cylinder** from the **Object Type** rollout and create a cylinder in the **Perspective** viewport. In the **Modify** panel > **Parameters** rollout, set **Radius** and **Height** to **5** and **60**, respectively. Now, place **Cylinder001** on the roof using the **Move** tool [see Fig. E11].

18. In the **Create** panel, choose **Cone** from the **Object Type** rollout and ensure **AutoGrid** is on. Create a cone on **Cylinder001**. Align **Cone001** and **Cylinder001**.

19. In the **Modify** panel > **Parameters** rollout, set **Radius 1**, **Radius 2**, and **Height** to **7.5**, **2**, and **13**, respectively [see Fig. E12].

20. Choose **Select All** from the **Edit** menu to select all objects in the scene. Choose **Group** from the **Group** menu to open the **Group** dialog box. In this dialog box, type **House** in the **Group name** field and click **OK** to create a group. Press **Ctrl+S** to open the **Save File As** dialog box. In this dialog box, navigate to the location where you want to save the file. Type the name of the file in the **File name** text box and then click **Save** to save the file.

Quiz

Evaluate your skills to see how many questions you can answer correctly.

Multiple Choice
Answer the following questions:

1. Which the following keys is used for a slower scroll rate in a spinner?

   [A] Alt   [B] Ctrl
   [C] Alt+Ctrl   [D] Shift

2. Which of the following keys is used to invoke the **Select Object** tool?

   [A] S   [B] Q
   [C] W   [D] R

3. Which of the following keys is used to switch any active viewport between its normal size and full-screen size?

   [A] Alt+X   [B] Alt+M
   [C] Alt+G   [D] Alt+W

4. Which the following keys is used to lock and unlock the selection?

   [A] Shift+Ctrl+N   [B] L
   [C] Alt+L   [D] Ctrl+L

5. Which of the following hotkeys are used to invoke the **SteeringWheel** gizmo?

   [A] Shift+S   [B] Shift+W
   [C] Shift+A   [D] Shift+X

Fill in the Blanks
Fill in the blanks in each of the following statements:

1. Press _____ to open the **Numeric Expression Evaluator** for a spinner.

2. _____ click on a spinner to set it to its default value.

3. The _____ command is used to reset 3ds Max default settings.

4. The _____ hotkeys are used to hold the scene. To recall the scene you can press _____.

5. To select all objects in a scene press _____.

6. The _____, _____, and _____ hotkeys are used to invoke **Select and Move**, **Select and Rotate**, and **Select and Scale** tools.

7. The _____ hotkeys are used to switch to the default **Perspective** view angle.

8. To deselect all objects in a scene press _____.

9. You can change the size of the transform gizmos using the _____ and _____ keys on the main keyboard.

10. Press _____ to turn off the selection brackets.

11. Press _____ to toggle the wireframe mode.

12. Press _____ to toggle the **Edged Faces** mode.

True or False
State whether each of the following is true or false:

1. You can use the **Ctrl** key for a faster scroll rate in a spinner.

2. Press **Ctrl+~** to toggle the visibility of all open dialogs in 3ds Max.

3. Toolbars can only be docked on the outer edge of the interface.

4. You can press **H** to turn off the grid in the active viewport.

5. The **S** key is used to cycle through snap options.

6. You can press **Ctrl+I** to invert the current selection.

7. The **Shift+Z** and **Shift+Y** hotkeys are used to undo and redo the scene view changes, respectively. [T/F]

Practice Activities

Interface elements: Spend time exploring the interface, menus, and toolbars. Create a floating viewport and change it to a four viewports arrangement and then move it to another monitor, if you have a two-monitor setup. Reset the scene and then configure the viewports using the **Viewport Layout** tab so that the three viewports are stacked on the right and one larger viewport on the left. From the top, set the stacked viewports to **Left**, **Front**, and **Top**, respectively. Then, set the larger one as **Perspective** viewport.

Workspaces: Detach the **Command** panel and doc it to the left of the interface. Expose a hidden toolbar and then doc it to the left of the **Command** panel. Detach the **Viewport Layout Tabs** toolbar and doc it to the right of the interface. Expose the hidden **Animation Layers** toolbar and doc it on the left of the **Command** panel. Save the workspace with the name **My Workspace** using the **Manage Workspaces** feature. Change the workspace to **Alt Menu and Toolbar** and notice the difference in the menubar when you choose this workspace. Explore various workspaces available in 3ds Max.

Explore Standard Primitives: From the **Command** panel > **Create** panel, choose **Geometry**, and then **Standard Primitives**. Pay attention to each object's parameters to get familiar with what each object is capable of.

Selection regions: Create few standard primitives in the viewport and then practice different types of region selection options: **Rectangular**, **Circular**, **Fence**, **Lasso**, and **Paint**.

Summary
The unit covered the following topics:

- Understanding workspaces
- Navigating the workspace
- Customizing the interface
- Understanding various UI components
- Working with the file management commands
- Setting preferences for 3ds Max
- Working with viewports
- Setting preferences for the viewports
- Creating objects in the scene
- Selecting objects
- Using the navigational gizmos
- Moving, rotating, and scaling objects
- Getting help
- Per-view Preferences, Asset Library, and Game Exporter

Multiple Choice
1. A, **2.** B, **3.** D, **4.** A, **5.** B

Fill in the Blanks
1. Ctrl+N, **2.** RMB, **3.** Reset, 4.Ctrl+H, Alt+Ctrl+F, **5.** Ctrl+A, **6.** W, E, R,
7. Alt+Home, **8.** Ctrl+D, **9.** -, =, **10.** Shift+J, **11.** F3, **12.** F4

True/False
1. T, **2.** T, **3.** T, **4.** F, **5.** T, **6.** T, **7.** T

- Creating clones and duplicates
- Understanding hierarchies
- Working with the **Scene** and **Layer** Explorers
- Understanding the **Mirror**, **Select and Place**, and **Select and Manipulate** tools
- Working with the **Align** and **Array** tools
- Working with precision and drawing aids
- Understanding modifiers, and normals

Unit 2: Introduction to 3ds Max - II

In the previous unit, I covered the interface as well as the tools that allow you to transform objects in the viewport. In this unit, I will cover the tools and procedures that will help you immensely during the modeling process. You will know about various explorers as well as various precision tools that 3ds Max offers. I have also covered the procedures for creating clones and duplicates.

Creating Copies, Clones, and References

The general term used for duplicating objects is cloning. To create a duplicate, clone, or reference, transform [move, rotate, or scale] the object with **Shift** held down. This process is generally called **Shift+Transform**. There are some other tools such as the **Mirror** tool available in 3ds Max that allows you to create clones.

What's is the difference between Copy, Instance, and Reference?
*There are three methods available in 3ds Max to clone the objects: **Copy**, **Instance**, and **Reference**. At the geometry level, clones created using any method are identical. However, they behave differently when used with the modifiers such as **Bend** or **Twist**.*

*The **Copy** method allows you to create a completely different copy of the original object. If you modify the original object, it will not affect the other. The **Instance** method creates a completely interchangeable clone of the original. If you modify the original or the instance, the change replicates in both objects.*

*The **Reference** method creates a clone dependent on the original up to the point when the object was created. If you apply a new modifier to the referenced object, it will affect only that object. Depending on the method used, the cloned objects are called copies, instances, or references.*

Cloning Techniques

3ds Max provides several techniques for creating clones. You can use any of these techniques on any selection. Here's the list:

- Clone
- Shift+Clone
- Snapshot
- **Array** tool
- **Mirror** tool
- **Spacing** tool
- **Clone and Align** tool
- Copy/Paste (**Scene Explorer**)

Table 1 summarizes these techniques:

Table 1: The list of cloning techniques	
Technique	**Description**
Clone	The easiest method for creating clones is to use the **Clone** command. To create a clone using this command, select the object[s] that you want to clone and then choose **Clone** from the **Edit** menu or press **Ctrl+V**. The **Clone Options** dialog box appears. Choose the method you want to use from the **Object** group of the dialog box and then specify a name for the cloned object using the **Name** text box. Next, click **OK** to create a clone. The clone will be superimposed on the original object at the same location. Use the **Move** tool to separate the two.
Shift+Drag	You can use this technique to clone objects while transforming them. This technique is the most used technique for cloning objects. To clone and transform objects, click **Move**, **Rotate**, or **Scale** in the **Main** toolbar and then select an object, multiple objects, group, or sub-objects in a viewport. Hold down **Shift** and then drag the selection. As you drag the selection, a clone is created and transformed. Now, release **Shift** and mouse button to open the **Clone Options** dialog box. Change the settings and click **OK** to create a clone.
Snapshot	You can use this feature to create an animated object over time. You can create a single clone on any frame or you can create clones on multiple frames along the animation path. The spacing between the clones is a uniform time interval.

Table 1: The list of cloning techniques	
Technique	Description
Array	You can use the **Array** tool to create repeating design patterns, for example, legs of a round coffee table, blades of a jet engine, text on the dial of a watch, and so on. The **Array** command allows you to precisely control the transformations in the 3D space.
Mirror	**Mirror** allows you to create a symmetrical copy along with any combination of axes. This tool also provides an option "**No Clone**" that allows you to perform a mirror operation without creating a clone.
Spacing tool	This tool distributes objects along a path defined by a spline. You can control the spacing between the objects.
Clone and Align tool	This tool allows you to distribute the source objects to a selection of destination objects. This tool is very useful when you work on an imported CAD file that contains lots of symbols. For example, you can replace the chair symbols in the CAD file with the actual chair geometry en masse.
Copy/Paste (Scene Explorer)	You can use the **Scene Explorer**'s **Edit** menu command to copy-paste nodes. The **Scene Explorer** should be in **Sort By Hierarchy** mode.

Working with the Mirror Tool

On clicking **Mirror** in the **Main** toolbar, the **Mirror** dialog box appears [see Fig. 1]. The parameters in this dialog box allow you to mirror the current selection about the center of the current coordinate system. You can also create a clone while mirroring a selection. To mirror an object, make a selection in a viewport. Click **Mirror** in the **Main** toolbar or choose **Mirror** from the **Tools** menu. In the **Mirror** dialog box that appears, set the parameters and click **OK** [refer to Fig. 2]. In Fig. 2, I first selected the left leg of the robot and then used the **Mirror** dialog box to create his right leg.

Notice in the **Mirror** dialog box, there are two options at the top: **Transform** and **Geometry**. These options control how the **Mirror** tool treats the reflected geometry. **Transform** uses the legacy mirror method. This method mirrors any word-space-modifiers [**WSM**] effect. **Geometry** applies a **Mirror** modifier to the object and does not mirror any **WSM** effect.

 Tip: Mirrored arrays
*You can create mirrored arrays using the **Mirror** and **Array** tools in succession.*

Tip: Animating the mirror operation
*To animate the mirror operation, enable **Auto Key** and then set a target frame for the transition to end. Now, mirror the object using the **Mirror** tool. The object will appear to flatten and then will reshape itself during the transition.*

Tip: Coordinate system
*The title bar of the **Mirror** dialog box shows the current coordinate system in use.*

Working with the Array Tool

The **Array** tool allows you to create an array of objects based on the current selection in the viewport. The **Array** button is not visible in the **Main** toolbar by default. The **Array** button is part of the **Extras** toolbar which is not visible by default.

To make it visible, **RMB** click on the empty gray area of **Main Toolbar** and then choose **Extras** from the popup to display the **Extras** toolbar [see Fig. 3].

Tip: Array command
*The **Array** command is also available in the **Tools** menu.*

Tip: Real-time update
*Click **Preview** in the **Array** dialog box to view the changes in the viewport as you change settings in the dialog box.*

To understand the functioning of this tool, reset 3ds Max, and create a teapot in the scene. Ensure teapot is selected in a viewport and then choose **Array** from the **Tools** menu to open the **Array** dialog box. Now, click **Preview** and set other parameters as shown in Fig. 4. Notice in Fig. 4, 3ds Max creates **4** copies of the teapot with **60** units distance between each copy.

Notice total distance is now **300** units, as shown in the **Totals** group of the dialog box indicating that **5** copies of the teapot are taking up **300** units space along the **X**-direction.

Now, if you want to distribute these teapots over a distance of say **400** units, click > on the right of the **Move** label and then set **X** to **400** [see Fig. 5]; the teapots are now spread over a distance of **400** units. Similarly, you can create an array using the **Rotate** and **Scale** transformations. Settings in Figs. 6 and 7 show how you can create a 2D or a 3D array using the **Array** dialog box.

You can also create a 360-degree array using the **Array** dialog box. Reset 3ds Max and then create a **Teapot** primitive with radius **10** at the top edge of the grid [see Fig. 8]. From the **Main** toolbar > **User Center** flyout, choose **Use Transform Coordinate Center** [see Fig. 9]. Choose **Array** from the **Tools** menu to open the **Array** dialog box. Now, specify the settings, as shown in Fig. 10 to create 12 teapots in a full circle [360 degrees].

Working with the Spacing Tool

This tool allows you to distribute the selected objects along a spline or along the distance specified by the two points. You can also control the spacing between two objects. This tool can be activated by choosing **Tools > Align > Spacing Tool** from the menu bar or choosing **Spacing Tool** from the **Array** flyout. Alternatively, you can press **Shift+I**.

To distribute objects along a path, select the objects in the scene, and then activate the **Spacing Tool** to open the **Spacing Tool** dialog box [see Fig. 11]. This dialog box provides you two methods for selecting path: **Pick Path** and **Pick Points**.

To use the **Pick Path** method, select the object and then click **Pick Path**. Place the cursor on a spline in the view and click to select the spline as a path. Now, specify the number of objects you want to distribute and then choose a distribution algorithm from the drop-down list available in the **Parameters** group [see Fig. 12]. Select **Follow**, if you want to align the pivot points of the object along the tangents of the spline [see Fig. 13].

If you click **Pick Points** from the **Spacing Tool** dialog box, you can specify the path by clicking on two places in the viewport. When you are done with the tool, 3ds Max deletes the spline.

Working with Clone and Align Tool

This tool lets you distribute the source objects based on the current selection to a selection of the target objects. You can activate this tool by choosing **Align > Clone and Align** from the **Tools** menu. Alternatively, choose **Clone and Align** tool from the **Array** flyout.

To use the **Clone and Align** tool, create four teapots and a cone in the viewport [see Fig. 14]. Select cone in a viewport and then choose **Align > Clone and Align** from the **Tools** menu to open the **Clone and Align** dialog box.

14

In this dialog box, click **Pick** and then click on each teapot to align the cone with the teapots [see Fig. 15]. If you want to pick multiple destination objects at once, click **Pick List** to open the **Pick Destination Objects** dialog box. In this dialog box, select the objects and then click **Pick**. This tool is very useful when you work on the CAD files. For example, you can replace the chair symbols in the CAD file with the actual chair geometry en masse using this tool.

Working With the Select and Place Tool

This tool is a cousin of the **AutoGrid** option found in the **Object Type** rollout. However, you can use it any time in your scene not just when you are creating an object. This tool can be activated by using one of the following four methods:

- Click the **Select and Place** icon in the **Main** toolbar.
- Choose **Placement** from the **Edit** menu.
- Press **Y** on the keyboard.
- **RMB** click on an object and then choose **Placement** from the **Transform** quadrant [see Fig. 16].

To place an object, you don't have to select it first. Pick the **Select and Place** tool, click-drag to place on another object [see Fig. 17].

As you drag the object, the orientation of the object changes based on the normals of the target object and object's **Up Axis** settings. The contact position of the target surface will be the object's pivot. To change the **Up Axis** settings, **RMB** click on the **Select and Place** tool in the **Main** toolbar to open the **Placement Settings** dialog box [see Fig. 18] and then select the axis from the **Object Up Axis** button array.

When **Rotate** is active in the **Placement Settings** dialog box, the translation of the object is prevented and the object rotates around the local axis specified using the **Object Up Axis** settings. **Use Base as Pivot** is useful in those cases when the pivot is not already located in the base of the object. **Pillow Mode** is very useful when you are trying to place an object on a target whose surface is uneven. This option prevents the intersection of the objects. When **Autoparent** is active, the placed object automatically becomes the child of the other object. This is a quick way to make a parent-child relationship.

Note: Select and Rotate tool
*If you just want to rotate the object, you can use the **Select and Rotate** tool from the*
***Main** toolbar.*

There are some more goodies associated with this tool:

* You can clone an object while dragging it by pressing **Shift**.
* Hold **Ctrl** and then drag to position an object vertically along the **Up Axis**.
* You can prevent an object from rotating while you place it by holding **Alt**.

You can also place several objects at one go. You can either select the desired objects before picking the **Select and Place** tool or you can select additional objects using **Ctrl** when this tool is active. Each object will move according to its own pivot unless objects are linked together.

Working With the Select and Manipulate Tool

The **Select and Manipulate** tool allows you to interactively edit the parameters of certain objects by dragging the manipulators in the viewports. The state of this tool is non-exclusive. You can manipulate objects as long as any of the select mode or one of the transform modes is active but if you want to select a manipulator helper, you must deactivate the **Select and Manipulate** tool. All those primitives with a **Radius** parameter have a built-in manipulator for the radius value. Let's see how it works:

Create a **Teapot** primitive in the scene. Pick the **Select and Manipulate** tool from the **Main** toolbar. A green ring appears beneath the teapot [see Fig. 19]. Click-drag the ring to interactively change the radius of the teapot. Click on **Select and Manipulate** on the **Main** toolbar to deactivate the tool. There are three types of custom manipulators available in 3ds Max: cone angle manipulator, plane angle manipulator, and slider manipulator. The cone angle manipulator is used by a spot light's **Hotspot** and **Falloff** parameters. To create a cone angle manipulator, choose **Create** panel > **Helpers** > **Manipulators** and then click **Cone Angle**. Click-drag in the viewport to create the helper [see Fig. 20]. To change its parameters, go to the **Modify** panel and change the values.

19   20

Now, let's work on a spotlight to see this manipulator in action:

Create a **Teapot** primitive in the scene. Now, create a spotlight and place it as shown in Fig. 21. Ensure the spotlight is selected and then click **Select and Manipulate** from the **Main** toolbar. Three rings appear on the spotlight [see Fig. 22].

The bottom inner ring controls **Hotspot** whereas the outer rings control **Falloff**. The center blue ring represents the roll angle. Using the **Select and Manipulate** tool, click-drag on these rings to interactively change parameters. The plane angle manipulator allows you to create a lever or joystick type shape. You can use its **Angle** parameter to create a custom control. You can use this control to drive the parameter of other objects. Let's see how it works.

Choose **Create** panel > **Helpers** > **Manipulators** and then click **Plane Angle**. In the **Front** viewport, click-drag to create a shape [see Fig. 23]. The **Plane Angle** manipulator always created vertically along the **Y**-axis of the viewport in which you are creating it. Create a **Teapot** in the **Perspective** viewport. Ensure the **Select and Manipulate** tool is not active and the manipulator is selected. Choose **Animation** > **Wire Parameters** > **Wire Parameters** from the menubar. In the popup that appears, choose **Object (Plane Angle Manipulator)** > **Angle** [Fig. 24]. A rubber band line appears. Click on the **Teapot**. In the popup that appears, choose **Object (Teapot)** > **Radius** [see Fig. 25].

In the **Parameter Wiring** dialog box, click **One-way connection** button and then the **Connect** button [see Fig. 26] to make the connection. Now, close the dialog box. Pick the **Select and Manipulate** tool and drag the manipulator in a circular motion to interactively change the radius of the **Teapot**.

The third type of manipulator, **Slider**, which creates a graphic control in the viewport. You can wire its value to a parameter of another object within the scene. Here's how:

Create a **Slider** manipulator in the **Front** viewport. Create a **Teapot** in the **Perspective** viewport [see Fig. 27]. Wire the **value** parameter of the manipulator to the **Radius** parameter of the **Teapot** as described above. Change the controls such as **Label**, **Minimum**, and **Maximum** values in the **Modify** panel [see Fig. 28]. Pick the **Select and Manipulate** tool and drag the manipulator's **Adjust** control to interactively change the shape of the teapot. Fig. 29 shows the components of a **Slider** control [**1.** Label, **2.** Value, **3.** Move, **4.** Show/hide, **5.** Slider bar, **6.** Adjust value, and **7.** Change width].

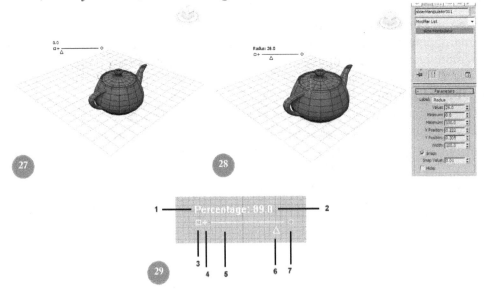

Scene Explorer

The **Scene Explorer** [see Fig. 30] is a modeless dialog box in 3ds Max that you can use to view, sort, filter, and select objects. Besides, you can rename, delete, hide, and freeze objects. You can also modify and edit object properties en masse. Each workspace in 3ds Max comes with a different **Scene Explorer** with the same name as its workspace. By default, the **Scene Explorer** is docked to the left of the viewports.

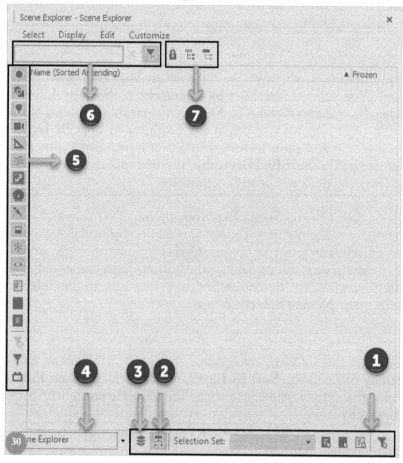

Several explorers in 3ds Max are different versions of the **Scene Explorer**. These includes **Layer Explorer**, **Container Explorer**, **MassFX Explorer**, and **Material Explorer**. The **Scene Explorer** comes with many toolbars [see Fig. 30]. Table 2 summarizes various toolbars available.

Table 2: The **Scene Explorer** toolbars	
Flag	**Toolbar**
1	Selection toolbar
4	View toolbar
5	Display toolbar
6	Find toolbar
7	Tools toolbar

Selection Toolbar

The **Scene Explorer** comes with two sorting modes: **Sort By Layer** mode and **Sort By Hierarchy** mode. You can use the **Sort by Hierarchy** or **Sort By Layer** button on the **Selection** toolbar [marked as 2 and 3 in Fig. 30] to use these modes. The **Sort By Layer** button [marked as 3 in Fig. 30] sets the **Scene Explorer** to **Sort By Layer** mode. In this mode, you can use drag and drop feature for editing layers. Some other options are also available in this mode. The **Sort By Hierarchy** [marked as 2 in Fig. 30] button allows you to edit hierarchies using drag and drop functionality.

If you click on an object in the **Scene Explorer**, the object is selected and the associated row in the explorer gets highlighted. To select multiple objects, click on objects with **Ctrl** held down. Press **Ctrl+A** to select all objects, **Ctrl+I** to invert the selection, and **Ctrl+D** to deselect. These commands are also available at the bottom-right corner of the **Scene Explorer** [marked as 1 in Figure 30]. The **Selection Set** drop-down list in the **Selection** toolbar lets you select objects using **Named Selection Sets**.

Tools Toolbar

The tools available in this toolbar [marked as 7 in Fig. 30] are dependent on whether the **Sort By Hierarchy** mode or the **Sort By Layer** mode is active. When **Lock cell editing** is active, you cannot change any name or settings. The **Pick Parent** button is only available in the **Sort By Hierarchy** mode. It allows you to change the parent. To make an object parent, select one or more objects and then click **Pick Parent**. Now, select the object that you want the parent of the selected object.

The **Create New Layer** button is available in the **Sort By Layer** mode. When you click **Create New Layer**, a new layer is created and the selection is automatically added to this layer. The new layer you create becomes the active layer and any subsequent objects you create are added to this layer automatically. If an existing layer is selected, and you click **Create New Layer**, the new layer becomes a child of the selected layer. **Add to Active Layer** is available in the **Sort By Layer** mode only. When you click on this button, all selected objects and layers are assigned to the active layer. **Select Children** allows you to select all child objects and layers of the selected items.

Tip: Selecting children
Double-clicking on a parent layer or object selects the parent and all its children.

The **Make Selected Layer Active** button is available in the **Sort By Layer** mode only. When you click on this button, 3ds Max makes the selected layer the active layer. Alternatively, click on the layer icon to make it the layer active.

Display Toolbar

The **Display** toolbar allows you to control the display of various objects in the **Scene Explorer**. It controls the type of objects that appear in the **Scene Explorer**'s listing. You can also solo the category by clicking on one of the category buttons with **Alt** held down. You can also turn on or off the categories by choosing **Display > Object Types** from the **Scene Explorer**'s menu bar.

View Toolbar

The **View** toolbar is located at the bottom-left corner of the **Scene Explorer**. This toolbar shows the name of the current **Scene Explorer**. When you click on the black triangle located in this toolbar, a menu appears. This menu gives access to all the local and global explorers.

Local and Global Scene Explorers

3ds Max comes with different **Scene Explorer** configurations. These configurations are available to every scene you create in 3ds Max. Therefore, they are referred to as **Global Scene Explorers**. On the other hand, the **Local Scene Explorers** live within a single scene and saved/loaded with the scene. The options to make a **Local** explorer **Global** are available in the menu located on the **View** toolbar [see Fig. 31].

How to delete objects?
*To delete one or more objects in the **Scene Explorer**, select them and then press **Delete** or **RMB** click on the list and then choose **Delete** from the **Quad** menu.*

How to hide and show objects?
Click the eye icon of the layer or object to hide. The eye icon turns gray. Click again to reveal.

How to create hierarchies in the Sort By Hierarchy mode?
To make a parent, drag and drop the child

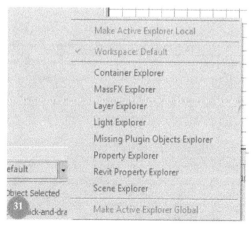

objects' name or icon onto the object that you want to act as a parent. To restore the child objects to the top level, drag them to an empty area of the **Scene Explorer**. Alternatively, you can **RMB** click on them and then choose **Unlink** from the **Quad** menu. You can use the same techniques on the layers as well.

How to freeze objects?

To freeze object, click on the corresponding cell of the **Frozen** column. Click again to unfreeze. If you want to freeze many objects, select them, and then click on the **Frozen** column of any selected objects.

How to change object properties?

To change the object properties, select one or more objects in the **Scene Explorer** and then **RMB**. Choose **Properties** from the **Quad** menu to open the **Object Properties** dialog box. You can use this dialog box to change the properties of the selected objects.

How to rename an object?

Select the object and then **RMB** click. Choose **Rename** from the **Quad** menu and then type a new name for the object.

Tip: Renaming objects

Slowly triple-click on the object name to rename the object if you don't want to use the **Quad** menu.

Can I add more columns next to the Frozen column?

Yes, you can. **RMB** click on any of the column head and then choose **Configure Columns** [see Fig. 32] from the context menu. The **Configure Column** window appears [see Fig. 33]. Double-click on the name of the column in this window that you want to add. Fig. 34 shows the **Has Material** column. A tick will appear in this column if a material has been assigned to the object.

Can I search objects by name?
*Yes, you can search an object by using the search text box available in the **Find** toolbar. Type the search string and then press **Enter**. For example, if you have many teapots in the scene and all have default names. Entering **tea** in the search field and then pressing **Enter** will select all teapots in the scene. You can also use the wild card characters such as **?** and * to create a broader search criteria.*

Working with the Precision Tools

3ds Max comes with several tools and objects that allow you to position and align objects efficiently. Two of the tools [**Select and Place** tool, and **Select and Manipulate** tool] I have already discussed that let you align and position objects. You have also seen the use of some helpers that are used with the **Select and Manipulate** tool.

Using Units

Units define the measurement system for the scene. The default unit system in 3ds Max is **Generic Units**. Besides **Generic Units**, you can also use feet and inches both decimal and fractional. The **Metric** system allows you to specify units from millimeters to kilometers. You can specify the unit system from the **Units Setup** dialog box [see Fig. 35].

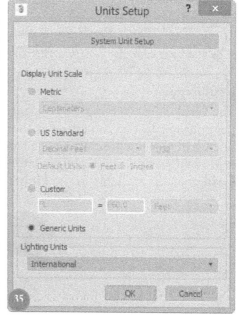

You can open this dialog box by choosing **Units Setup** from the **Customize** menu. On clicking **System Unit Setup** in this dialog box, the **System Unit Setup** dialog box appears from where you can specify the **System** units.

What is the difference between the Scene and System units?
The system units only affect how geometry appears in the viewports whereas the system units control the actual scale of the geometry.

Caution: System units
*The system units should only be changed before you create your scene or import a **unitless** file. Do not change the system units in the current scene.*

If you change units for a scene, 3ds Max automatically changes the values for the parameters. For example, if you are using **Centimeters** and value in a spinner is **30** cm, when you change units to **Decimal Inches**; 3ds Max will change the value to **11.811** inches. Now, if you type **50cm** in the spinner and press **Enter**, 3ds Max changes the value to **19.685** inches. Similarly, if you type **2'** in the spinner, the value changes to **24.0** inches.

Using Grids

Grids are two-dimensional arrays that you can use to position the objects accurately. You can use grids to visualize space, scale, and distance. You can use it as a construction plane for creating objects as well use it for snapping objects using the snap feature. I will discuss about snap features later in this unit. 3ds Max provides two types of grids: **Home** grid and **Grid** objects.

Home Grid

The **Home** grid is defined by three intersecting planes along the world **X**, **Y**, and **Z** axes. These planes intersect at the origin defined by **0,0,0**. The **Home** grid is fixed, you cannot move or rotate it.

Tip: Home Grid
*Press **G** to toggle the visibility of the **Home** grid.*

Grid Object

The **Grid** object [see Fig. 36] is a helper object that you can use to create a reference grid as per your needs. You can create as many **Grid** objects as you want in a scene. However, only one **Grid** object will be active at a time. When a **Grid** object is active, it replaces the **Home** grid in all viewports. You can rename and delete the **Grid** objects like any other object. The **Grid** object is available in the **Helpers** category in the **Create** panel.

Tip: Activating the Home grid and the Grid object
*You can activate the **Home** grid by choosing **Tools > Grids and Snaps > Activate Home Grid** from the menubar. When you choose this command, it activates the **Home** grid in all viewports and deactivates the current active **Grid** object. Similarly, you*

can activate a **Grid** object by choosing **Tools > Grids and Snaps > Activate Grid Object** from the menubar.

 Tip: Aligning a Grid object to the view
*To align a **Grid** object with the current view, make sure it is selected and then choose **Tools > Grids and Snaps > Activate Grid Object** from the menubar. The **Grid** object is aligned and will be coplanar with the current view.*

Auto Grid

The **Auto Grid** feature lets you create objects on the surface of other objects. The **Auto Grid** option is available in the **Object Type** rollout of any category. It is also available in the **Extras** toolbar. When you activate this option and drag the cursor on the surface of an object, a construction plane is created temporarily on the surface of the object.

 Tip: Select and Place tool
*The **Select and Place** tool discussed earlier provides a similar mechanism to align the objects.*

Aligning Objects

3ds Max provides six different tools for aligning the objects in a scene. These tools are available in the **Align** flyout on the **Main** toolbar.

Using with Align Tool

The **Align** tool in 3ds Max allows you to align the current selection to a target selection. You can pick the **Align** tool from the **Align** flyout in the **Main** toolbar. You can also activate this tool by choosing **Align > Align** from the **Tools** menu or by pressing **Alt+A**. Using this tool, you can align the position and orientation of the bounding box of a source object to the bounding box of a target object. A bounding box is the smallest box that encloses the extents (maximum dimensions) of an object. A bounding box appears when you set a viewport to a non-wireframe mode. Fig. 37 shows the extents of a teapot model.

To toggle the display of the bounding box, select the object and then press **Shift+J**. You can also enable the display of the bounding boxes by turning on **Selection Brackets** from the **Viewport Setting and Preference** dialog box > **Per-View Preferences** panel [see Fig. 38]. Refer to **Explore More** section of **Unit 1** for more information on the **Viewport Setting and Preference** dialog box.

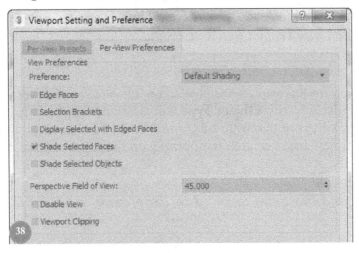

Let's dive in and align some objects. Create three boxes and assign them red, green, and blue colors [see Fig. 39]. Use the following dimensions:

Red Box: Length=52, Width=61, and Height=32
Green Box: Length=35, Width=40, and Height=12
Blue Box: Length=50, Width=40, and Height=30

RMB click on the red box and choose **Object Properties** from the **Quad** menu. In the **General** panel > **Display Properties** group, select **See-Through** and click **OK**; this will help you better see the alignment process. Now, let's center align the red and blue boxes along the **X** and **Y** axes.

Make sure the red box is selected and then pick the **Align** tool from the **Main** toolbar. Click the blue box. In the **Align Selection** dialog box > **Align Position (World)** group, select **X Position** and **Y Position**. Turn off **Z Position**. Make sure **Center** is selected in the **Current Object** and **Target Object** groups. You will see that both the objects are center-aligned [see Fig. 40]. Click **OK** to accept changes.

Now, let's see how to place the blue box on the top of the red box.

Select the blue box and then pick the **Align** tool from the **Main** toolbar. Click the red box. You have already performed alignment along the **X** and **Y** axes. Therefore, turn off **X Position** and **Y Position** and select **Z Position**. You will see that now the blue box is at the center of the red box. Select **Maximum** from the **Target Object** group. Notice the blue box's center is aligned to the center of the red box [see Fig. 41]. Now, select **Pivot Point** from the **Current Object** group. The blue box sits on the top of the red box [see Fig. 42]. Click **OK** to accept changes.

Now, let's align one corner of the green box with the blue box.

Select the green box and then pick the **Align** tool from the **Main** toolbar. Click the blue box. Select **X Position**, **Y Position**, and **Z Position**. Select **Minimum** from the **Current Object** and **Target Object** groups [see Fig. 43]. Click **OK** to accept changes. With the green box selected, click the blue box using the **Align** tool. Now, select **Z Position** and turn off **X Position** and **Y Position**. Select **Minimum** from the **Current Object** group and then select **Maximum** from the **Target Object** group. Next, click **OK**; the boxes are now stacked over each other [see Fig. 44].

Using the Quick Align Tool

The **Quick Align** tool instantly aligns an object with the target object. The hotkeys associated with this tool are **Shift+A**. To align an object, select the source object and press **Shift+A** to activate the tool. Now, click on the target object to align two objects [see Fig. 45]. If the current selection contains a single object, this tool uses the pivot points of the two objects for alignment. If multiple objects are selected, the selection center of the source objects is aligned with the pivot of the target objects.

Using the Normal Align Tool

This tool allows you to align the two objects based on the directions of the normals of the selected faces. The hotkeys associated with this tool are **Alt+N**. To understand the functioning of this tool, create a sphere and teapot in the scene [see Fig. 46]. Select the teapot, the source object in this case. Press **Alt+N** to activate the tool and then drag across the surface of the teapot, a blue arrow indicates the location of the current normal [see Fig. 47].

Keep dragging on the surface until you find the normal you are looking for. Now, click and drag on the surface of the sphere until you find the normal to which you want to align the source object. Release the mouse button; the teapot gets aligned with the sphere [see Fig. 48] and the **Normal Align** dialog box appears. Using the parameters available in this dialog box, you can offset the position and orientation of the teapot.

What are normals?

A normal is a vector that defines the inner and outer surfaces of a face in a mesh. The direction of the vector indicates the front [outer] surface of a face or vertex. Sometimes, normals are flipped during the modeling process. To fix this issue, you can use the **Normal** *modifier to flip or unify normals. Fig. 49 shows the vertex and face normals, respectively.*

Using the Place Highlight Tool

You can use this tool to align an object or light to another object so that its highlight [reflection] can be precisely positioned. To position a light to highlight a face, make sure the viewport that you want to render is active. Choose **Place Highlight** from the **Align** flyout and drag the mouse pointer on the object to place the highlight. Now, release the mouse button when the normal indicates the face on which you want to place the highlight [see Fig. 50].

Note: Light type and highlights

With the omni, free spot, or directional light, 3ds Max displays face normal. With a target spotlight, 3ds Max displays the target of the light and base of its cone.

Using the Align Camera Tool

This tool lets you align the camera to a selected face normal. The functioning of this tool is similar to the **Place Highlight** tool but it does not change the camera position interactively. You need to release the mouse button and then 3ds Max aligns the camera with the selected face.

Using the Align View Tool

When this tool is picked from the **Align** flyout, it opens the **Align to View** dialog box that lets you align the local axis of the selection or sub-object selection with the current viewport [see Fig. 51]. To use this tool, select the objects or sub-objects to align and then choose **Align to View** from the **Align** flyout. 3ds Max opens the **Align to View** dialog box. Choose the options from the dialog box as desired. If you want to flip the direction of alignment, select **Flip** in this dialog box.

Drawing Assistants

3ds Max provides several tools and utilities that help you in drawing objects with precession. Let's have a look.

Measuring Distances

The **Measure Distance** tool allows you to quickly calculate the distance between two points. The calculated distance appears in the **Status Bar** in scene [display] units. To measure distance, choose **Measure Distance** from the **Tools** menu. Now, click on the point in the viewport from where you want to measure the distance. Click again in the viewport where you want to measure to. The distance between the two points is displayed in the **Status Bar**.

The **Measure** utility available in the **Utilities** panel displays the measurement of a selected object or spline. To display measurement of an object, select the object and then on the **Utilities** panel, click **Measure**. The measurements are displayed in the **Measure** rollout [see Fig. 52].

There is one more utility called **Rescale World Units** that you can use to rescale the word units. You can scale the entire scene or the selected objects. To rescale an object, select it, and then on the **Utilities** panel click **More** to open the **Utilities** dialog box. Select **Rescale World Units** from the dialog box and then click **OK**. The **Rescale World Units** rollout appears in the **Utilities** panel. Click **Rescale** from this rollout to open the **Rescale World Units** dialog box [see Fig. 53].

Set **Scale Factor** in this dialog box and then select **Scene** or **Selection** from the **Affect** group. Click **OK** to apply the scale factor to the selected object or the entire scene. For example, you specify **Scale Factor** as **2** and select **Selection** from the dialog box, the selected object will be scaled to double its current size.

The Snap tools in 3ds Max allow you to precisely control the dimensions and placement of the objects when you create or transform them. You can invoke these tools using the **Snap** buttons available on the **Main** toolbar. You can also invoke these tools by choosing **Grids and Snaps** from the **Tools** menu.

2D Snap, 2.5 Snap, and 3D Snap

The hotkey for activating snap is **S**. The **2D Snap** tool snaps the cursor to the active construction grid including the geometry on the plane of the grid. The **Z**-axis is ignored by this tool. The **2.5D Snap** tool snaps the cursor to the vertices or edges of the projection of an object onto the active grid. The **3D snap** is the default tool. It snaps the cursor directly to any geometry in the 3D space. **RMB** click on the snap toggle button to open the **Grid and Snap Settings** dialog box [see Fig. 54].

You can specify which type of snap you want active from the **Snaps** panel of this dialog box. For example, if you want the cursor to snap to the pivot or vertices of the object, select **Pivot** and **Vertex** from this panel. To see snap feature in action, select **Pivot** and **Vertex** from the **Grid and Snap Settings** dialog box. Now, create a box and teapot in the viewport [see of Fig. 55]. Pick the **Move** tool from the **Main** toolbar and move the teapot to one of the vertex of the box or its pivot [see Fig. 56].

Angle Snap Toggle

You can use **Angle Snap Toggle** to rotate an object around a given axis in the increment you set. This snap toggle also works with the **Pan/Orbit** camera controls, **FOV** and **Roll** camera settings, and **Hotspot/Falloff** spotlight angles. The hotkey for invoking this tool is **A**.

To rotate an object, click **Angle Snap Toggle** in the **Main** toolbar and then rotate the object using the **Rotate** tool. By default, the rotation takes place in five-degree increments. You can change this default value by specifying a new value for the **Angle** parameter in the **Options** panel of the **Grid and Snap Settings** dialog box.

Percent Snap Toggle

Percent Snap Toggle lets you control the increments of scaling by the specified percentage. The default percentage value is **10**. You can change this default value by specifying a new value for the **Percent** parameter in the **Options** panel of the **Grid and Snap Settings** dialog box.

Spinner Snap Toggle

This toggle allows you to set single-increment or decrement value for all the spinners in 3ds Max. The default value is **1**. To change this value, **RMB** click on **Spinner Snap Toggle** on the **Main** toolbar to open the **Preferences Settings** dialog box. In the **Spinners** group of the **General** panel, specify a value for the **Snap** parameter.

Modifiers

The modifiers in 3ds Max provide a way to edit and sculpt objects. You can change the shape of an object using the modifier's properties. Fig. 57 shows the original box [first image] and the modified geometry after applying the **Bend**, **Twist**, and **Taper** modifiers, respectively.

You can apply modifiers from the **Modifier** drop-down list available in the **Modify** panel of the **Command** panel [see Fig. 58]. The modifiers you apply to an object are stored in a stack called modifier stack. Modifiers are described in detail in a later unit.

Quiz

Evaluate your skills to see how many questions you can answer correctly.

Multiple Choice
Answer the following questions:

1. Which of the following keys is used to invoke the **Select and Place** tool?

   [A] X   [B] S
   [C] Y   [D] P

2. Which of the following systems is the default unit system in 3ds Max?

   [A] Generic Units   [B] Metric
   [C] Imperial   [D] Custom

3. Which of the following keys is used to toggle the visibility of the home grid?

   [A] H   [B] Shift+H
   [C] G   [D] Alt+G

4. Which of the following key is used to invoke the **Align** tool?

   [A] Alt+T   [B] Alt+A
   [C] Ctrl+T   [D] Ctrl+A

Fill in the Blanks
Fill in the blanks in each of the following statements:

1. To create a clone, select the object[s] that you want to clone and then choose _____
   from the _____ menu or press _____.

2. The _____ is used to distribute objects along a path or between two points.

3. The _____ method in the **Clone Options** dialog box allows you to create a clone dependent on the original up to the point when the object was created.

4. The _____ tool allows you to interactively edit the parameters of certain objects by dragging the manipulators in the viewports.

5. Press _____ to invoke the **Quick Align** tool.

6. A _____ is a vector that defines the inner and outer surfaces of a face in a mesh.

True or False
State whether each of the following is true or false:

1. The **Mirror** tool can be used to just create a mirror reflection.

2. The **Transform** option in the **Mirror** dialog box allows you to mirror any word-space-modifiers [WSM] effect.

3. You can not animate the mirror operation.

4. The **Clone and Align** tool lets you distribute the source objects based on the current selection to a selection of the target objects.

5. Double-clicking on a parent layer or object in the **Scene Explorer** selects the parent and all its children.

6. The system units only affect how geometry appears in the viewports whereas the system units control the actual scale of the geometry.

Practice Activities

Note: Project folder
*The name of the project folder for this chapter is **intro-2**.*

Apply a modifier: Create a teapot in the viewport. Apply the **Melt** modifier to it. Now, change the **Melt > Amount** and **Solidity** to melt the teapot. Add a **Noise** modifier and then change **Strength** on all three axes. Finally, apply a **TurboSmooth** modifier and set **Iterations** to **2** [see Fig. A1]. Keep in mind that the final result depends on the order in which the modifiers appear in the modifier stack.

Make a clone: Select the teapot from the previous activity and create two clones: one as **Instance** and another as **Reference**. Select the referenced teapot and apply the **Spherify** modifier to it [see Fig. A2]. Notice in the viewport that only the referenced clone is affected by the **Spherify** modifier because the **Reference** cloning method creates a clone dependent on the original up to the point when the object was created.

Work with the Mirror tool: Create a **Box** primitive in the **Perspective** viewport and then in the **Modify** panel, set it's **Length, Width, Height,** and **Length Segs** to **130, 20, 20,** and **20,** respectively. Apply the **Bend** modifier to it. Change the value of **Bend > Angle** and **Bend Axis**. Create a copy of the box using the **Mirror** tool and set the **Offset** value so that the boxes don't overlap [see Fig. A3].

Work with the Array tool: Create a **Box** in the **Perspective** viewport and then set its **Length, Width,** and **Height** to **10, 8,** and **45,** respectively. In the **Hierarchy** panel, scroll down to the **Use Working Pivot** rollout and then enable **Use Working Pivot**. Now, create an array of **12** boxes using the **Array** tool. Create a **20** degrees incremental rotation (z-axis) and apply a **500%** total scale (z-axis) to the clones [see Fig. A4]. If you want to create a full circular array, use **30** degrees for incremental rotation (**12** clones * **30** degrees= total **360** degrees) or simply enter **360** for the total rotation along the z-axis.

Work with the Spacing tool: Open **\practice-activities\spacing-tool.max** and then distribute the glass object along the two splines present in the scene [see Fig. A5]. Experiment with various options that the **Spacing** tool offers.

Work with Clone and Align tool: Open **\practice-activities\clone-n-align.max** and then place and align the teapot on the top of each box [see Fig. A6]. Use the local **Z** position offset to align the teapot. Select the **Link to Destination** checkbox to link each clone as a child of the destination object.

A5   A6

Work with Select and Place tool: Create a sphere and a teapot in the scene. Align the teapot to the surface of the sphere using the **Select and Place** tool. Now, only using the **Select and Place** tool, rotate the teapot along the z-axis without changing its position.

Summary
The unit covered the following topics:

- Creating clones and duplicates
- Understanding hierarchies
- Working with the **Scene** and **Layer** Explorers
- Understanding the **Mirror**, **Select and Place**, and **Select and Manipulate** tools
- Working with the **Align** and **Array** tools
- Working with precision and drawing aids
- Understanding modifiers, and normals

Answer to Quiz
Multiple Choice
1. C, **2.** A, **3.** C, **4.** B

Fill in the Blanks
1. Clone, Edit, Ctrl+V, **2.** Spacing Tool, **3.** Reference, **4.** Select and Manipulate,
5. Shift+A, **6.** Normal

True/False
1. F, **2.** T, **3.** F, **4.** T, **5.** T, **6.** T

- Creating and modifying the **Standard** Primitives
- Creating and modifying the **Extended** Primitives
- Working with the **Architectural** objects
- Setting the project folder
- Using the **Align** and **Mirror** tools
- Creating clones
- Using the **Scene Explorer**
- Creating a group
- Setting grid spacings
- Using the **Transform Type-In** dialog box
- Using the **Array** dialog box
- Specifying the units for the scene

Unit 3: Geometric Primitives and Architectural Objects

The 3D objects in the scene and the objects that are used to create them are known as geometries. Most of the 3D applications offer basic building blocks for creating geometries called geometric primitives. You can use these primitives and some modifiers to create basic models. In this unit, you will work with the **Standard** and **Extended** primitives as well as the **Architectural** objects.

You can edit these geometric primitives at sub-object levels to create complex models. This process is known as surface modeling that I've covered in the next unit. In this unit, I will explain **Standard** and **Extended** primitives and how you can use them to create some basic models. Geometric primitives in 3ds Max are divided into two categories: **Standard** and **Extended**. Let's first start exploring the **Standard** primitives.

Standard Primitives

3ds Max offers eleven standard primitives, see Fig. 1. You can combine **Standard** primitives into more complex objects. You can then further refine them by using modifiers. You can interactively create primitives in the viewport using the mouse. Primitives can also be created by entering precise values using the keyboard. You can specify the parameters before creating the primitives and as well as modify them later from the **Parameters** rollout in the **Modify** panel. Let's take a look at different **Standard** primitives.

Box

Box is the simplest of the primitives. You can use it to create the rectangular as well as cubical geometries [see Fig. 2]. To create a **Box** primitive, in the **Create** panel, click **Geometry**, and then in the **Object Type** rollout, click **Box**.

To create a box, click and drag in a viewport to specify the length and width of the box. Now, release the mouse button and drag the mouse up or down [without holding any button] to specify the height of the box and then click to complete the process.

Whenever you choose a tool from the **Object Type** rollout, the **Name and Color**, **Creation Method**, **Keyboard Entry**, and **Parameters** rollouts appear in the **Command** panel. You can use these rollouts to specify the initial properties of the objects.

Tip: Navigating between the steps
*If you are creating a primitive that requires two or more steps [for example **Cylinder** or **Torus**], you can pan and orbit the viewport between the steps. To pan the viewport, **MMB** drag. To orbit, hold **Alt** and then **MMB** drag.*

Name and Color Rollout

The parameters in the **Name and Color** rollout allow you to rename the objects and change their colors. Whenever you create an object, 3ds Max assigns it a default name and color. For example, if you reset the scene and create a box in the viewport, 3ds Max assigns it the name **Box001**. To change the name of the object, type a new name in the text box available in the **Name and Color** rollout. The color swatch to the right of the text box lets you change the color of the object.

On clicking the color swatch, the **Object Color** dialog box appears. You can click on one of the color swatches and then click **OK** to assign the color to the object. If you want to specify a custom color, select a color swatch associated with the **Custom Colors** parameter, and then click **Add Custom Colors**. In the **Color Selector: Add Color** dialog box that appears, specify a color and then click **Add Color** to add the chosen color to the selected swatch in the **Object Color** dialog box. Now, click **OK** to close the dialog box and apply the selected color to the object.

Tip: Scene Explorer
*As discussed in Unit 2, you can easily rename objects using the **Scene Explorer**.*

Creation Method Rollout

There are two parameters available in this rollout: **Cube** and **Box**. **Box** creates a standard box primitive with different settings for length, width, and height. **Cube** creates a cube with equal width, height, and length. Creating a cube is one step operation. Click and drag the mouse pointer in the viewport to create a cube.

Parameters Rollout

The default settings in this rollout produce a box with one segment on each side. Table 1 summarizes the controls in the **Parameters** rollout.

Table 1: The parameters in the **Box**'s **Parameters** rollout	
Parameters	**Description**
Length, Width, Height	The **Length**, **Width**, and **Height** parameters set the length, width, and height of the box, respectively. These controls also act as readouts when you interactively create a box.
Length Segs, Width Segs, Height Segs	The **Length Segs**, **Width Segs**, and **Height Segs** parameters set the number of segments [divisions] along each axis of the object. You can set these parameters before and after the creation of the box. The default value for these parameters is **1, 1, 1**.
Generate Mapping Coords	The **Generate Mapping Coords** checkbox is on by default for most objects. It generates coordinates for applying a material to the box.
Real-World Map Size	The **Real-World Map Size** checkbox lets you create a material and specify the actual width and height of a 2D texture map in the material editor. The scaling values are controlled from the map's [for example the **Diffuse** map] **Coordinates** rollout.

Note: Default values
Whatever values you specify for these parameters become the default for the current session.

Tip: Resolution
*If you are planning to use the modifiers such as **Bend** on a primitive object, increase the values for the **Length Segs**, **Width Segs**, and **Height Segs** parameters to get some extra resolution on the objects. The higher the resolution, the smoother the bend will be.*

Keyboard Entry Rollout

You can use the parameters in this rollout to define both the size of the box as well as its position in 3D space in a single operation. The method for creating objects through the keyboard is generally the same for all primitives; differences might occur in the type and number of parameters. The **X**, **Y**, and **Z** parameters define the position of the object. The default value is **0, 0, 0** which is the center of the active grid.

Cone

You can use this primitive to create round upward or inverted cones [see Fig. 3]. To create a cone, click **Cone** in the **Object Type** rollout. In the viewport, drag to define the base of the cone and then release the mouse button. Now, move the mouse pointer up or down in the viewport to define the height.

The height can be negative or positive. Click to set the height. Move the mouse pointer vertically to define the radius of the other end of the cone. If you want to create a pointed cone, set this radius to zero.

Creation Method Rollout

Two creation methods are available for the **Cone** primitive: **Edge** and **Center**. **Edge** draws a cone from edge to edge. **Center** draws from the center out.

Parameters Rollout

The default settings in this rollout produce a smooth cone with 24 sides, 1 cap segment, and 5 height segments. Table 2 summarizes the parameters in the **Parameters** rollout.

Parameters	Description
Table 2: The parameters in the **Cone**'s **Parameters** rollout	
Radius 1, Radius 2	**Radius 1** and **Radius 2** define the first and second radii of the cone. You can use these two parameters to create pointed or flat-topped cones.
Height	**Height** sets the dimension of the cone along the central axis. If you set a negative value, the cone will be created below the construction plane.
Height Segments	**Height Segments** parameter sets the number of divisions along the major axis of the cone.
Cap Segments	**Cap Segments** sets the number of concentric divisions at the top or bottom of the cone.
Sides	**Sides** determines the number of sides around the cone.

Table 2: The parameters in the **Cone**'s **Parameters** rollout

Parameters	Description
Smooth	**Smooth** is on by default. It blends the faces of the cone on rendering, therefore, producing smooth looking renders.
Slice From, Slice To	You can use the **Slice From** and **Slice To** parameters to slice the cone. These two parameters set the number of degrees around the local Z-axis. To activate these two parameters, select **Slice On**.

Caution: Minimum and negative values
*If you specify negative values for **Radius 1** and **Radius 2**, these values will be converted to **0**. The minimum value for these parameters is **0**.*

Note: Same value for Radius 1 and Radius 2
*If you specify the same value for **Radius 1** and **Radius 2**, a cylinder will be created. If these two values are close in size, an object is created which resembles the effect as if a **Taper** modifier applied to a cylinder.*

Tip: Pointed cones
For improved rendering on smooth pointed cones, increase the number of height segments.

Sphere

You can use the **Sphere** primitive to create a full sphere, a hemisphere, a slice of a sphere, or some part of a sphere [see Fig. 4]. To create a sphere, in the **Create** panel, click **Geometry**, and then in the **Object Type** rollout, click **Sphere**.

In the viewport, drag the mouse pointer to define the radius of the sphere, release the mouse button to set the radius. To create a hemisphere, create the sphere of the desired radius and then set **Hemisphere** to **0.5** in the **Parameters** rollout.

Creation Method Rollout

There are two methods available for creating a sphere: **Edge** and **Center**. **Edge** draws the sphere from edge to edge. **Center** draws a sphere from the center out.

Parameters Rollout

The default values in this rollout produce a smooth sphere with **32** divisions. Table 3 summarizes the parameters in the **Parameters** rollout.

Table 3: The parameters in the **Sphere**'s **Parameters** rollout	
Parameters	**Description**
Radius	**Radius** specifies the radius of the sphere.
Segments	**Segments** defines the number of segments for the sphere.
Hemisphere	**Hemisphere** lets you create a hemisphere. It cuts off the sphere to create a partial sphere. You can use this parameter to create an animation in which the sphere will be cut off starting from its base to top.
Chop, Squash	**Chop** and **Squash** determine the number of vertices and faces when you create a hemisphere. **Chop** reduces the number of vertices and faces by chopping them out whereas **Squash** maintains the number of vertices and faces by squashing the geometry toward the top of the sphere. Fig. 5 shows the effect of **Chop** [left] and **Squash** [right] on a hemisphere with **16** segments.
Base To Pivot	If you select **Base to Pivot**, the sphere moves upward along its local Z-axis and places the pivot point at its base. Fig. 6 shows the pivot at the center [left], which is the default, and at the base of the sphere [right].

[+][Perspective][Wireframe]

GeoSphere

You can use the **GeoSphere** primitive to create spheres and geo-hemispheres based on three classes of polyhedrons: **Tetra**, **Octa**, and **Icosa** [see Fig. 7].

The **GeoSphere** primitive produces more regular shape than the **Sphere** primitive. Unlike the **Sphere** primitive, the geometry produced by the **GeoSphere** primitive has no poles which is an

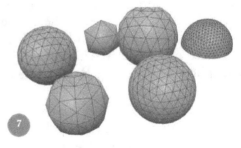

advantage is in certain modeling scenarios. Also, they appear slightly smoother than the standard sphere when rendered. To create a **GeoSphere**, in the **Create** panel, click **Geometry**, and then in the **Object Type** rollout, click **GeoSphere**. In the viewport, drag the mouse pointer to define the radius of the sphere, release the mouse button to set the radius. To create a hemisphere, create a hemisphere of the desired radius and then select the **Hemisphere** checkbox in the **Parameters** rollout.

Creation Method rollout

There are two methods available for creating a geosphere: **Diameter** and **Center**. **Diameter** draws the geosphere from edge to edge whereas **Center** draws from the center out.

Parameters Rollout

Table 4 summarizes the parameters in the **Parameters** rollout.

Table 4: The parameters in the **GeoSphere**'s **Parameters** rollout	
Parameters	**Description**
Radius	**Radius** sets the radius of the geosphere.
Segments	**Segments** defines the number of faces in the geosphere.
Tetra, Octa, Icosa	The parameters in the **Geodesic Base Type** group let you choose one of the regular polyhedrons for geosphere geometry. **Tetra** creates a four-sided tetrahedron. The facets can vary in shape and size. The geosphere can be divided into four equal segments. **Octa** creates an eight-sided tetrahedron. The facets can vary in shape and size. The geosphere can be divided into eight equal segments. **Icosa** creates a 20-sided tetrahedron. The facets are equal in size. The geosphere can be divided into any number of equal segments.

Cylinder

Cylinder creates a cylinder that can be sliced along its major axis [see Fig. 8]. To create a cylinder, in the **Create** panel, click **Geometry**, and then in the **Object Type** rollout, click **Cylinder**. In the viewport, drag the mouse pointer to define the radius, release the mouse button to set the radius. Now, move the mouse pointer up or down to define the height, click to set it.

Parameters Rollout

The default parameters in the **Parameters** rollout produce an **18** sided smooth cylinder with the **5** height segments, **1** cap segment, and the pivot point at its base. Table 5 summarizes the parameters in the **Parameters** rollout.

Table 5: The parameters in the **Cylinder**'s **Parameters** rollout

Parameter	Description
Radius	**Radius** sets the radius of the cylinder.
Height	**Height** defines the height of the cylinder along the cylinder's major axis.
Height Segments	**Height Segments** defines the number of divisions along the cylinder's major axis.
Sides	**Sides** sets the sides around the cylinder.
Cap Segments	**Cap Segments** sets the number of concentric divisions around the top and bottom of the cylinder.

Tip: Resolution
*If you are going to use the cylinder with a modifier such as **Bend**, increase the number of height segments. If you are planning to modify the end of the cylinder, increase the number of cap segments.*

Tube

The **Tube** primitive produces a cylinder with hole in it [see Fig. 9]. You can use this primitive to use both the round and prismatic tubes. To create a **Tube**, in the **Create** panel, click **Geometry**, and then in the **Object Type** rollout, click **Tube**. In the viewport, drag the mouse pointer to define the first radius, which can be either the inner or the outer radius of the tube, release the mouse button to set the first radius. Move the mouse pointer to create the second radius, and then click to set it. Move the pointer up or down to create the height [positive or negative] and then click to set the height of the tube.

a

9

Tip: Prismatic tube
*To create a prismatic tube, set the number of **Sides** according to the type of the prismatic tube you want to create. Clear the **Smooth** checkbox and then create the tube.*

Parameters Rollout

Radius 1 and **Radius 2** are used to specify the inside and outside radii of the tube. The larger among the two values defines the outside radius of the tube.

Torus

You can use the **Torus** primitive to create a doughnut-like shape which is a ring with the circular cross-section [see Fig. 10]. To create a torus, in the **Create** panel, click **Geometry**, and then in the **Object Type** rollout, click **Torus**. In the viewport, drag the mouse pointer to define a torus; the torus emerges from its center. Release the mouse button to set the radius of the torus ring. Now, move the mouse pointer to define the radius of the cross-section, and then click to complete the creation process.

Parameters Rollout

The default values in this rollout produce a smooth torus with **12** sides and **24** segments. The pivot point of the torus is located at the center of the torus on the plane which cuts through the center. **Rotation** sets the degree of rotation. The vertices are uniformly rotated about the circle running through the center of the torus ring. **Twist** defines the degree of twist. 3ds Max twists the cross-sections about the circle running through the center of the torus.

 Caution: Twisting a close torus
*Twisting a close torus will create a constriction in the first segment. To overcome this, you can either twist the torus in the increments of **360** or select **Slice** and then set both **Slice From** and **Slice To** to **0**.*

The parameters in the **Smooth** group control the level of smoothing. The default **All** parameter produces smoothing on all surfaces of the torus. **Sides** smoothes the edges between the adjacent segments thus producing smooth bands that run around the torus. **None** turns off the smoothing and produces prism-like facets on the torus. **Segments** smoothes each segment individually and produces ring-like segments.

Pyramid

The **Pyramid** primitive is used to create a pyramid-like shape with the square or rectangle face and triangular sides [see Fig. 11]. To create a pyramid, in the **Create** panel, click **Geometry**, and then in the **Object Type** rollout, click **Pyramid**. In the viewport, drag the mouse pointer to define the base of the pyramid. Click to set it and then drag the mouse pointer up to define the height.

 Tip: Constrain the base of the pyramid to a square
*To constrain the base of the pyramid to a square, drag with the **Ctrl** key held down.*

Plane

The **Plane** primitive creates a flat plane that you can enlarge to any size [see Fig. 12]. To create a **Plane**, in the **Create** panel, click **Geometry**, and then in the **Object Type** rollout, click **Plane**. In the viewport, drag the mouse pointer to create a plane.

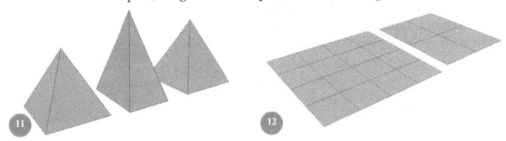

Parameters Rollout

The parameters in the **Render Multipliers** group are used to set the multipliers at the render time. You can use **Scale** to specify the factor by which both length and width will be multiplied at the render time. **Density** specifies a factor by which the number of segments in both length and width are multiplied at the render time.

Teapot

The **Teapot** primitive is used to create a parametric teapot object [see Fig. 12A]. This object is comprised of a lid, body, handle, and spout. You can create the whole teapot [which is default] or a combination of the parts. You can even control which parts to display after creation. To create a **Teapot**, in the **Create** panel, click **Geometry**, and then in the **Object Type** rollout, click **Teapot**. In the viewport, click and drag to define the radius. Release the mouse button to set the radius and create a teapot. You can control which part of the teapot you want to create by turning on the required parameters from the **Teapot Parts** group of the **Parameters** rollout.

TextPlus

The **TextPlus** primitive is used to create an all-in-one text object. You can use this primitive to create a spline outline as well as solid, extruded beveled geometry. It allows you to apply different fonts and styles on a per-character basis and add animation and special effects. It is a very useful tool for producing motion graphics elements. To create the text, in the **Create** panel, click **Geometry**, and then in the **Object Type** rollout, click **TextPlus**. Click on the viewport to create the **TextPlus** object. If you want to create a region of text, click-drag in the viewport to define the region.

Layout Rollout

From this rollout, you can define the plane onto which you will type the text. The default option is **Auto**. Also, you can set whether you want to create a region of text or text just starting from a point [see Fig. 13].

Parameters Rollout

From this rollout, you can set the font and other global parameters such as tracking and leading for the text. If you click on **Open Large Text Window**, the **Enter Text** window appears [see Fig. 14].

This window lets you easily type and format text. If you want to interactively change global parameters in the viewport, click **Manipulate Text** in the **Parameters** rollout; some symbols appear on the text in the viewport [see Fig. 15]. You can use these symbols to manipulate the global parameters. When you are manipulating the text, you can use the following:

- To select more than one letter, use **Ctrl**+click.
- If you click a letter with **Shift** held down, the clicked letter will be selected, all other previously selected letters will be de-selected.
- The tracking symbols only appear when you select more than one letter.
- You can change the font and font type for individual characters.
- When you select letters in the **Text** field, letters are also selected in the viewport [see Fig. 16].

To reset the parameters, click **Reset Parameters**, the **Reset Text** dialog box appears [see Fig. 17]. Select the options that you want to reset and then click **Reset**.

Geometry Rollout
The parameters in this rollout allow you to create depth using the **Extrude** and **Bevel** functions.

Values As Strings
You can also use the **TextPlus** object to display the value of an object's parameter in the viewport. You can also show any value that can be returned from a script or expression. The value will dynamically update in the viewport when it changes.

To see this feature in action, create a **TextPlus** object in a viewport and then type **radius:** in the **Text** field of the **Parameters** rollout. Create a sphere in a viewport. In the **Parameters** rollout of the **TextPlus** object, click **Set Value as Text** to open the **Edit Value As Text** dialog box. In this dialog box, select **Script** from the **Value Options** group [see Fig. 18] and then click **Pick Value From Scene**. Now, click on the sphere and then choose **Object (Sphere) > Radius** from the popup [see Fig. 19] to make the connection.

Select **Real Number** from the drop-down list available in the **Display As** group and then set **Decimals** to **2**. Now, put the cursor at the end of the text typed in the **Text** field and click **Insert In Text** from the **Edit Value As Text** dialog box. Close the dialog box. The string **%[Value1]** is appended in the **Text** field [see Fig. 20]. Now, if you change the value of the **Radius** parameter, the value will be dynamically updated in the **TextPlus** object.

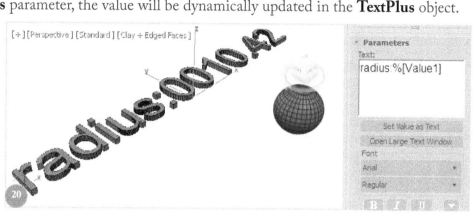

Extended Primitives

Extended primitives are a little complex than **Standard** primitives. 3ds Max offers thirteen extended primitives, see Fig. 21. You can combine the **Extended** primitives with the **Standard** primitives and modifiers to create refined models. You can interactively create **Extended** primitives in the viewport using the mouse and most of the primitives can be generated by entering precise values using the keyboard. You can specify the

parameters before creating the **Extended** primitives as well as modify them later from the **Parameters** rollout in the **Modify** panel. Let's take a look at the commonly used **Extended** primitives. Experiment with the primitives that are not covered in this section. They are straight forward and you can easily understand their parameters by changing them from the **Parameters** rollout.

Hedra
You can use this primitive to create a different types of polyhedra objects [see Fig. 22]. Table 6 summarizes the controls in the **Parameters** rollout.

Table 6: The parameters in the **Hedra**'s **Parameters** rollout	
Group	**Description**
Family Group	The parameters in this group allow you to choose the type of polyhedral you want to create. **Tetra** creates a tetrahedron. **Cube/Octa** creates a cubic or octahedral polyhedron. **Dodec/Icos** creates a dodecahedron or icosahedron. **Star 1** and **Star 2** create two different star-shaped polyhedron.
Family Parameters Group	The **P** and **Q** parameters in this group change the geometry back and forth between the vertices and faces. In Fig. 23, the left polyhedron has **P** and **Q** values set to **0** each whereas the polyhedron on the right has the **P** and **Q** values set to **0.3** each. The combined value of **P** and **Q** can be equal to or less than **1**.
Axis Scaling Group	The **P**, **Q**, and **R** parameters in this group allow you to push or pull the corresponding facets in or out. The polyhedron at the left in Fig. 24 is created with the default parameters. For the polyhedron at the right, I have changed the **Q** and **R** values to **120** and **150**, respectively. On clicking **Reset**, the axes return to their default values.
Vertices Group	The parameters in this group determine the internal geometry of each facet of the polyhedron.
Radius	Sets the radius of the polyhedron.

Note: Creating extended primitives
*To save some space, I am not writing the process to create the **Extended** primitives. You can easily create them using the standard click-drag methods as done in the **Standard Primitives** section.*

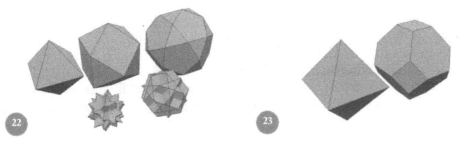

ChamferBox

You can use this primitive to create a box with beveled or round edges [see Fig. 25]. Most of the parameters in the **Parameters** rollout are similar to that of the **Box** primitive. Table 7 lists the parameters that are unique to **ChamferBox**.

Table 7: The parameters in the **ChamferBox**'s **Parameters** rollout	
Parameter	**Description**
Fillet	Slices the edges of the box. Higher the value you specify, the more refined fillet you will get.
Fillet Segs	Determines the number of segments in the filleted edges.
Smooth	Blends the display of the faces of the box. As a result, when rendered, the box appears smooth in the rendered results.

ChamferCylinder

This primitive creates a cylinder with beveled or rounded cap edges [see Fig. 26].

Most of the parameters in the **Parameters** rollout are similar to that of the **Cylinder** primitive. Table 8 lists the parameters that are unique to **ChamferCylinder**.

Table 8: The parameters in the **Chamfer Cylinder**'s **Parameters** rollout	
Parameter	**Description**
Fillet	It chamfers the top and bottom cap edges of the cylinder. The higher the value you specify, the more refined fillet will be.
Fillet Segs	Determines the number of segments in the filleted edges of the cylinder.

Architectural Objects

3ds Max provides several architectural objects that you can use as basic building blocks for architectural models such as home, offices, and so on. Table 9 summarizes the architectural objects that 3ds Max offers.

Table 9: The architectural objects	
Types	**Objects**
AEC Extended Objects	**Foliage**, **Railing**, and **Wall**
Stairs	**L-Type Stair**, **Spiral Stair**, **Straight Stair**, and **U-Type Stair**
Doors	**Pivot**, **Bifold**, and **Sliding**
Windows	**Awning**, **Casement**, **Fixed**, **Pivoted**, **Projected**, and **Sliding**

You can access all **AEC** objects from the **AEC Objects** sub-menu of the **Create** menu. You can also access these objects from the **Create** panel. Let's explore these objects.

Doors

The door objects allow you to quickly create a door. You can also set the door to be partially open even you can animate the opening. 3ds Max offers three types of doors. Table 10 summarizes these types.

Table 10: The door types	
Type	**Description**
Pivot	This door is hinged on one side only [see Fig. 27]. You can also make the door double-door, each hinged on its outer edge.
Bifold	This door is hinged in the middle as well as on the side. You can use this object to model a set of double doors [see Fig. 28].
Sliding	This type of door has a fixed half and a sliding half [see Fig. 29].

27

Tip: Navigating viewport
*If while creating **AEC** objects, you need to navigate the interface between clicks, drag **MMB** to pan the viewport, **Alt+MMB** drag to orbit the viewport, and **Alt+Ctrl+Scroll** to zoom the viewport.*

To create a door, click **Command** panel > **Create** panel > **Geometry** and then choose **Doors** from the drop-down list. In the **Object Type** rollout, choose the type of the door you want to create and then set the desired create options from the rollouts. Drag the mouse in the viewport to create the first two points to define the width and angle of the base of the door. Now, release the mouse button and drag to define the depth of the door and click to set. Drag the mouse to define the height of the door and then click to finish.

Assigning Material to Doors

By default, 3ds Max assigns five different IDs to the door you create. The default **Door-Template Multi-Subobject** material is found in the **Ace Templates.mat** material library. Fig. 30 shows the ID numbers and their associated parts in the door. 3ds Max does not assign a material to the door object. If you want to use the default material, you need to open the library in the material editor and then assign the material to your object. Table 11 summarizes the material IDs assigned to doors.

Table 11: The material IDs	
ID	Component
1	Font
2	Back
3	Inner Bevel. This ID is used for glazing when you set **Panels** to **Glass** or **Beveled**.
4	Frame
5	Inner Door

Tip: The Ace Template.mat library
You can find this library at the following location:
C:\Program Files\Autodesk\3ds Max 2021\materiallibraries.

Windows

The window objects in 3ds Max allow you to create the appearance of a window. You can also set the window to be partially open even you can animate the opening. 3ds Max offers six types of windows. Table 12 summarizes the window types.

Table 12: The window types	
Type	Description
Casement	It is two-door like sashes arrangement that can swing inward or outward [see Fig. 31].
Pivoted	It pivots vertically or horizontally at the center of its sash [see Fig. 32].

Table 12: The window types

Type	Description
Projected	It has three sashes two of which open like awning in opposite directions [see Fig. 33].
Sliding	It has two sashes one of which slides vertically or horizontally [see Fig. 34].
Fixed	It does not open [see Fig. 35].
Awning	It has a sash that is hinged at the top [see Fig. 36].

To create a window, click **Command** panel > **Create** panel > **Geometry** and then choose **Windows** from the drop-down list. In the **Object Type** rollout, choose the type of the window you want to create and then create the window in the viewport using click-drag operations.

Assigning Material to Windows

By default, 3ds Max assigns five different IDs to the window you create. The default **Window-Template Multi-Subobject** material is found in the **Ace Templates.mat** material library. Fig. 37 shows the ID numbers and their associated parts in a window. 3ds Max does not assign a material to the window object. If you want to use the default material, you need to open the library in the material editor and then assign the material to your object. Table 13 summarizes the material IDs assigned to the windows.

Table 13: The material IDs

ID	Component
1	Front Rails
2	Back Rails
3	Panels. The Opacity is set to 50%.
4	Front Frame
5	Back Frame

37

Stairs

3ds Max allows you to create four different types of stairs. The following table summarizes the types of stairs.

Table 14: The stairs types

Type	Description
Spiral Stair	It allows you to create a spiral staircase. You can specify the radius and number of revolutions. You can also add stringers, center pole, and more to the stairs [see Fig. 38].
Straight Stair	It allows you to create simple straight stairs [see Fig. 39].
L-Type Stair	It lets you create the L-Type stairs [see Fig. 40].
U-Type Stair	It lets you create the U-Type stairs [see Fig. 41].

To create a stair, click **Command** panel > **Create** panel > **Geometry** and then choose **Stairs** from the drop-down list. In the **Object Type** rollout, choose the type of the stair you want to create and then create the stair in the viewport using click-drag operations.

Assigning Material to Stairs

By default, 3ds Max assigns five different IDs to the stairs you create. The default **Stairs-Template Multi-Subobject** material is found in the **Ace Templates.mat** material library. 3ds Max does not assign a material to the stairs object. If you want to use the default material, you need to open the library in the material editor and then assign the material to your object. Table 15 summarizes the material IDs assigned to the stairs.

Table 15: The material IDs	
ID	**Component**
1	Treads of the stairs.
2	Front riser of the stairs.
3	Bottom, back, and sides of the risers of the stairs.
4	Center pole of the stairs.
5	Handrails of the stairs.
6	Carriage of the stairs.
7	Stringers of the stairs.

AEC Extended Objects

AEC stands for **Architecture Engineer Construction**. These objects are designed for use in the architectural, engineering, and construction fields. To create an **AEC** object, click **Command** panel > **Create** panel > **Geometry** and then choose **AEC Extended** from the drop-down list. In the **Object Type** rollout, choose the type of object you want to create and then create the object in the viewport using click-drag operations.

Railing

This tool allows you to create railings in a 3ds Max scene. The railing object includes rails, posts, and fencing [see Fig. 42]. You can create railing by specifying the orientation and height. You can also use a spline object to create railing along with it. If you edit the spline, the railing object updates to follow the path. You can use the railing object with the stair object to create a complete stair.

To create a railing, click **Command** panel > **Create** panel > **Geometry** and then choose **AEC Extended** from the drop-down list. In the **Object Type** rollout, click **Railing** and then create the railing in the viewport using click-drag operations.

Assigning Material to Railings

By default, 3ds Max assigns five different IDs to the railings you create. The default **Rail-Template Multi-Subobject** material is found in the **Ace Templates.mat** material library. 3ds Max does not assign a material to the railing objects. If you want to use the default material, you need to open the library in the material editor and then assign the material to your object. Table 16 summarizes the material IDs assigned to railings.

ID	Component
Table 16: The material IDs	
1	Lower rails
2	Posts of the railing
3	Solid fill of the railing
4	Top of the railing
5	Pickets of the railing

Foliage

You can use this tool to place various kinds of tree species in a scene [see Figs. 43 and 44]. This tool can produce good looking trees efficiently. You can define the height, density, pruning, seed, canopy display, and level of detail for the **Foliage** object.

To create a tree, click **Command** panel > **Create** panel > **Geometry** and then choose **AEC Extended** from the drop-down list. In the **Object Type** rollout, click **Foliage.** In the **Favorite**

Plants rollout, either drag a tree to add to the scene or select the plant and then click on the viewport to place it. You can also double-click on a plant in the **Favorite Plants** rollout.

Tip: Placing plants in the scene
*You can use the **Spacing** tool to place plants along a path.*

Wall

The **Wall** tool is used to create walls [see Fig. 45] in 3ds Max. The wall object is made up of three sub-object types: **Vertex**, **Segment**, and **Profile** that you can use to edit it.

You can create the wall in any viewport but for vertical walls, you should use a **Perspective**, **Camera**, or **Top** viewport. To create a wall, set the **Width** and **Height** parameters, and then click in a viewport. Now, release the mouse button and then drag to specify the length, click again.

If you want to create a single wall component, **RMB** click, else continue clicking. To finish creating a room, click on an end segment; 3ds Max displays the **Weld Point** dialog box. You can use the options in this dialog box to either weld the two end vertices into a single vertex or you can keep the two end vertices distinct. **RMB** click to finish the wall.

Assigning Material to Walls

By default, 3ds Max assigns five different IDs to the walls you create. The default **Wall-Template Multi-Subobject** material is found in the **Ace Templates.mat** material library. 3ds Max does not assign a material to the wall object. If you want to use the default material, you need to open the library in the material editor and then assign the material to the object.

Table 17 summarizes the material IDs assigned to the walls.

Table 17: The material IDs assigned to the walls

ID	Component
1	Vertical ends of the wall.
2	Outside of the wall.
3	Inside of the wall.
4	Top of the wall, including any edges cut out of the wall.
5	Bottom of the wall.

Note: ID 2 and 3
The definitions of ID 2 and 3 is interchangeable because the inside and outside of the wall depend on your point-of-view and how you created the wall object.

Note: Inserting doors and windows in a wall
3ds Max automatically makes the opening for doors and windows in a wall object. It also makes the linked doors and windows children of the wall object. To do this, directly create doors and windows on the wall by snapping to its faces, vertices, or edges.

Tip: Making opening using Boolean operations
*You can also make openings in a wall using the **Boolean** operations. Single wall with many doors and windows can slow down your system. To speed up, use multiple walls instead of a single wall. You can also collapse the stack to speed up the performance of your system.*

Hands-on Exercises

Exercise 1: Creating a Sofa
In this exercise, we will model a sofa using the **Box** primitive [see Fig. E1]. Table E1 the exercise.

Table E1	
Skill level	Beginner
Time to complete	30 Minutes
Topics	• Specifying the Units for the Exercise • Creating One Seat Section of the Sofa • Creating Corner Section of the Sofa
Resources folder	**prim-arch-objects**

Table E1	
Units	**US Standard – Decimal Inches**
Final file	**sofa-finish.max**

Specifying the Units for the Exercise

Follow these steps:

1. From the **Customize** menu choose **Units Setup**. In the **Units Setup** dialog box that appears, select **US Standard** from the **Display Unit Scale** group. Next, choose **Decimal Inches** from the drop-down list located below **US Standard** [see Fig. E2] and then click **OK** to accept the change.

What just happened?
*Here, I have set the display units for the scene. The units that you set here are used to measure geometry in the scene. You can also set the lighting units using this dialog box. Apart from the display units, you can also set the system units that 3ds Max uses for the internal mechanism. To view parameters available for changing system units, click **System Unit Setup** in the **Units Setup** dialog box.*

2. **RMB** click on any snap toggle button in the **Main** toolbar. In the **Grid and Snap Settings**
dialog box that appears, choose the **Home Grid** panel and then set **Grid Spacing** to **3**,
Major Lines every Nth Grid Line to **4**, and **Perspective View Grid Extent** to **10**. Close
the **Grid and Snap Settings** dialog box.

3. From the **File** menu, choose **Save** to open the **Save File As** dialog box. In the **File name**
text box type **sofa-finish.max** and then click **Save** to save the file.

Creating One Seat Section of the Sofa
Follow these steps:

1. In the **Create** panel 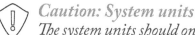, click **Geometry** , and then in the **Object Type** rollout, click
Box. In the **Perspective** viewport, drag out a box of any size. Go to the **Modify** panel
and then in the **Parameters** rollout, set **Length** to **25.591**, **Width** to **25.591**, and
Height to **1**.

2. **RMB** click on the **Select and Move** tool ⊕ in the **Main** toolbar to open the **Move Transform Type-In** dialog box and then set **X** to **0**, **Y** to **0**, and **Z** to **11.42** in the **Absolute: World** group. Close the dialog box. Click **Zoom Extents All** 🔍 to zoom on **Box001** in all viewports [see Fig. E3].

What just happened?

*Here, I have set the position of the box using the **Move Transform Type-In** dialog box. This dialog box allows you to enter precise values for the move, rotate, and scale transforms. To open this dialog box, **RMB** click on the **Select and Move** ⊕, **Select and Rotate** 🔄, or **Select and Scale** 🔳 tool in the **Main** toolbar. You can also press **F12** while one of the aforesaid tools is active to open the dialog box.*

Tip: Transform Type-In boxes

*You can also use the **Transform Type-In** boxes in the **Status Bar**. To transform objects, ensure they are selected. Type the values in the **Transform Type-In** boxes and then press **Enter**. You can toggle between the absolute transform and relative transform by clicking the button available to the right of the **Selection Lock Toggle** button.*

3. In the **Create** panel, click **Geometry**, and then in the **Object Type** rollout, click **Box**. Activate the **Top** viewport. Expand the **Keyboard Entry** rollout, and set **Length** to **25.591**, **Width** to **1**, and **Height** to **11.417**. Click **Create**. Click **Align** 🔲 on the **Main** toolbar. Now, click **Box001**. In the **Align Selection** dialog box that appears, set the parameters, as shown in Fig. E4. Click **OK** to accept the changes made [see Fig. E5].

4. Align **Box001** and **Box002** using **Select and Move** [see Fig. E6]. Click **Mirror** 🔳 on the **Main** toolbar to open the **Mirror** dialog box. In this dialog box, make sure **X** is

selected in the **Mirror Axis** group. Select **Copy** from the **Clone Selection** group and then set **Offset** to **24.591**. Click **OK** to accept the changes made and create a mirror copy of **Box002** [see Fig. E7].

5. Activate the **Top** viewport. In the **Create** panel, click **Geometry**, and then in the **Object Type** rollout, click **Box**. Expand the **Keyboard Entry** rollout and then set **Length** to **1**, **Width** to **25.591**, and **Height** to **25.984**. Click **Create** to create a box with the name **Box004**. Make sure **Box004** is selected.

6. Activate the **Top** viewport. Click **Align** 📇 on the **Main** toolbar and then click **Box001**. In the **Align Selection** dialog box that appears, set the parameters shown in Fig. E8 and click **OK** to align the objects [see Fig. E9].

7. Activate the **Top** viewport. In the **Create** panel, click **Geometry**, and then in the **Object Type** rollout, click **Box**. Expand the **Keyboard Entry** rollout and then set **Length** to **1**, **Width** to **23.591**, and **Height** to **11.417**. Click **Create** to create a box with the name **Box005**. Next, align it as shown in Fig. E10.

[+][Perspective][Standard][Clay + Edged Faces]

E10

8. Select **Box001** to **Box005** in the **Scene Explorer**. RMB click on the selection to open a **Quad** menu. Choose **Add Selected To > New Group** from the menu. In the **Group** dialog box that appears, type the group name as **oneSeat** and click **OK**.

Creating Corner Section of the Sofa

Follow these steps:

1. Collapse **oneSeat** in the **Scene Explorer**, if no already collapsed, **RMB** click on it and select **Clone** from the **Quad** menu. In the **Clone Options** dialog box that appears, select **Copy** from the **Object** group. Change the **Name** to **cornerSeat** and click **OK**.

2. In the **Perspective** viewport, move the **cornerSeat** to the right of **oneSeat**. Select **cornerSeat** in the **Scene Explorer**. Next, choose **Group > Open** from the menubar to open the group.

3. Select the right-most box. Go to the **Modify** panel, and then on the **Parameters** rollout, set **Height** to **25.984**. Choose **Group > Close** from the menubar to close the group. Fig. E11 shows the **cornerSeat** and **oneSeat** objects. Now, make various combinations of **oneSeat** and **cornerSeat** by making copies of them [see Fig. E12]. Press **CTRL+S** to save the file.

[+][Perspective][Standard][Clay + Edged Faces]

E11   E12

Exercise 2: Creating a Coffee Table

In this exercise, you will model a coffee table using the **Cylinder** and **Torus** primitives [see Fig. E1]. Table E2 summarizes the exercise.

E1

Table E2	
Skill level	Beginner
Time to complete	20 Minutes
Topics	• Specifying the Units for the Exercise • Creating the Coffee Table
Resources folder	**prim-arch-objects**
Units	**Metric - Centimeters**
Final file	**coffee-table-finish.max**

Specifying the Units for the Exercise

Follow these steps:

1. Reset 3ds Max. From the **Customize** menu choose **Units Setup**. In the **Units Setup** dialog box that appears, select **Metric** from the **Display Unit Scale** group. Next, select **Centimeters** from the drop-down list located below **Metric**, if already not selected. Click **OK** to accept the change.

2. **RMB** click on any snap toggle button in the **Main** toolbar. In the **Grid and Snap Settings** dialog box that appears, choose the **Home Grid** panel and then set **Grid Spacing** to **3**, **Major Lines every Nth Grid Line** to **4**, and **Perspective View Grid Extent** to **10**. Close the **Grid and Snap Settings** dialog box.

3. From the **File menu**, choose **Save** to open the **Save File As** dialog box. In the **File name** text box type **coffee-table-finish.max** and click **Save** to save the file.

Creating the Coffee Table

Follow these steps:

1. In the **Create** panel, click **Geometry**, and then in the **Object Type** rollout, click **Cylinder**. Activate the **Top** viewport. Expand the **Keyboard Entry** rollout, and set **Radius** to **37.5** and **Height** to **2**. In the **Parameters** layout, set **Height Segments** to **1**, **Cap Segments** to **1**, and **Sides** to **64**. Click **Create** from the **Keyboard Entry** rollout.

2. In the **Create** panel, click **Geometry**, and then in the **Object Type** rollout, click **Torus**. Create a torus in the **Top** viewport. Go to the **Modify** panel and then in the **Parameters** rollout set **Radius 1** to **37.5**, **Radius 2** to **1.581**, **Segments** to **100**, and **Sides** to **12**.

3. Click **Select and Place** [⊕] tool on the **Main** toolbar and then drag torus onto the cylinder to align the two objects [see Fig. E2]. If required, use the **Move** tool to align the two objects.

4. Select **Torus001** and **Cylinder001** and then activate the **Front** viewport by **MMB** clicking on it. Click **Select and Move** in the **Main** toolbar and then press **Shift**, move the selection down by **30** units along the negative **Y** direction. In the **Clone Options** dialog box that appears, choose **Copy** from the **Object** group and click **OK** to create a copy of the selected objects [see Fig. E3].

5. In the **Create** panel, click **Geometry**, and then in the **Object Type** rollout, click **Cylinder**. Create a cylinder in the **Top** viewport. Go to the **Modify** panel and then in the **Parameters** rollout, set **Radius** to **1.2**, **Height** to **41**, **Height Segments** to **1**, and **Sides** to **18**.

6. Make sure that **Select and Move** tool is active and then in the **Status Bar**, enter **-40.246**, **0**, and **-35.352** in the **Transform Type-In** boxes to place the cylinder [see Fig. E4].

7. In the **Hierarchy** panel of the **Command** panel, click **Use Working Pivot** from the **Working Pivot** rollout.

8. Choose **Array** from the **Tools** menu. Set the parameters in the **Array** dialog box, as shown in Fig. E5 and click **OK** to create two more copies of the cylinder [see Fig. E6].

9. Select all objects from the **Scene Explorer** and then choose **Group > Group** from menubar. Name the group **coffeeTable**. Press **CTRL+S** to save the file.

Exercise 3: Creating a Foot Stool

In this exercise, you will model a foot stool using the **ChamferBox** and **OilTank** extended primitives [see Fig. E1]. Table E3 summarizes the exercise.

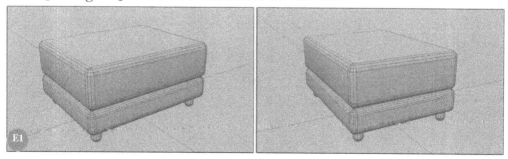

Table E3	
Skill level	Beginner
Time to complete	20 Minutes
Topics	• Specifying the Units for the Exercise • Creating the Stool

Table E3	
Resources folder	**prim-arch-objects**
Units	**US Standard – Decimal Inches**
Final file	**foot-stool-finish.max**

Specifying the Units for the Exercise
Follow these steps:

1. Reset 3ds Max. From the **Customize** menu choose **Units Setup**. In the **Units Setup** dialog box that appears, select the **US standard** option from the **Display Unit Scale** group. Next, select **Decimal Inches** from the drop-down list located below the **US Standard** option, if already not selected. Click **OK** to accept the change.

2. **RMB** click on any snap toggle button on the **Main** toolbar. In the **Grid and Snap Settings** dialog box that appears, choose the **Home Grid** panel and then set **Grid Spacing** to **3**, **Major Lines every Nth Grid Line** to **4**, and **Perspective View Grid Extent** to **10**. Close the **Grid and Snap Settings** dialog box.

Creating the Stool
Follow these steps:

1. In the **Create** panel, click **Geometry**, and then select **Extended Primitives** from the drop-down list located below **Geometry**. In the **Object Type** rollout, click **ChamferBox**. Create a chamfer box in the **Top** viewport.

2. Go to the **Modify** panel and then in the **Parameters** rollout set **Length** to **24.8**, **Width** to **31.5**, **Height** to **5**, **Fillet** to **1.2**, and **Fillet Segs** to **5**. Rename the chamfer box to **baseGeo**.

3. Click **Select and Move** in the **Main** toolbar and then enter **0** in all **Transform Type-In** boxes in the **Status Bar** to place the box at the origin. Press **Shift+Ctrl+Z** to zoom the chamfer box to its extents.

4. In the **Perspective** viewport, press **Shift** and drag **baseGeo** along the **+Z** axis about **5** units. In the **Clone Options** dialog box that appears, make sure **Copy** is selected from the **Object** group. Type **seatGeo** in the name text box and click **OK**.

5. Go to the **Modify** panel and then in the **Parameters** rollout set **Height** to **8**, **Fillet** to **0.72**, and **Fillet Segs** to **3**. Align the boxes [see Fig. E2].

6. In the **Create** panel, click **Geometry**, and then select **Extended Primitives** from the drop-down list located below **Geometry**. In the **Object Type** rollout, click **OilTank**. Create an oil tank in the **Top** viewport.

7. Go to the **Modify** panel and then in the **Parameters** rollout set **Radius** to **1.1**, **Height** to **5**, **Sides** to **25**, and **Cap Height** to **0.9**. Rename oil tank as **legGeo** and then align it [see Fig. E3].

8. Create three more copies of **legGeo** and align it viewports [see Fig. E4].

Exercise 4: Creating a Bar Table

In this exercise, you will model a bar table using the **ChamferBox** and **ChamferCyl** extended primitives [see Fig. E1]. Table E4 summarizes the exercise.

Table E4	
Skill level	Beginner
Time to complete	40 Minutes
Topics	• Specifying the Units for the Exercise • Creating the Bar Table
Resources folder	**prim-arch-objects**
Units	**US Standard – Decimal Inches**
Final file	**bar-table-finish.max**

Specifying the Units for the Exercise
Follow these steps:

1. Reset 3ds Max. From the **Customize** menu choose **Units Setup**. In the **Units Setup** dialog box that appears, select the **US standard** option from the **Display Unit Scale** group. Next, select **Decimal Inches** from the drop-down list located below the **US Standard** option, if already not selected. Click **OK** to accept the change.

2. **RMB** click on any snap toggle button on the **Main** toolbar. In the **Grid and Snap Settings** dialog box that appears, choose the **Home Grid** panel and then set **Grid Spacing** to **3**, **Major Lines every Nth Grid Line** to **4**, and **Perspective View Grid Extent** to **4**. Close the **Grid and Snap Settings** dialog box.

Creating the Bar Table
Follow these steps:

1. In the **Create** panel, click **Geometry**, and then select **Extended Primitives** from the drop-down list located below **Geometry**. In the **Object Type** rollout, click **ChamferCyl**.

2. Create a cylinder in the **Top** viewport. Go to the **Modify** panel and then in the **Parameters** rollout set **Radius** to **13.78**, **Height** to **1.5**, **Fillet** to **0.15**, **Fillet Segs** to **5**, and **Sides** to **50**. Rename the cylinder as **topGeo**.

3. Click **Select and Move** in the **Main** toolbar and then enter **0** in all **Transform Type-In** boxes in the **Status Bar** to place **topGeo** at the origin. Create another chamfer cylinder in the **Top** viewport and rename it as **supportGeo**.

4. Go to the **Modify** panel and then in the **Parameters** rollout set **Radius** to **1.3**, **Height** to **38**, **Fillet** to **0**, **Fillet Segs** to **1**, and **Sides** to **18**. Now, align **topGeo** and **supportGeo** in viewports [see Fig. E2].

5. In the **Create** panel, click **Geometry**, and then choose **Standard Primitives** from the drop-down list located below **Geometry**. In the **Object Type** rollout, click **Tube**. Create a tube in the **Top** viewport. Go to the **Modify** panel and then in the **Parameters** rollout set **Radius 1** to **4**, **Radius 2** to **1.3**, **Height** to **3**, and **Sides** to **50**. Rename tube as **tubeGeo**. Align the tube, as shown in Fig. E3.

6. In the **Create** panel, click **Geometry**, and then select **Extended Primitives** from the drop-down list located below **Geometry**. In the **Object Type** rollout, click **ChamferBox**. Create a box in the **Top** viewport. Go to the **Modify** panel and then in the **Parameters** rollout set **Length** to **2.1**, **Width** to **12.8**, **Height** to **1.6**, **Fillet** to **0.1**, and **Fillet Segs** to **6**. Rename the box as **legGeo**.

7. From the **Object-Space Modifiers** section of the **Modifier** list, select **Taper**. In the **Parameters** layout, set **Amount** to **-0.64**. Set **Primary** to **X** in the **Taper Axis** area. Now, align **legGeo** with **tubeGeo** [see Fig. E4].

8. Create another chamfer box in the **Top** viewport. Go to the **Modify** panel and then in the **Parameters** rollout set **Length** to **1.57**, **Width** to **5.6**, **Height** to **0.64**, **Fillet** to **0.07**, **Width Segs** to **32**, and **Fillet Segs** to **3**.

9. From the **Object-Space Modifiers** section of the **Modifier** list, select **Bend**. In the **Parameters** layout, set **Angle** to **213**. Select **X** radio button in the **Bend Axis** area [see Fig. E5].

10. Create a chamfer cylinder in the **Top** viewport. Go to the **Modify** panel and then in the **Parameters** rollout set **Radius** to **1.362**, **Height** to **1.72**, **Fillet** to **0.1**, **Fillet Segs** to **5**, and **Sides** to **50**.

11. Align the cylinder with the box and then group them with the name **grpRoller**. Align **grpRoller** with **legGeo** [see Fig. E6] and then group them as **grpLeg**.

12. Ensure **grpLeg** is selected and activate the **Perspective** viewport. Select **Use Transform Coordinate Center** ![icon] from the **Use Center** flyout the **Main** toolbar. Choose **Array** from the **Tools** menu. Now, set the values in the **Array** dialog box, as shown in Fig. E7, and then click **OK** to create **3** more copies [see Fig. E8].

Quiz

Evaluate your skills to see how many questions you can answer correctly.

Fill in the Blanks
Fill in the blanks in each of the following statements:

1. You can use the **GeoSphere** primitive to create spheres and geo-hemispheres based on three classes of polyhedrons: _____, _____, and _____.

2. To constrain the base of the pyramid to a square, drag with the _____ key held down.

3. The default **Window-Template Multi-Subobject** material is found in the _____ material library.

True or False

State whether each of the following is true or false:

1. You can change the name of an object from the **Name and Color** rollout.

2. You can create a cube object using the **Box** tool.

3. The **GeoSphere** tool produces a smooth shape than the **Sphere** tool.

Practice Activities

Explore Extended primitives: From the **Command** panel > **Create** panel, choose **Geometry**, and then **AEC Extended**. Pay attention to each object's parameters to get familiar with what each object is capable of.

Explore Architectural objects: From the **Command** panel > **Create** panel, choose **Geometry**, and then **Extended Primitives**. Pay attention to the parameters of **Wall** and **Railing** to get familiar with what each object is capable of.

Work with the Foliage object: Create few **Foliage** objects in the scene and then use the placement and alignment tools that you learned in **Introduction to 3ds Max - II** chapter to place and align them.

Create a roadside sign: Using the **Box**, **Pyramid**, and **Box** primitives, create the road sign as shown in Fig. A1.

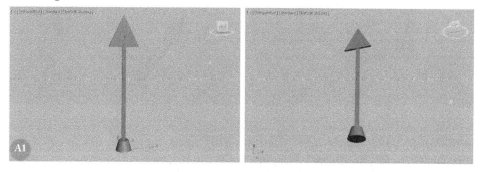

Create a robot model: Using the **Standard** primitives, create the model of the robot, as shown in Fig. A2.

Hints:

- *The primitives used in the model shown in Fig. A2 are **Box**, **Sphere**, **Cylinder**, **Pyramid**, **Cone**, **Torus**, and **Pipe**.*
- *The fingers are created using **Torus** primitives. Select **Slice On** in the **Parameters** rollout of the torus to create an opening in the torus.*
- *Use the **Auto Grid** and **Select and Place** features of 3ds Max to align and place body parts.*
- *Create one leg and then use the **Mirror** tool to create a copy on the other side. Apply the same concept on eyes and hands. Create a group before applying the **Mirror** tool.*
- *Create layers for different parts in **Layer Explorer**. For example, keep all geometries that make a hand in the hands layer, and so on.*
- *Try to use various features of the **Scene Explorer**.*

Create a coffee table: Create the model of the table using the **Box** primitive, as shown in A3.

Dimensions:
1: Length=35.433", Width=21.654", Height=1.5"
2: Length=34.037", Width=20.8", Height=1.5"
3: Length=2", Width=2", Height=13.78"

Create an 8-drawer model: Create the model of the 8-drawer model using the **Box** primitive, as shown in Fig. A4. Create the knobs using the **Sphere** and **Cylinder** primitives.

Dimensions:
1: *Length=65", Width=21", Height=1.5"*
2: *Length=2", Width=2", Height=35"*
3: *Length=60.997", Width=18.251", Height=30"*
4: *Length=27.225", Width=19.15", Height=11"*
5: *Length=27.225", Width=19.15", Height=7"*
6: *Length=12.871", Width=19.15", Height=5"*

Create a footstool model: Create the model of the footstool using the **ChamferCyl** primitive, as shown in Fig. A5.

Dimensions:
1: *Radius=14", Height=5.91", Fillet=0.32", Sides=24, and Fillet Segs=3*
2: *Radius=14", Height=7.5", Fillet=0.74", Sides=24, and Fillet Segs=3*
3: *Radius=1.104", Height=2.238", Fillet=0.276", and Fillet Segs=3*

Hint:
*Check **Slice On** for the cylinders and set **Slice To** to **–180**. Apply the **Taper** modifier to the legs of the stool.*

Create a sofa model: Create the sofa model using the **Chamfer Box** primitive, as shown in Fig. A6. Assume the dimensions.

Summary
The unit covered the following topics:

- Creating and modifying the **Standard** Primitives
- Creating and modifying the **Extended** Primitives
- Working with the **Architectural** objects
- Setting the project folder
- Using the **Align** and **Mirror** tools
- Creating clones
- Using the **Scene Explorer**
- Creating a group
- Setting grid spacings
- Using the **Transform Type-In** dialog box
- Using the **Array** dialog box
- Specifying the units for the scene

- Working with the polygon modeling tools
- Using the polygon modeling techniques
- Selecting polygon sub-objects
- Transforming sub-objects
- Soft selecting sub-objects

Unit 4: Polygon Modeling

In Unit 3, you have modeled objects using parametric modeling techniques. In parametric modeling, you create primitives from the **Create** panel and modify them using the creation parameters. Then, you transform the primitives using the transformation tools to create the shape of the models. **Parametric** modeling is powerful and easy but it has some limitations when it comes to creating complex models. **Surface** modeling, on the other hand, is more flexible and allows you to create any object that you can imagine. Once you convert an object to an editable object such as an editable poly, editable mesh, editable patch, or NURBS object; 3ds Max provides a specialized toolset to create the models.

Editable Poly Object

An editable poly object is an editable object with five sub-object levels: **Vertex**, **Edge**, **Border**, **Polygon**, and **Element**. Sub-objects such as vertices and edges are the basic building blocks of an object. Vertices are points in 3D space. They define the structure for other sub-objects such as edges and polygons. An edge is a line connecting two vertices. The connection forms one side of the polygon. An edge cannot be shared by more than two polygons. Also, the normals of the two polygons should be adjacent. When three or more edges combine together, they form a polygon. **Elements** are groups of contiguous polygons. A border can be described as the edge of a hole in the object. Fig. 1 shows various sub-object levels available for an editable poly object.

You can convert an object to an editable poly object by using one of the following methods:

1. Select an object in a viewport and then go to the **Modify** panel. Next, **RMB** click on the object entry in the stack display and then choose **Editable Poly** from the popup menu displayed [see Fig. 2].
2. Select the object in a viewport and then **RMB** click. Choose **transform** quadrant> **Convert To: > Convert to Editable Poly** [see Fig. 3].
3. Apply a modifier to a parametric object that makes the object a poly object. For example, the **Turn to Poly** modifier.
4. Apply the **Edit Poly** modifier.

Caution: Limitations of the Edit Poly modifier

*The **Edit Poly** modifier offers most of the capabilities of the **Editable Poly** object except the **Vertex Color Information**, the **Subdivision Surface** rollout, the **Weight** and **Crease** settings, and the **Subdivision Displacement** rollout.*

Note: Graphite modeling tools

*The option to convert an object to an editable poly is also available in the **Graphite Modeling Tools**. You will learn about these tools in a later unit.*

Selecting Sub-objects **UPDATED**

You can select sub-objects using one of the following ways:

1. Expand the object's hierarchy [by clicking the triangle] in the stack display and then choose a sub-object level [see Fig. 4]. The selected sub-object will be highlighted in the stack display.
2. Click a selection button from the **Selection** rollout [see Fig. 5].
3. **RMB** click on an object in a viewport and then choose the sub-object level from the upper-left quadrant [**tools 1**] of the **Quad** menu [see Fig. 6].
4. Choose a selection or transform tool and then click on the sub-objects in a viewport using the standard selection techniques.

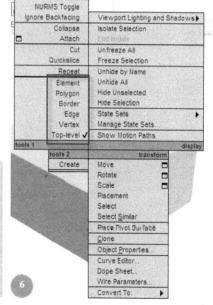

Note: Adding and removing from the selection

*To select a vertex, edge, polygon, or element, click it. To add to the sub-object selection, press and hold **Ctrl** and click. You can also drag a selection region to select a group of* *sub-objects. To subtract from the sub-object selection, press and hold **Alt** and click. You can also drag a selection region to deselect a group of sub-objects.*

 Tip: Locking selection ▌UPDATED

Once you make the sub-object selection, you can lock the selection by pressing **Shift+Ctrl+N**. *Locking the selection helps in unintentionally selecting other sub-objects. To release the lock, press* **Shift+Ctrl+N** *again. You can also lock the selection using the* **Lock Quad** *menu. To invoke this menu, press* **Spacebar**.

Tip: Keyboard shortcuts ▌UPDATED

You can use the numeric keys from **1** *to* **5** *to activate the* **Vertex**, **Edge**, **Border**, **Polygon**, *and* **Element** *sub-object levels, respectively. Press the key again to return to the* **Object** *level. For example, if you press* **1**, *the* **Vertex** *mode becomes active; press* **1** *again if you want to return to the* **Object** *level.*

Creating and Modifying Selections

The parameters available in the **Selection** and **Soft Selection** rollouts let you access different sub-object levels, as well as, give you the ability to create and modify selections. Let's have a look at the tools available in these two rollouts.

Selection Rollout

There are five buttons at the top of the **Selection** rollout. These buttons allow you to select the sub-object levels. Table 1 summarizes the functioning of these buttons:

Table 1: The sub-object buttons		
Button	**Icon**	**Description**
Vertex		It activates the **Vertex** sub-object level and allows you to select the vertex beneath the mouse pointer. Draw a region selection to select the vertices within the region.
Edge		It activates the **Edge** sub-object level and allows you to select the edge beneath the mouse pointer. Draw a region selection to select the edges within the region.
Border		It activates the **Border** sub-object level and allows you to select a set of edges that borders a hole in the geometry. In other words, you can select the edges that are on the border.
Polygon		It activates the **Polygon** sub-object level and allows you to select the polygon beneath the mouse pointer. Draw a region selection to select the polygons within the region.

Table 1: The sub-object buttons		
Button	**Icon**	**Description**
Element		It activates the **Element** sub-object level and allows you to select all contiguous polygons. Draw a region selection to select multiple elements within the region.

 Note: Border edges

*If the concept of border edges is not clear to you, I would recommend a simple exercise. Create a **Cylinder** primitive in the scene and then convert it to **Editable Poly**. Select the **Polygon** sub-object level and then click on the top face of the cylinder to select it. Press **Delete** to delete the top face. Now, activate the **Border** sub-object level, and click on the border to select the border element [see Fig. 7]. There is now only one border edge in the geometry that borders the hole in the cylinder.*

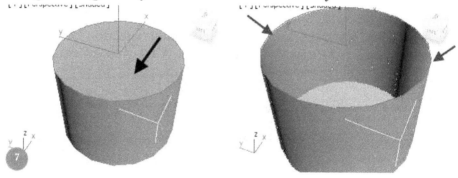

Working with Selection Sets

The **Named Selection Sets** list allows you to name a selection set [both at the object level as well as at the sub-object level] that you can recall later during the modeling process. For example, if you are modeling a face, you might want to select different sub-objects for various parts of the face. In such a case, you can create a selection set for a particular area of the face [nose, for example] and recall it later. It will save you a lot of time as you do not have to recreate the selection later during the modeling process.

Caution: Selection Set Names
The selection set names are case-sensitive.

Keep the following in mind while working with the named selection sets:

- You can transfer sub-objects selection from one modifier to another. You can also transfer the sub-object selection from one level to another in the modifier stack.
- You can transfer named selection sets only between the same types of sub-objects. For example, you cannot transfer a **Vertex** selection to a **Face** selection.

- You are only allowed to transfer selection sets between the modifiers that work on the same geometry type. For example, you cannot transfer a selection set from an **Edit Spline** modifier to an **Edit Poly** modifier.
- You can copy and paste selection sets between two modifiers assigned to two different objects. However, both modifiers should handle the same types of geometry.

 Caution: Changing Topology
If you modify the topology of the object, you might get unpredictable results when you use the named selection set.

To create a named selection set, select the objects or sub-objects that you want part of the set and then type the name of the selection set in the **Named Selection Sets** field [see Fig. 8] in the **Main** toolbar. Press **Enter** to create the selection set.

To recall a selection, select the name from the **Named Selection Sets** list. If you want to select more than one selection sets from the list, press **Ctrl** while selecting names. To remove a name from the selection, press and hold **Alt** and then click the name in the list.

Once you make a sub-object selection, you can perform the following tasks:

- You can move, rotate, and scale sub-objects using the standard transformation tools.
- You can apply the object-space modifiers.
- You can bind a space warp to the selection.
- If you have made the polygon selection, you can use the **Align**, **Normal Align**, and **Align To View** tools from the **Align** flyout of the **Main** toolbar.

Transforming a Sub-object Selection

If you are working with an editable object such as mesh, poly, patch, or spline, you can directly manipulate the selection using the transformations tools. However, if you are using a selection modifier such as **Mesh Select** or **Spline Select**, you need to use an **XFrom Modifier** to transform the selection.

Here's how it works:

1. Create a polygon primitive such as **Box** and then convert to an **Editable Poly** object.
2. Make a sub-object selection and move it using the **Select and Move** tool. You will notice that you can easily move the selection [see Fig. 9]. Press **Ctrl+Z** to undo the last operation and deselect everything. Now, apply the **Mesh Select** modifier [see Fig. 10] and then make a selection. Notice that the transformation tools are inactive on the **Main** toolbar.

3. Apply the **XFrom** modifier to the object. Expand the **XFrom** modifier in the stack display and select **Gizmo** [see Fig. 11]. Now, you can move the selection as required.

Cloning Sub-objects

When you **SHIFT**+transform [move, scale, or rotate] a sub-object selection, the **Clone Part of Mesh** dialog box appears [see Fig. 12]. This dialog box gives you two options: **Clone to Object** and **Clone to Element**. When you select **Clone To Object**, 3ds Max creates a separate object comprises the selected sub-objects. If you select **Clone to Element**, the selection is cloned and it becomes an element of the current object.

Converting Sub-Object Selections

If you make a sub-object selection, for example, a vertex selection, you can convert it to a different sub-object selection such as edge or face using the **Ctrl** and **Shift** keys:

- To convert a selection to a different sub-object selection, click on the sub-object level button in the **Selection** rollout with **Ctrl** held down [see Fig. 13].
- If you press **Ctrl+Shift** while clicking the sub-object level button, only those sub-objects will be selected whose source components were originally selected [see Fig. 14].
- If you press **Shift** while clicking the sub-object level button, only those sub-objects will be selected that border the selection [see Fig. 15].

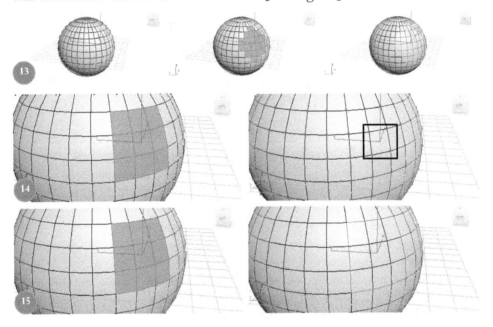

Note: Quad menu

The conversion commands are also available for the **Quad** *menu. To convert a selection,* **RMB** *click and then choose the desired option from the upper left quadrant* [***tools 1***] *of the* **Quad** *menu with* **Ctrl**, **Shift**, *or* **Ctrl+Shift** *held down.*

Now, let's explore the other options available in the **Selection** rollout. When **By Vertex** is selected, you can select the sub-objects that share the clicked vertex [see Fig. 16]. When **Ignore Backfacing** is selected, you can only select those sub-objects that are facing you. When off, you can select any sub-object beneath the mouse pointer.

When **By Angle** is selected and you select a polygon, all neighboring polygons are also selected based on the angle value specified by the spinner to the right of **By Angle** [see Fig. 17].

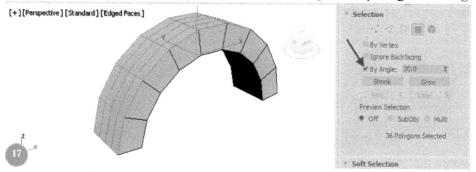

Shrink reduces the selection area by deselecting the outermost sub-objects [see Fig. 18]. On the other hand, **Grow** expands the selection in all possible directions [see Fig. 19].

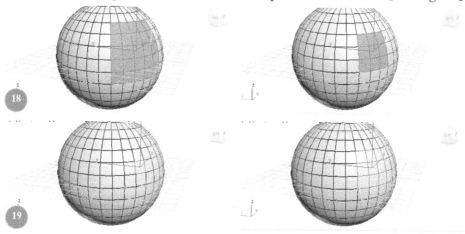

Ring lets you select an edge selection by selecting all edges parallel to the selected edges. To select an edge ring, select an edge[s] and then click **Ring** to select edges parallel to the selected edges [see Fig. 20].

💡 *Tip: Quickly selecting a ring/loop*
*Select an edge and then hover over another edge with **Shift** held down. This edge should be directly next to the previous selection (a consecutive edge). A yellow highlight will show the ring or loop to be selected. Now, click on the neighboring edge to select a ring.*

The spinner next to **Ring** allows you to move the selection in either direction to other edges in the same ring. The left image in Fig. 21 shows the two edges selected. When I clicked on the up arrow of the spinner the selection moved, as shown in the right image of Fig. 21. This feature works with only the **Edge** and **Border** sub-object types.

 Tip: Loop
If you have selected a loop, you can use the spinner to select the neighboring loop.

Loop allows you to expand edge selection as far as possible. The selection only propagates through four-way junctions. To select a loop, select an edge and then click **Loop** [see Fig. 22].

 Tip: Loop selection shortcut
You can quickly select a loop by double-clicking on an edge.

The spinner to the right of **Loop** allows you to move the selection in either direction to other edges in the same loop. If you have selected a ring, it allows you to move the ring selection. This feature works with the **Edge** and **Border** sub-objects. The parameters in the **Preview Selection** group allow you to preview a selection before actually selecting. When **Off** is selected, no preview will be available. When **SubObj** is selected, you can preview the selection at the current sub-object level. The preview appears in yellow color [see Fig. 23].

When **Multi** is selected, you can switch between various sub-object levels. For example, you can place the mouse pointer on an edge, the edge highlights, and clicking on the edge activates the **Edge** sub-object level and selects the edge. To select multiple sub-objects at the current level, press and hold **Ctrl** and move the mouse pointer[do not click] to add highlighted sub-objects to the preview. Now, to make the selection, click.

To remove sub-objects from the current selection, press and hold **Ctrl+Alt**. Now, move the mouse to highlight more sub-objects and then click a selected sub-object that you want to remove from the selection. This action deselects all highlighted sub-objects. The area below these parameters shows the information about the selected or highlighted polygons [see Fig. 24].

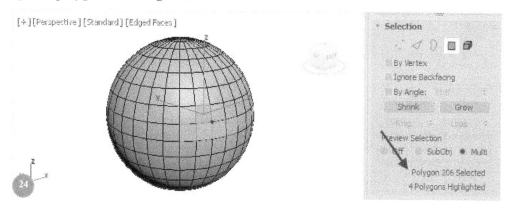

Soft Selection Rollout

The parameters in the **Soft Selection** rollout let you partially select the sub-objects in the vicinity of the selected sub-objects. As you transform the sub-objects, the sub-objects in the vicinity will be transformed smoothly [see Fig. 25]. The falloff appears in the viewport as a color spectrum [**ROYGB**: red, orange, yellow, green, and blue]. The sub-objects that you explicitly select coded in red color.

When **Edge Distance** is selected, 3ds Max limits the selection to a certain number of edges specified by the spinner to the right of **Edge Distance**. Fig. 26 shows the selection with the **Edge Distance** value set to **1** and **7**, respectively.

When **Affect Backfacing** is selected, those deselected faces whose normals face in the opposite direction to the average normal of the selected sub-objects are affected by the soft-selection. **Falloff** defines the distance in current units from the center to the edge of a sphere that defines the region of influence. The falloff curve appears below **Bubble**. **Pinch** affects the top point of the curve. **Bubble** lets you expand or shrink the falloff curve along the vertical axis. Experiment with these settings to get a better understanding of how these parameters affect the falloff curve. **Shaded Face Toggle** displays a color gradient in the viewport [see Fig. 27].

The gradient represents the weight on the faces of the geometry. This feature is only available when you are working with the editable poly or patch objects. **Lock Soft Selection** locks the soft selection to prevent any changes in the procedural selection.

The parameters in the **Paint Soft Selection** group, let you paint soft selection on the object using a brush. Click **Paint** and then drag the mouse pointer on the surface to paint the selection. **Blur** lets you soften the edges of the selection whereas **Revert** reverses the selection.

Object Level
When no sub-object level is active, you are at the **Object** level. The parameters available at the **Object** level are also available at all sub-object levels.

Edit Geometry Rollout
The **Edit Geometry** rollout provides global parameters for modifying a poly object. Let's have a look at these parameters:

Repeat Last
When clicked, 3ds Max repeats the most recently used command. For example, if you apply a command such as **Bevel** to some polygons and then want to apply the same settings to another set of polygons, select them, and then click **Repeat Last**. The same bevel settings will be applied to the last selected polygons.

Caution: Which commands are repeated?
Repeat Last *does not repeat all commands, for example, transformations. To check which command in 3ds Max will repeat, hover the mouse pointer on* **Repeat Last**. *A tooltip appears indicating which command will be repeated when you click this button [see Fig. 28].*

 Tip: Keyboard shortcut
You can also use the keyboard shortcuts to repeat the last command. If you are using the **3ds Max** *mode, press semicolon (;), and if you are using the* **Maya** *mode, press* **G**.

Constraints

The parameters in this rollout let you constrain the sub-objects transformations to edges, faces, or normals of the existing geometry. Table 2 summarizes the types of constraints.

Table 2: The Constraints types	
Type	**Description**
None	This is the default option. No constraints will be applied.
Edge	It constrains transformations to the edge boundaries [see Fig. 29].
Face	It constrains transformations to the face boundaries.
Normal	It allows the transformations along the normals.

Preserve UVs

When **Preserve UVs** is selected, 3ds Max allows you to edit the sub-objects without affecting the UV mapping. The image at the left of Fig. 30 is the original vertex position. The middle image shows the result when **Preserve UVs** is selected. I scaled the selected vertices inward to show the function of **Preserve UVs**. The image at the right of Fig. 30 shows the result when **Preserve UVs** is off.

Create

It allows you to create new geometry in the scene. The result produced by **Create** depends on which sub-object level is active. Table 3 summarizes the behavior of this command.

Table 3: Creating new geometry	
Level	**Description**
Object, Polygon, Element	Adds polygons by clicking existing or new vertices.
Vertex	Adds vertices.
Edge, Border	Adds edges between the pairs of the non-adjacent vertices on the same polygon.

To create geometry, activate a sub-object level, and then click **Create**. Now, in the active viewport click to create the geometry [see Fig. 31]. **RMB** click or press **Esc** to exit the tool.

Collapse

It allows you to collapse contiguous selection of the vertices, edges, borders, or polygons by welding their vertices to a vertex. The welded vertex is placed at the center of the selection [see Figs. 32 and 33].

Attach

Attach allows you to attach other geometries to the selected poly object. To attach the objects, select a poly object, and then click **Attach**. Now, click on the object that you want to attach; the **Attach** command remains active. If required, keep clicking on other objects to attach them to the selected object. **RMB** click or click **Attach** again to terminate the command.

You can also attach splines, patch objects, and NURBS surfaces to a poly object. If you attach a non-mesh object it is converted to an editable format. It becomes an element of the poly object [see Fig. 34].

On clicking **Attach List** available to the right of **Attach**, the **Attach List** dialog box appears. You can use this dialog box to attach multiple objects to the selected poly object.

Detach

Detach allows you to separate the selected sub-objects and corresponding polygons to an object or element. To detach sub-objects, select them and then click **Detach**. In the **Detach** dialog box that appears, type the name of the object in the **Detach as** field and then click **OK**.

There are two parameters in the **Detach** dialog box that let you detach sub-objects as an element or a clone. These parameters are **Detach To Element** and **Detach As Clone**. Select the required parameter and then click **OK**.

Slice Plane

This option is available at the sub-objects levels only. The parameters in the group are known as knife tools. These tools subdivide along a poly plane [slice] or in a specific area [cut]. When you click **Slice Plane**, a gizmo appears in viewports. Also, the **Slice** and **Reset Plane** tools become active in the rollout. Transform the **Gizmo** in a viewport and then click **Slice** to create the edges where the gizmo intersects the edges [see Fig. 35]. Click **Slice Plane** to deactivate the command. Click **Reset Plane** to reset the position of the gizmo.

If you select **Split**, 3ds Max creates double sets of vertices that allow you to create a hole in the geometry [see Fig. 36].

QuickSlice

QuickSlice allows you to quickly sub-divide a geometry without making adjustments to the gizmo. To slice a geometry, make a selection and then click **QuickSlice**. Now, drag the cursor in a viewport to create a slicing line. Release the mouse button to slice the selection [see Fig. 37]. You can continue slicing the geometry or **RMB** click to exit the command.

You can use **QuickSlice** in any viewport including **Perspective** and camera. 3ds Max also shows you the preview of the slice before you commit the command.

 Caution: Polygons and elements
*If you are at the **Polygon** or **Element** level, only selected sub-objects are sliced. If you want to slice the entire object, use any sub-object level other than **Polygon** or **Element**.*

Cut

Cut allows you to subdivide polygons by creating edges from one polygon to another or within the polygons. It is available at the object level as well as at all the sub-object levels. To create edges, click **Cut** and then click at the start point. Move the mouse pointer and then click on another point to create connected edges [see Fig. 38]. You can continue moving and clicking to create the edges. **RMB** click to exit the command.

 Tip: Mouse pointer
The shape of the mouse pointer shows the type of sub-object it is over. Fig. 39 shows the shape of the mouse pointer when you are cutting to a vertex, edge, or polygon, respectively.

MSmooth

Applies smoothing to the selected area of the poly object [see Fig. 40]. Click **Settings** to the right of **MSmooth** to open the **MeshSmooth** caddy control [see Fig. 41] that allows you to adjust the settings used by the **MSmooth** command. Table 4 summarizes the **MeshSmooth** caddy control.

Table 4: The **MeshSmooth** caddy control	
Control	**Description**
Smoothness	**Smoothness** in a poly mesh is created by adding polygons to it. It determines how sharp the corners of the mesh are. A value of **1** adds polygons to all vertices of the mesh. If you set **Smoothness** to **0**, no polygons will be created.
Separate by Smoothing Groups	When on, the polygons are created at the edges that share at least one smoothing group.
Separate by Materials ID	When on, the polygons are created at the edges that share the material IDs.

Tessellate

It subdivides the polygons based on the tessellate settings that can be accessed by clicking **Settings** on the right of **Tessellate**. Fig. 42 shows the **Tessellate** caddy control. Table 5 summarizes the **Tessellate** caddy control.

Table 5: The **Tessellate** caddy control	
Control	**Description**
Type	There are two tessellation types available: **Edge** and **Face**. When **Edge** is selected, 3ds Max inserts vertices at the center of each edge and then connect them. The polygons created are the number of sides of the original polygon [see Fig. 43]. On selecting the **Face** type, a vertex is created at the center of each polygon and then that vertex is connected to the original vertices. The number of polygons created is equal to the number of sides of the original polygon [see Fig. 44].
Tension	It is available only for the **Edge** type. It determines the edge tension value. A positive value pulls the edges outward whereas a negative value pulls them inward [see Fig. 45].

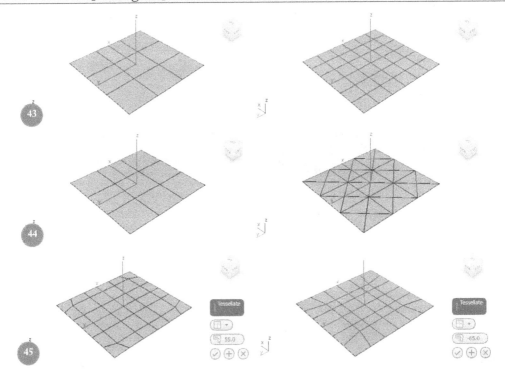

Make Planar

Makes all selected sub-objects to be coplanar. The sub-objects are forced to be coplanar along the average surface normal of the selection [see Fig. 46]. If you are at the **Object** level, all vertices of the object will be forced to be coplanar. The **X**, **Y**, and **Z** buttons let you align the plane with the local coordinate system of the object. For example, if you click **Z**, the selection will be aligned according to the local **XY** axis [see Fig. 47].

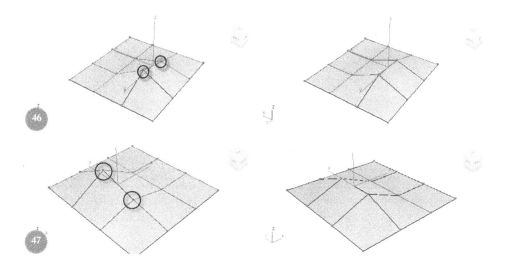

View Align

It aligns all vertices of the object to the plane of the active viewport. It affects vertices only.

Grid Align

It aligns all vertices to the construction plane of the current view. Also, it moves them to that plane. If a **Perspective** or a camera viewport is active, this command aligns vertices to the home grid [see Fig. 48] otherwise the current construction plane is the active grid. For example, if you make the **Front** viewport active before clicking **Grid Align**, the **XZ** plane will be used for the aligning process. If you are using a grid object, the current plane will be the active grid object.

Relax

It relaxes [normalizes mesh spacing] the current selection by moving each vertex towards the average location of its neighboring vertices [see Fig. 49]. If you are at the **Object** level, 3ds Max applies smoothing to whole mesh otherwise the **Relax** function is applied to the current sub-object selection. The settings for the **Relax** command can be accessed by clicking **Settings** on the right of **Relax**. The **Relax** caddy control appears. Table 6 summarizes the **Relax** caddy control.

49

Table 6: The **Relax** caddy control	
Control	**Description**
Amount	It determines how far the vertex moves each iteration relax function. It defines a percentage of the distance from the original location to the average location of the neighbors.
Iterations	It determines how many times you want to repeat the **Relax** operation.
Relax Hold Boundary Points	When on [default], determines whether vertices at the edges of open meshes are moved or not.
Relax Hold Outer Points	When on, 3ds Max preserves the original position of the vertices that are farthest away from the center of the object. Fig. 50 shows a mesh when **Hold Outer Points** is off.

50

Hide Selected, Unhide All, Hide Unselected

These parameters are available at the **Vertex**, **Polygon**, and **Element** sub-object levels. Table 7 summarizes the functions of these parameters.

Table 7: Sub-object visibility	
Parameter	**Description**
Hide Selected	Hides the selected sub-objects.
Unhide All	Unhides the hidden sub-objects.

Table 7: Sub-object visibility	
Parameter	**Description**
Hide Unselected	Hides unselected sub-objects.

Copy, Paste

These parameters allow you to copy and paste named selection sets from one object to another. These commands use sub-object IDs. Therefore if there is some difference between the source and target meshes, on pasting, the selection may comprise of different sub-object selected.

Delete Isolated Vertices

It is selected by default. As a result, when you delete a selection of contiguous sub-objects, the isolated vertices are deleted. If off, deleting sub-object selection leaves the vertices intact.

Full Interactivity

It allows you to toggle feedback on and off for dialog boxes and caddies as well as for the **Quick Slice** and **Cut** parameters. When on, 3ds Max updates the viewports in real-time as you use the mouse in the viewport or change values numerically using the keyboard.

Vertex Level `UPDATED`

Edges and **Polygons** make a poly object. Vertices are the basic building blocks for edges and polygons. You can manipulate vertices at the **Vertex** sub-object level. The parameters available for modifying the geometry at the **Vertex** level are found in the **Edit Vertices** and **Vertex Properties** rollouts.

Edit Vertices Rollout

Let's discuss the controls available in this rollout.

Remove: Remove lets you delete selected vertices. The polygons that are using these vertices are combined [see the middle image of Fig. 51]. The keyboard shortcut for the **Remove** function is **Backspace**.

Caution: Using Delete
*If you use the **Delete** key instead of **Backspace**, 3ds Max can create holes in the poly mesh [see the image at the right of Fig. 51].*

Break: Creates a new vertex for each connected polygon to the original selection that allows you to move the corners of polygons [see Fig. 52].

Extrude: You can use this parameter to extrude the vertices along a normal. 3ds Max creates new polygons that form the sides of the extrusion [see Fig. 53]. The number of polygons in the extrusion will be equal to the number of polygons that were associated with the selected vertex. To extrude a vertex, select it and then click **Extrude**. Drag the selected vertex vertically to set the extent of the extrusion. Drag horizontally to set the size of the base. If you have selected multiple vertices, all are affected in the same way by the **Extrude** function. **RMB** click to end the **Extrude** operation.

Clicking **Settings** on the right of **Extrude** opens the **Extrude** caddy control. Table 8 summarizes the **Extrude** caddy control.

Table 8: The **Extrude Vertices** caddy control	
Parameter	**Description**
Height	Determines the extent of the extrusion in scene units.
Width	Determines the size of the base of the extrusion.

Weld: This parameter lets you combine the contiguous selected vertices that fall within a threshold specified using the **Weld** caddy control. To weld vertices, make a selection and then click **Settings** on the right of **Weld** to open the **Weld Vertices** caddy control. Set **Weld Threshold** and then click **OK** to weld the vertices [see Fig. 54].

Chamfer: This parameter allows you to chamfer the vertices. To chamfer a vertex, select it and then click **Chamfer**. Now, drag the vertex in a viewport to apply chamfering. If you have selected multiple vertices, all vertices will be chamfered identically [see the middle image in Fig. 55]. On clicking **Settings** on the right of **Chamfer**, the **Chamfer** caddy control appears. Table 9 summarizes the **Chamfer** caddy control.

Table 9: The **Chamfer** caddy control	
Parameter	**Description**
Vertex Chamfer Amount	Determines the extent of the chamfer.
Open Chamfer	When on, you can create open space around the chamfered vertices [see the last image in Fig. 56]

55

Target Weld: It allows you to select a vertex and then weld it to a contiguous target vertex. This tool works on those vertices that are connected with a single edge. Also, this parameter does not allow to cross newly created edges.

To weld a vertex, click **Target Weld**. When you hover the mouse pointer over the vertex, the shape of the mouse pointer changes to a plus shape. Click and drag on the vertex, a rubber band line gets attached to the mouse pointer. Now, position the mouse pointer on the neighboring vertex and when the shape of the mouse changes to a plus sign, click to weld the vertices [see Fig. 56].

56

Connect: **UPDATED** It allows you to create new edges between pairs of the selected vertices [see Fig. 57]. However, it does not let the new edges cross. For example, if you select all four vertices of a polygon and then click **Connect**, only two of the vertices will be connected. If you want to connect all four vertices, use the **Cut** tool.

Remove Isolated Vertices: It deletes all vertices that do not belong to any polygon of the selected object.

Remove Unused Map Verts: If there are some unused map vertices that are appearing in the **Unwrap UVW** editor but cannot be used for mapping, click this parameter to remove them.

Weight: You can use this parameter to assign a weight to the selected vertices. The specified weight is used by the **NURMS** subdivision function and the **MeshSmooth** modifier. The vertices with larger weights pull the smoothened result towards them.

Crease: It sets the crease value for the selected vertices. This value is used by the **OpenSubdiv** and **CreaseSet** modifiers. On increasing the crease weight, 3ds Max pulls the smoothened result towards the vertices and creates a sharp point.

Vertex Properties Rollout

The parameters in this rollout are only available for the **Editable Poly** object. They are unavailable for the **Edit Poly** modifier.

Edit Vertex Colors Group: The parameters in this group allow you to set the color and illumination color of the selected vertices. Click the **Color** swatch to change their color. **Illumination** allows you to change the illumination color of the vertices without changing their color. The **Alpha** parameter lets you set the alpha values for the vertices. These values are used when you export the data containing a full RGBA set for the color values.

Select Vertices By Group: You can select **Color** or **Illumination** from this group to determine whether to select vertices by using the vertex color or vertex illumination values. You can also specify a custom color for selecting vertices by using the color swatch available in this group. On clicking **Select**, 3ds Max selects the vertices depending on the selection parameter that you had turned on. The **Range** parameter allows you to specify a range for the color match.

Edge Level

The edge connects two vertices. This section covers the parameters available at the **Edge** sub-object level. These parameters are available in the **Edit Edges** rollout.

Insert Vertex

It allows you to subdivide the edges. To insert a vertex, click **Insert Vertex** and then click on an edge [see Fig. 58]. You can continue adding vertices as long as the command is active. **RMB** click to exit the command.

Remove

Removes the selected edges and combines the polygons [see Fig. 59]. The keyboard shortcut is **Backspace**. When you remove edges, the vertices remain intact [see the left image in Fig. 60]. To remove the corresponding vertices, press and hold **Ctrl** when you click **Remove** [see the right image in Fig. 60].

Split

It divides the mesh along the selected edges [see Fig. 61].

Extrude

This parameter allows you to extrude the edges manually or using the precise values. The precise values can be entered using the **Extrude Edges** caddy control. The parameters in the **Extrude Edges** caddy control are similar to that of the **Extrude Vertices** caddy at the **Vertex** level, refer to Table 8.

To extrude an edge, select it and then click **Extrude**. Drag the selected edge vertically to set the extent of the extrusion. Drag horizontally to set the size of the base [see Fig. 62]. If you have selected multiple edges, all are affected in the same way by the **Extrude** function. **RMB** click to end the extrude operation.

Weld, Target Weld

Refer to the **Vertex Level** group for understanding the functioning of these parameters. You need to select edge instead of vertex when dealing with edge-welding.

Chamfer `UPDATED`

This parameter allows you to chamfer an edge creating two or more edges for each chamfered edge. When you click on **Settings** on the right of **Chamfer**, the **Chamfer** caddy control appears. The options in this caddy control are discussed next.

Mitering

The **Mitering** drop-down allows you to choose one of the following mitering methods:

Quad: This method creates new quadrilateral polygons around each chamfered edge. The higher the **Segments** value used, the more the chamfer that can be rounded off, depending on the **Tension** value you specify. Fig. 63 shows the chamfered edges with the **Quad** mitering type.

Tri: This mitering method generates both triangular and quadrilateral polygons. However, triangular polygons may cause mesh issues when you smooth or subdivide them. Fig. 64 shows the chamfered edges with the **Tri** mitering type.

Uniform: This mitering method creates a uniform corner with quadrilateral intersections. The corner generated can be smoothed or sharpened using the **Edge Depth** value. Fig. 65 shows the chamfered edges with **Edge Depth** set to **0** and **-0.1**, respectively.

Radial: This metering method creates an arc in the corners. It helps in avoiding connecting bevel edge vertices to non-bevel edge vertices, see Fig. 66.

Patch: This mitering method also creates quadrilateral intersections. However, with this method, you get better higher resolutions results. Also, it helps in removing artifacts, see Fig. 67.

Edge Tension

It determines the angle between the new polygons. At the value of **1**, all polygons will be coplanar. Fig. 68 shows the chamfered edges with **Edge Tension** set to **0**, **0.5**, and **1**, respectively.

Table 10 summarizes rest of the caddy controls.

Table 10: The **Chamfer** caddy control	
Parameter	**Description**
Edge Chamfer Amount	Determines the amount of chamfer in scene units.
Connect Edge Segments	Adds a number of polygons over the region of the chamfer.

Table 10: The **Chamfer** caddy control

Parameter	Description
End Bias	This parameter works only with the **Quad** and **Uniform** mitering types. It controls the ends of the chamfers that do not involve a corner and moves the end point towards the next edge [see Fig. 69].
Radius Bias	This parameter works only with the **Quad** and **Uniform** mitering types and controls the radius of the chamfered corners. Fig. 70 shows the chamfered edges with **Radius Bias** set to **0** and **1**, respectively.
Open Chamfer	Deletes the faces created after the chamfer operation.
Invert Open	It deletes all faces except those created by the chamfering operation. It is available only when the **Open Chamfer** option is active.
Smooth	When on, it applies smoothing groups after chamfering. Also, it enables the **Smooth Type** function.
Smooth Type	There are two types of smoothing methods available. **Smooth Entire Object** applies smoothing groups to the entire object. **Smooth Chamfers Only** applies smoothing groups to the newly created polygons.
Smooth Threshold	If a smooth type is applied to the chamfered edges, it places two adjacent faces in the same smoothing group if the angle between their normals is less than the value specified using the **Smooth Threshold** parameter.

Bridge

You can use the **Bridge** parameter to bridge the border edges to create a polygon bridge between them. Keep in mind that **Bridge** only connects the edges of the borders. To create a bridge between the edges, select two or more border edges, and then click **Bridge**. A bridge will be created using the existing **Bridge** settings [see Fig. 71]. To set **Bridge** settings, click **Settings** on the right of **Bridge**; the **Bridge Edges** caddy control appears. Table 11 summarizes the **Bridge Edges** caddy control.

Table 11: The **Bridge Edges** caddy control	
Parameters	**Description**
Segments	It specifies the number of polygons along the length of the bridge.
Smooth	It sets the maximum angle for smoothing to occur.
Bridge Adjacent	It controls the minimum angle between the adjacent edges across which bridging can occur. The edges that are at less than this angle will not be bridged.
Reverse Triangulation	When you are bridging two borders, each of which contains different numbers of edges, you can use this parameter to define the method of triangulation. Fig. 72 shows the bridge when **Reverse Triangulation** is **On** and **Off**, respectively.
Use Edge Selection	It allows you to choose between two methods. Either you can use the existing selection or you can choose the edges using the caddy control. When you choose **Use Specific Edges**, the **Pick Edge 1**, and **Pick Edge 2** parameters become available.
Pick Edge 1, Pick Edge 2	Click **Pick Edge 1** and then click a border edge in a viewport. Select the other border edge using **Pick Edge 2**, the bridge will be created between the two border edges.

Connect

It allows you to refine selected edges by creating new edges between them. To create new edges, select the edges of the active object that you want to connect and then click **Connect** [see Fig. 73].

Caution: Connecting edges
*You can connect edges on the same polygon. The **Connect** command will stop the new edges to cross. For example, if you select all edges of a polygon face and apply this function, only neighboring edges are connected. The new edges will not cross each other [see Fig. 74].*

Clicking on the **Settings** on the right of **Connect** opens the **Connect Edges** caddy control that allows you to change settings for the **Connect** command and also preview the changes before committing them [see Fig. 75].

Table 12 summarizes the **Connect Edges** caddy control.

Table 12: The **Connect Edges** caddy control	
Parameter	**Description**
Segments	Defines the number of new edges between each adjacent pair of selected edges.

Table 12: The **Connect Edges** caddy control	
Parameter	**Description**
Pinch	Controls the relative spacing between the new and connecting edges.
Slide	Controls the relative positioning of the new edges.

Create Shape from Selection

This parameter allows you to create a shape [spline] from the selected edges. The pivot of the shape will be created at the geometric center of the poly object. To create a shape, select the edges of the active object, and then click **Create Shape from Selection** to open the **Create Shape** dialog box. Type the new name in the **Curve Name** field and then choose **Shape Type**. Next, click **OK** to create the shape [see Fig. 76].

Edit Tri

This parameter gives you the ability to modify the triangulation for the polygons. To enable triangulation, click **Edit Tri**. The hidden edges appear on the object [see left image in Fig. 77]. Now, to change the triangulation for a polygon, click a vertex; a rubber band line appears attached to the mouse pointer. Now, click on an adjacent vertex to create a new triangulation [see the right image in Fig. 77].

Turn

It allows you to modify the polygon triangulation by clicking on the diagonals. To change triangulation, click **Turn**. The current triangulation appears on the object. Click on the diagonals to change the triangulation.

Border Level

A border can be described as the edge [boundary] of a hole. As discussed earlier, if you create a cylinder and delete its caps, the adjacent row of edges form a border. You can manipulate borders using the parameters available in the **Edit Borders** rollout. Most of the parameters are similar to that of the edge and vertex controls. Select border edges and experiment with these parameters. One additional parameter appears in the **Edit Borders** rollout called **Cap**. It caps an entire border loop with a polygon. You can use it to fill holes in an object.

Polygon/Element Level

A polygon is formed by connecting three or more edges. Polygons form a surface that you can render. At the **Polygon** sub-object level, you can select polygons and then apply various polygon modeling functions to them. At the **Element** sub-object level, you can edit groups of contiguous polygons.

Tip: Highlighting polygons
*When you select a polygon, it is highlighted in red in the viewport. You can toggle this feature by pressing the **F2** key.*

You can edit polygons and elements using the parameters available in the **Edit Polygons** and **Edit Elements** rollouts, respectively.

Edit Polygons Rollout

Let's first explore the tools available in the **Edit Polygons** rollout.

Insert Vertex

It allows you to subdivide a polygon manually. It also works at the **Element** sub-object level. To subdivide the polygon, click **Insert Vertex** and then click on a polygon to subdivide it. You can continue subdividing the polygons as the command remains active until you **RMB** click [see Fig. 78].

Extrude

Extruding is a process in which polygons move along the normal and new polygons are created. This command lets you extrude the polygons. To do so, select them in a viewport and then click **Extrude**. Position the mouse pointer on the polygons. The shape of the cursor changes to the **Extrude** cursor. Drag the cursor vertically to specify the extent of extrusion and horizontally to set the base [see Fig. 79]. On clicking **Settings** on the right of **Extrude**, the **Extrude Polygons** caddy control appears that allows you to specify settings for the extrusion. Table 13 summarizes the **Extrude Polygons** caddy control.

Table 13: The **Extrude Polygons** caddy control	
Parameter	**Description**
Extrusion Type	This drop-down list provides three methods for extrusion: **Group**, **Local Normal**, and **By Polygon**. On selecting **Group**, 3ds Max extrudes polygons along the average normal of each contiguous group of polygons [see the left image in Fig. 80]. When **Normal** is selected, the extrusion takes place along each normal of the selected polygon [see the middle image in Fig. 80]. On selecting **By Polygon**, 3ds Max extrudes each polygon individually [see the right image in Fig. 80].
Height	Determines the amount of extrusion in scene units.

Outline

This command lets you increase or decrease the outside edge of each group of contiguous polygons. It does not scale, it just changes the size of the outside edge of the selected polygons. To change the size of the outside edge of the polygons, select a group of contiguous polygons and then click **Outline**. Now, position the mouse pointer on the selected polygons and drag the pointer to outline the polygons [see Fig. 81]. Notice in Fig. 81 that the inner polygons are not affected by the **Outline** operation. If you want to manually specify the outline amount, then click **Settings** on the right of the **Outline** to open the **Outline** caddy control and specify the value using the **Amount** parameter.

Bevel

It allows you to perform bevel function on a group of contiguous selected polygons. To bevel the polygons, select them in a viewport and then click **Bevel**. Position the mouse pointer on the polygons; the shape of the cursor changes to the **Bevel** cursor. Drag the cursor vertically to define the height and horizontally to define the outline amount [see Fig. 82].

On clicking **Settings** on the right of **Bevel**, the **Bevel** caddy control appears that allows you to specify settings for the bevel. Table 14 summarizes the **Bevel** caddy control.

Table 14: The **Bevel** caddy control	
Parameter	**Description**
Bevel Type	This drop-down list provides three methods for beveling: **Group**, **Local Normal**, and **By Polygon**. On selecting **Group**, 3ds Max bevels polygons along the average normal of each contiguous group of polygons. When **Normal** is selected, the beveling takes place along each normal of the selected polygon. On selecting **By Polygon**, 3ds Max bevels each polygon individually.
Height	Determines the amount of extrusion in scene units.
Outline	Lets you make the outer border of the selection bigger or smaller.

Inset

This command performs a bevel with no height. To inset polygons, select them, and then click **Inset**, position the cursor over the polygons, and then drag to define the **Inset** amount [see Fig. 83].

On clicking **Settings** on the right of **Inset**, the **Inset** caddy control appears that allows you to specify settings for inset. Table 15 summarizes the **Inset** caddy control.

Table 15: The **Inset** caddy control	
Parameter	**Description**
Inset Type	This drop-down list provides two methods for insetting: **Group**, and **By Polygon**. On selecting **Group**, 3ds Max insets polygons across each selection of multiple, contiguous polygons. On selecting **By Polygon**, 3ds Max insets each polygon individually.
Amount	Determines the extent of inset in scene units.

Bridge

You have seen how you have applied the **Bridge** function on the edges. It works similarly at the **Polygon** sub-object level. Here, you have to select polygons instead of edges [see Fig. 84]. Fig. 84 shows an external bridge [right] as well as an internal bridge [left].

To specify settings for the **Bridge** function, click **Settings** on the right of **Bridge** to open the **Bridge Polygons** caddy control. Table 16 summarizes the **Bridge Polygons** caddy control.

Table 16: The **Bridge Polygons** caddy control	
Parameter	**Description**
Segments	Determines the number of polygons along the length of the bridge.
Taper	Allows you to taper the bridge length towards its center. Negative values make the bridge center smaller whereas the positive values make the center bigger.
Bias	Defines the location of the maximum taper amount.
Smooth	Sets the angle for smoothing.
Twist 1, Twist 2	Allow you to twist each end of the bridge.
Use Specific Polygons, Use Polygon Selection	It allows you to choose between two methods. Either you can use the existing selection or you can choose the polygons using the caddy control. When you choose **Use Specific Polygons**, the **Pick Polygon 1** and **Pick Polygon 2** parameters become available.

Table 16: The **Bridge Polygons** caddy control	
Parameter	**Description**
Pick Polygon 1, Pick Polygon 2	Click **Pick Polygon 1** and then click a polygon in a viewport. Select the other polygon using **Pick Polygon 2**, the bridge will be created between the two border edges.

Flip

It allows you to reverse the direction of normals on the selected polygons.

Hinge From Edge

This command allows you to perform a hinge operation in the viewport. Make a polygon selection in a viewport and then click **Hinge From Edge**. Now, drag on an edge to hinge the selection [see Fig. 85]. On clicking **Settings** on the right of **Hinge From Edge**, the **Hinge From Edge** caddy control appears that allows you to specify settings for extrusion. Table 17 summarizes the **Hinge From Edge** caddy control.

85

Table 17: The **Hinge From Edge** caddy control	
Parameter	**Description**
Angle	Sets the rotation angle around the hinge [see Fig. 86].
Segments	Specifies the number of polygons along the extruded side.
Pick Hinge	Click it and then click on an edge to specify the hinge edge.

86

Unit 4: Polygon Modeling

Extrude Along Spline

It allows you to extrude a selection along a spline. To extrude, create a spline and then select the polygons that you want to extrude. Click **Extrude Along Spline** and then click the spline in a viewport to extrude the polygons [see Fig. 87].

87

On clicking **Settings** on the right of **Extrude Along Spline**, the **Extrude Along Spline** caddy control appears that allows you to specify settings for the extrusion. Table 18 summarizes the **Extrude Along Spline** caddy control.

Parameter	Description
Table 18: The **Extrude Along Spline** caddy control	
Segments	Determines the number of polygons along the extrusion [see Fig. 88].
Taper Amount	Sets the taper amount for the extrusion.
Taper Curve	Defines the rate at which tapering occurs.
Twist	Applies a twist along the length of the taper.
Extrude Along Spline Align	Aligns the extrusion along the face normal [see Fig. 89].
Rotation	Sets the rotation of extrusion.
Pick Spline	Allows you to pick a spline along which the extrusion will occur.

Edit Triangulation/Turn

Refer to the **Edge Level** group for understanding the functioning of these parameters.

Retriangulate

When clicked, 3ds Max automatically performs the best triangulation on the selected polygon[s].

Edit Elements Rollout

Refer to **Edit Polygons** rollout for the parameters available in this rollout.

Hands-on Exercises

Exercise 1: Creating a Circular Hole in the Geometry

In this exercise, you will learn to create a perfectly circular hole in a geometry [see Fig. E1]. Table E1 summarizes the exercise.

Table E1	
Skill level	Beginner
Time to complete	40 Minutes
Topics	• Specifying the Units for the Exercise • Creating the Hole
Resources folder	**polygon-modeling**
Units	**Generic**
Final file	**hole-finish.max**

Specifying the Units for the Exercise

Follow these steps:

1. From the **Customize** menu choose **Units Setup**. In the **Units Setup** dialog box that appears, select **Generic Units** from the **Units Setup** dialog box. Click **OK** to accept the changes made.

2. From the **File** menu, choose **Save** to open the **Save File As** dialog box. In the **File name** text box type **hole-finish.max** and then click **Save** to save the file.

Creating the Hole

Follow these steps:

1. In the **Create** panel, click **Geometry**, and then in the **Object Type** rollout, click **Plane**. In the **Perspective** viewport, create a plane. Switch to the **Modify** panel and then in the **Parameters** rollout, change **Length** to **50**, **Width** to **50**, **Height Length Segs** to **2**, and **Width Segs** to **2**. Place the plane at the origin.

2. **RMB** click on the plane and then choose **transform** quadrant > **Convert To:** > **Convert to Editable Poly**. In the **Modify** panel > **Selection** rollout, click **Vertex** to activate the vertex sub-object level.

3. Select the vertices, as shown in Fig. E2 and then in the **Modify** panel > **Edit Vertices** rollout, click **Connect** [see Fig. E3]. Similarly, connect the other vertices diagonally [see Fig. E4].

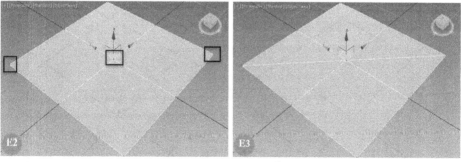

4. Select the center vertex and then in the **Modify** panel > **Edit Vertices** rollout, click **Chamfer** > **Settings** to open the **Chamfer** caddy control. Change **Vertex Chamfer Amount** to **10** and **Vertex Chamfer Segments** to **0**. Then, click **OK** [see Fig. E5].

5. In the **Modify** panel > **Selection** rollout, click **Polygon** to activate the polygon sub-object level. Select the center polygon and then delete it [see Fig. E6]. In the **Modify** panel > **Selection** rollout, click **Border** to activate the border sub-object level. Select the border, as shown in Fig. E7.

6. Invoke the **Move** tool and then drag the border along to **-Z** axis to create the extrusion [see Fig. E8]. Invoke the **Scale** tool and then scale border inwards with the **Shift** key [see Fig. E9].

7. In the **Modify** panel > **Selection** rollout, **Ctrl**+click on **Vertex** to convert selection to vertices. Now, in the **Modify** panel > **Edit Geometry** rollout, click **Collapse** [see Fig. E10]. Select the edges [see Fig. E11] and then in the **Modify** panel > **Selection** rollout, click **Loop**.

8. In the **Edit Edges** rollout, click **Chamfer > Settings** to open the **Chamfer** caddy control. Change **Edge Chamfer Amount** to **0.3** and **Connect Edge Segments** to **1**. Now, click **OK** [see Fig. E12].

9. Invoke the **Move** tool and then double-click on the outer edges of the plane to select the loop. Now, hold down **Shift** and then drag the loop along **-Z** axis to create the extrusion [see Fig. E13].

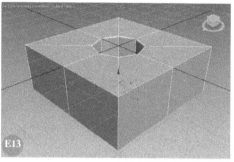

10. In the **Modify** panel > **Selection** rollout, click **Border** to activate the border sub-object level. Now, in the **Edit Borders** rollout, click **Cap** [see Fig. 14].

11. From the **Object-Space Modifiers** section of the **Modifier** list, select **MeshSmooth**. In the **Subdivision Amount** rollout, change **Iterations** to **3** [see Fig. E15].

Exercise 2: Creating a Circular Hole in a Cube

In this exercise, you will create a hole in a cube [see Fig. E1]. Table E2 summarizes the exercise.

Table E2	
Skill level	Beginner
Time to complete	40 Minutes
Topics	• Specifying the Units for the Exercise • Creating the Hole
Resources folder	**polygon-modeling**
Units	**Generic Units**
Final file	**hole-cube-finish.max**

Specifying the Units for the Exercise

Follow these steps:

1. From the **Customize** menu choose **Units Setup**. In the **Units Setup** dialog box that appears, select **Generic Units** from the **Units Setup** dialog box. Click **OK** to accept the changes made.

2. From the **File** menu, choose **Save** to open the **Save File As** dialog box. In the **File name** text box type **hole-cube-finish.max** and then click **Save** to save the file.

Creating the Hole

Follow these steps:

1. In the **Create** panel, click **Geometry**, and then in the **Object Type** rollout, click **Box**. In the **Perspective** viewport, create a box. Switch to the **Modify** panel and in the **Parameters** rollout, change **Length** to **40**, **Width** to **40**, and **Height** to **40**. Change **Length Segs**, **Width Segs**, and **Height Segs** to **2** each [see Fig. E2].

2. **RMB** click on the cube and then choose **transform** quadrant **> Convert To: > Convert to Editable Poly**. Now, create holes in the opposite faces of the box, as done in the previous exercise [see Fig. E3].

3. In the **Modify** panel > **Selection** rollout, click **Border** to activate the border sub-object level. Select the border edges, refer to Fig. E4. Now, in the **Edit Edges** rollout, click **Bridge** to connect the edges [see Fig. E5].

4. Chamfer all the border edges and then apply the **MeshSmooth** modifier.

Exercise 3: Creating a Solid Model

In this exercise, you will create a solid model [see Fig. E1].

Table E3 summarizes the exercise.

Table E3	
Skill level	Beginner
Time to complete	30 Minutes
Topics	• Specifying the Units for the Exercise • Creating the Model
Resources folder	**polygon-modeling**
Units	**Generic Units**
Final file	**solid-1-finish.max**

Specifying the Units for the Exercise
Follow these steps:

1. From the **Customize** menu choose **Units Setup**. In the **Units Setup** dialog box that appears, select **Generic Units** from the **Units Setup** dialog box. Click **OK** to accept the changes made.

2. From the **File** menu, choose **Save** to open the **Save File As** dialog box. In the **File name** text box type **solid-1-finish.max** and then click **Save** to save the file.

Creating the Model
Follow these steps:

1. In the **Create** panel, click **Geometry**, and then choose **Standard Primitives** from the drop-down list located below **Geometry**. In the **Object Type** rollout, click **Tube**. Create a tube in the **Top** viewport. Place the tube at the origin. Switch to the **Modify** panel and then in the **Parameters** rollout, change **Radius 1** to **30**, **Radius 2** to **50**, **Height** to **15**, **Height Segments** to **1**, **Cap Segments to 2**, and **Sides** to **24** [see Fig. E2].

2. **RMB** click on the tube and then choose **transform** quadrant > **Convert To:** > **Convert to Editable Poly**. In the **Modify** panel > **Selection** rollout, click **Polygon** to activate the polygon sub-object level. Select the polygons, as shown in Fig. E3. Press **Ctrl+I** to invert the selection and then press **Delete** to delete the polygons [see Fig. E4].

3. In the **Modify** panel > **Selection** rollout, click **Vertex** to activate the vertex sub-object level. Select the center vertex and then in the **Modify** panel > **Edit Vertices** rollout, click **Chamfer** > **Settings** to open the **Chamfer** caddy control. Change **Vertex Chamfer Amount** to **7.5** and **Vertex Chamfer Amount** to **0**. Then, click **OK** [see Fig. E5].

4. In the **Modify** panel > **Selection** rollout, click **Edge** to activate the edge sub-object level. Now, connect the newly created edges [see Fig. E6]. In the **Modify** panel > **Edit Geometry** rollout, click **Cut** and then create edges, as shown in Fig. E7.

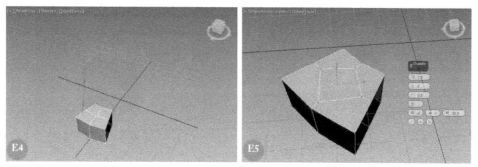

5. In the **Modify** panel > **Selection** rollout, click **Polygon** to activate the polygon sub-object level. Select the polygons, as shown in Fig. E8 and then press **Delete**. In the **Modify** panel > **Selection** rollout, click **Vertex** to activate the vertex sub-object level. Now, select the vertices as shown in Fig. E9 and then scale them using the **Scale** tool [see Fig E10].

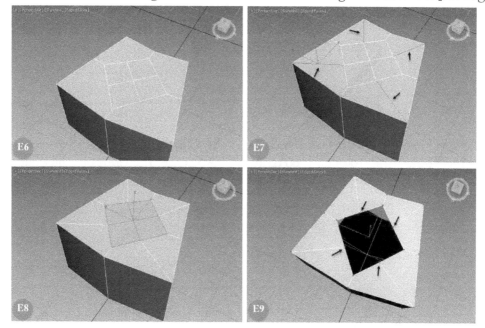

6. Select all vertices associated with the hole and then from the **Object-Space Modifiers** section of the **Modifier** list, select **Spherify** [see Fig. E11]. **RMB** click on the mesh and then choose **transform** quadrant > **Convert To:** > **Convert to Editable Poly**. Now, create the rest of the hole, as done earlier [see Fig. E12].

Caution: Chamfer
*Use the **Quad** mitering method to avoid distortions in the mesh. It will help you to get the clean geometry when you will smooth the mesh.*

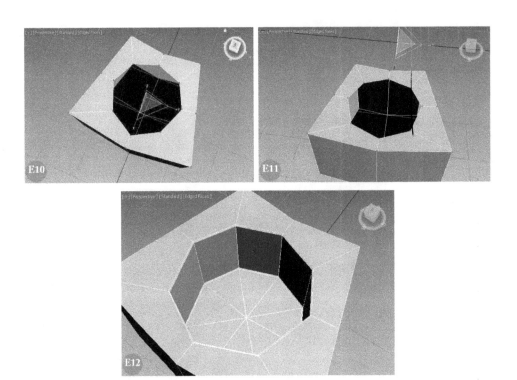

7. Make sure mesh is selected and you are in the **Object** mode and then choose **Array** from the **Tools** menu to open the **Array** dialog box. Set the values in the dialog box, as shown in Fig. E13 and then click **OK** [see Fig. 14].

8. In the **Modify** panel > **Edit Geometry** rollout, click **Attach** > **Settings** to open the **Attach List** dialog box. Now, select all objects and click **Attach**.

9. In the **Modify** panel > **Selection** rollout, click **Vertex** to activate the vertex sub-object level. Select all boundary vertices [use the **Paint Selection Region** tool], as shown in Fig. E15. In the **Modify** panel > **Edit Vertices** rollout, click **Weld**.

10. In the **Modify** panel > **Selection** rollout, click **Edge** to activate the edge sub-object level. Select all border edges, as shown in Fig. E16. Now, chamfer these edges [see Fig. E17]. From the **Object-Space Modifiers** section of the **Modifier** list, select **MeshSmooth**. In the **Subdivision Amount** rollout, change **Iterations** to **3** [see Fig. E18].

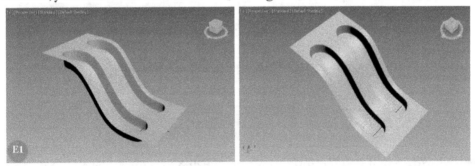

Exercise 4: Creating a Solid Model

In this exercise, you will create a solid model [see Fig. E1]. Table E4 summarizes the exercise.

Table E4	
Skill level	Beginner
Time to complete	30 Minutes
Topics	• Specifying the Units for the Exercise • Creating the Model
Resources folder	**polygon-modeling**
Units	**Generic Units**

Table E4	
Final file	**solid-2-finish.max**

Specifying the Units for the Exercise

Follow these steps:

1. From the **Customize** menu choose **Units Setup**. In the **Units Setup** dialog box that appears, select **Generic Units** from the **Units Setup** dialog box. Click **OK** to accept the changes made.

2. From the **File** menu, choose **Save** to open the **Save File As** dialog box. In the **File name** text box type **solid-2-finish.max** and then click **Save** to save the file.

Creating the Model

Follow these steps:

1. In the **Create** panel, click **Geometry**, then click **Plane**. In the **Top** viewport, create a plane. In the **Modify** panel > **Parameters** rollout, change **Length** to **150** and **Width** to **200**. Also, change **Length Segs** and **Width Segs** to **1** each. Place the plane at the origin.

2. **RMB** click on the plane and then choose **transform** quadrant > **Convert To:** > **Convert to Editable Poly**. In the **Modify** panel > **Selection** rollout, click **Edge** to activate the edge sub-object level. Select the edge, as shown in Fig. E2 and then extrude the edge using **Shift** [see Fig. E3]. Again, extrude the edge, as shown in Fig. E4.

3. Select the edge ring, as shown in Fig. E5 and then in the **Modify** panel > **Edit Edges** rollout, click **Connect > Settings** to open the **Connect Edges** caddy control. Now, change **Segments** to **2** and **Pinch** to **80** [see Fig. E6]. Click **OK**.

4. Select the edge ring, as shown in Fig. E7 and then in the **Modify** panel > **Edit Edges** rollout, click **Connect > Settings** to open the **Connect Edges** caddy control. Now, change **Segments** to **2** and **Pinch** to **-16** [see Fig. E8]. Click **OK**.

5. Select the edge rings as shown in Fig. E9 and then in the **Modify** panel > **Edit Edges** rollout, click **Connect > Settings** to open the **Connect Edges** caddy control. Now, change **Segments** to **1** and **Pinch** to **0** [see Fig. E10].

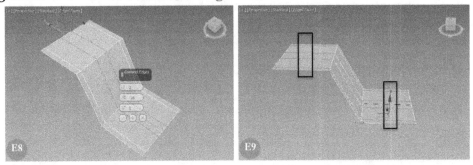

6. Select the edges, as shown in Fig. E11 and then in the **Modify** panel > **Edit Edges** rollout, click **Connect > Settings** to open the **Connect Edges** caddy control. Now, change **Segments** to **6** and **Pinch** to **0** [see Fig. E12].

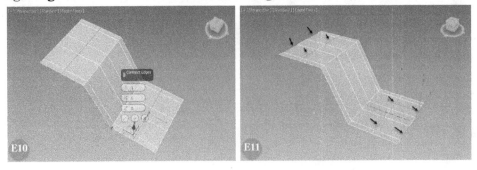

7. In the **Modify** panel > **Selection** rollout, click **Vertex** to activate the edge sub-object level and then using the **Move** tool, create shape, as shown in Fig. E13. In the **Modify** panel > **Selection** rollout, click **Polygon** to activate the polygon sub-object level and then select polygons, as shown in Fig. E14.

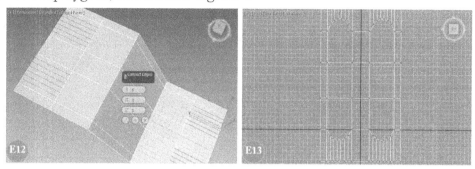

8. In the **Modify** panel > **Edit Polygons** rollout, click **Extrude > Settings** to open the **Extrude Polygons** caddy control. In the caddy control, change extrusion type to **Local Normal**, and **Height** to **-35** [see Fig. E15].

9. In the **Modify** panel > **Selection** rollout, click **Edge** to activate the edge sub-object level and then select the edges, as shown in Fig. E16.

10. In the **Modify** panel > **Edit Edges** rollout, click **Chamfer > Settings** to open the **Chamfer** caddy control. In the caddy control, change **Mitering** to **Quad**, **Edge Chamfer Amount** to **1.5**, and then click **OK** [see Fig. E17].

11. From the **Object-Space Modifiers** section of the **Modifier** list, select **MeshSmooth**. In the **Subdivision Amount** rollout, change **Iterations** to **3** [see Fig. E18].

Exercise 5: Creating a Solid Model

In this exercise, you will create a solid model [see Fig. E1].

Table E5 summarizes the exercise.

Table E5	
Skill level	Beginner
Time to complete	30 Minutes
Topics	• Specifying the Units for the Exercise • Creating the Model
Resources folder	**polygon-modeling**
Units	**Generic Units**
Final file	**solid-3-finish.max**

Specifying the Units for the Exercise

Follow these steps:

1. From the **Customize** menu choose **Units Setup**. In the **Units Setup** dialog box that appears, select **Generic Units** from the **Units Setup** dialog box. Click **OK** to accept the changes made.

2. From the **File** menu, choose **Save** to open the **Save File As** dialog box. In the **File name** text box type **solid-3-finish.max** and then click **Save** to save the file.

Creating the Model

Follow these steps:

1. In the **Create** panel, click **Geometry**, and then choose **Standard Primitives** from the drop-down list located below **Geometry**. In the **Object Type** rollout, click **Tube**. Create a tube in the **Top** viewport. Switch to the **Modify** panel and then in the **Parameters** rollout, change **Radius 1** to **20**, **Radius 2** to **30**, **Height** to **2**, **Height Segments** to **1**, **Cap Segments to 1**, and **Sides** to **8**.

2. **RMB** click the **Move** tool to open the **Move Transform Type-In** dialog box. In the **Absolute: World** group of the dialog box, change **X, Y**, and **Z** to **0, 65**, and **0**, respectively. **RMB** click and then choose **transform** quadrant > **Convert To:** > **Convert to Editable Poly**. In the **Modify** panel > **Selection** rollout, click **Polygon** to activate the polygon sub-object level. Select all polygons except the top polygons [see Fig. E2] and then press **Delete** to delete selected polygons [see Fig. E3].

3. Switch to the **Object** mode. Select **Use Transform Coordinate Center** from the **Use Center** flyout. Make sure the mesh is selected and then choose **Array** from the **Tools** menu to open the **Array** dialog box. Set the values in the dialog box, as shown in Fig. E4 and then click **OK** [see Fig. E5]. Select **Pivot Point Center** from the **Use Center** flyout.

4. In the **Modify** panel > **Edit Geometry** rollout, click **Attach** > **Settings** to open the **Attach List** dialog box. Now, select all objects and click **Attach**.

5. Select the edges, as shown in Fig. E6 and then in the **Modify** panel > **Edit Edges** rollout, click **Bridge** to bridge the edges [see Fig. E7]. Similarly, connect all edges [see Fig. E8]. Use the **;** hotkey to repeat the **Bridge** command.

6. Select the edges, as shown in Fig. E9 and then in the **Modify** panel > **Edit Edges** rollout, click **Connect** [see Fig. E10]. Similarly, connect all edges [see Fig. E11].

7. In the **Modify** panel > **Selection** rollout, click **Vertex** to activate the vertex sub-object level. Select the vertices, as shown in Fig. E12 and then uniformly scale them using the **Scale** tool [see Fig. E13].

8. In the **Modify** panel > **Selection** rollout, click **Border** to activate the border sub-object level and then select the border, as shown in Fig. E14. Extrude the border using the **Scale** tool and **Shift** [see Fig. E15].

9. Select the borders, as shown in Fig. E16 and then type **Borders** in the **Named Selection Sets** drop-down list in the **Main** toolbar [see Fig. E17]. Extrude selected borders downwards using the **Move** tool and **Shift** [see Fig. E18].

E16

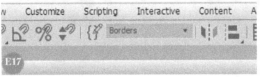

E17

10. Select **Borders** from the **Named Selection Sets** drop-down list. In the **Modify** panel > **Edit Edges** rollout, click **Chamfer > Settings** to open the **Chamfer** caddy control. In the caddy control, change **Mitering** to **Quad**, **Amount** to **1.5**, and then click **OK** [see Fig. E19].

E18

E19

11. From the **Object-Space Modifiers** section of the **Modifier** list, select **MeshSmooth**. In the **Subdivision Amount** rollout, change **Iterations** to **3** [see Fig. E20].

E20

Exercise 6: Creating a Serving Bowl

In this exercise, you will create a model of a bowl [see Fig. E1].

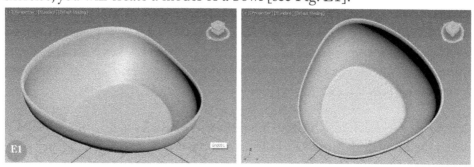

Table E6 summarizes the exercise.

Table E6	
Skill level	Beginner
Time to complete	20 Minutes
Topics	• Specifying the Units for the Exercise • Creating the Bowl
Resources folder	**polygon-modeling**
Units	**Metric - Centimeters**
Final file	**bowl-finish.max**

Specifying the Units for the Exercise

Follow these steps:

1. From the **Customize** menu choose **Units Setup**. In the **Units Setup** dialog box that appears, select **Metric** from the **Display Unit Scale** group. Next, select **Centimeters** from the drop-down list located below **Metric**, if already not selected. Click **OK**.

2. In the **Create** panel, click **Helpers** and then in the **Object Type** rollout, click **Grid**. Create a grid on the **Top** viewport. Set the **Transform Type-In** boxes in the **Status Bar** to **0** to place the grid at the origin. Go to the **Modify** panel and then in the **Parameters** rollout, set **Length**, **Width**, and **Grid** to **60**, **60**, and **5**, respectively. Press **X** to open the **3ds Max Commands** list and type **Acti** in the **Search All Actions** field.

3. Select **Activate Grid Object** from the list to hide the **Home** grid and activate the grid that you just created [see Fig. E2].

What just happened?
*Here, I've created a **Grid** object that will act as a construction plane for the objects. A **Grid** object is a parametric object. You can create any number of grid objects in the scene. They are saved with the scene. When you select **Activate Grid Object** command, the **Home** grid is deactivated and the selected **Grid** object becomes the active construction plane. Here, I have created a **60x60** cm grid and each grid square represents the size of the smallest square in the grid [5 cm].*

4. From the **File** menu, choose **Save** to open the **Save File As** dialog box. In the **File name** text box type **bowl-finish.max** and then click **Save** to save the file.

Creating the Bowl
Follow these steps:

1. In the **Create** panel, click **Geometry**, select **Standard Primitives** from the drop-down list, and then in the **Object Type** rollout, click **Cylinder**. Create a cylinder in the **Top** viewport. Go to the **Modify** panel and then in the **Parameters** rollout, set **Radius** to **25.591**, **Height** to **13**, **Sides** to **36**, and **Height Segments** to **2**. Set the **Transform Type-In** boxes in the **Status Bar** to **0** to place the cylinder at the origin [see Fig. E3]. Now, rename the cylinder as **bowlGeo**.

2. **RMB** click on **bowlGeo**. In the **transform** quadrant of the **Quad** menu that appears, choose **Convert To: Convert to Editable Poly**. Click **Polygon** in the **Modify** panel > **Selection** rollout and then select the top polygon of **bowlGeo**. Press **Delete** to remove the polygon.

3. Click **Select and Uniform Scale** on the Main toolbar. Select the bottom set of vertices and uniformly scale them down about **70%** [see Fig. E4]. You can use the **Scale Transform Type-In** dialog box to precisely enter the scale value.

Tip: Percent Snap Toggle
*You can activate **Percent Snap Toggle** from the Main toolbar to increment the scale values by an increment of **10%** [default value]. You can change the percentage value from the **Grid and Snap Settings** dialog box.*

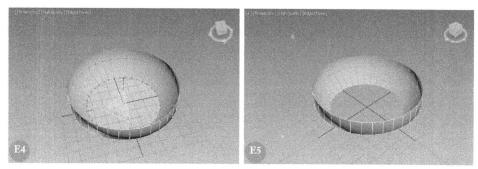

4. Select the bottom polygon and then press **Delete** to delete it [see Fig. E5]. Now, select the edges, as shown in Fig. E6 and then in the **Modify** panel > **Edit Edges** rollout, click **Bridge** to bridge the edges [see Fig. E7].

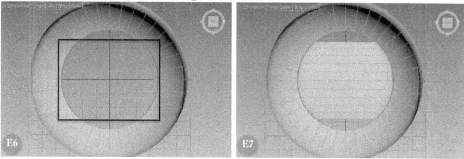

5. Select the edge ring, as shown in Fig. E8 and then in the **Modify** panel > **Edit Edges** rollout, click **Connect > Settings** to open the **Connect Edges** caddy control. Now, change **Segments** to **7** [see Fig. E9]. Now, bridge the edges [see Fig. E10].

6. Press **3** to activate the border sub-object level and then select the borders [see Fig. E11]. In the **Modify** panel > **Edit Borders** rollout, click **Cap** [see Fig. E12].

7. Select the edge ring, as shown in Fig. E13 and then in the **Modify** panel > **Edit Edges** rollout, click **Connect > Settings** to open the **Connect Edges** caddy control. Now, change **Segments** to **1** [see Fig. E14]. Similarly, connect the edges on the opposite side [see Fig. E15].

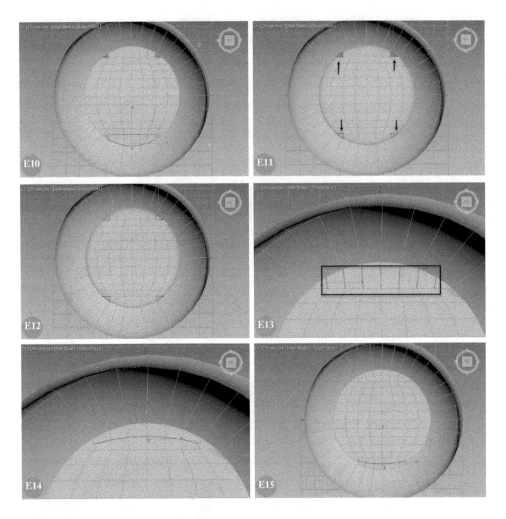

8. Select the vertices, as shown in Fig. E16 and then scale them in to maintain the topology [see Fig. E17]. Select newly created polygons and then click **Settings** on the right of **Extrude** in the **Modify** panel > **Edit Polygons** rollout. In the **Extrude's** caddy, set **Height** to **1** and click **OK** [see Fig. E18].

9. From the **Modifier** list > **Object-Space Modifiers** section, choose **Shell**. In the **Parameters** rollout, set **Outer Amount** to **0.5**.

10. From the **Modifier** list > **Object-Space Modifiers** section, choose **CreaseSet**. Similarly, add the **OpenSubdiv** modifier. In the **Modify** panel > **General Controls** rollout, set **Iterations** to **2**.

What just happened?
*Here, I've added the **OpenSubdiv** modifier. This modifier performs subdivision and smoothing operations on a mesh object. It can read the crease values from underlying stack entities [creases defined using the **CreaseSet** modifier] and applies them to the smooth mesh. The **Iterations** parameter controls the number of times a mesh is sub-divided.*

11. Expand the **CreaseSet** modifier in the modifier stack and select **Edge**. Now, select the top two loops using **Ctrl** double-clicking [see Fig. E19].

12. In the **Modify** panel > **Crease Sets** rollout, type name as **top_crease** and then click **Create Set** to create a new crease set [see Fig. E20]. Now, enter **0.5** in the spinner besides **top_crease** to round the edges [see Fig. E21].

What just happened?
*Here, I have used the **CreaseSet** modifier to create a crease set. This modifier provides various options for creating and managing creases in conjunction with the **OpenSubdiv** modifier. A crease set is a collection of edges and vertices having the same crease value.*

13. Similarly, create crease sets for the bottom and inner edges [see Figs. E22 and E23].

14. From the **Modifier** list > **Object-Space Modifiers** section, choose **Edit Poly**. From the **Modifier** list > **Object-Space Modifiers** section, choose **Taper**. In the modifier stack display, expand **Taper** and click on the **Gizmo** sub-object. Click **Select and Uniform Scale** on the **Main** toolbar and then scale down the gizmo [see Fig. E24]. Exit **Taper's** sub-object level.

15. In the **Parameters** rollout, set **Amount** to **0.26** and **Curve** to **-0.93**. Also, set **Primary** to **X** and **Effect** to **Y** [see Fig. E25].

What just happened?
*I have applied the **Taper** modifier to change the shape of the bowl. This modifier produces a tapered contour by scaling the ends of the geometry. The **Taper's** gizmo allows you to manipulate the result. **Amount** defines the extent of scaling. The parameters in the **Primary** group define the central axis for taper. **Effect** determines the direction of the taper.*

Exercise 7: Creating a Kitchen Cabinet

In this exercise, you will create the model of a kitchen cabinet [see Fig. E1].

Table E7 summarizes the exercise.

Table E7	
Skill level	Beginner
Time to complete	20 Minutes
Topics	• Specifying the Units for the Exercise • Creating the Kitchen Cabinet
Resources folder	**polygon-modeling**
Units	**Metric - Centimeters**
Final file	**kitchen-cabinet-finish.max**

Specifying the Units for the Exercise

Follow these steps:

1. From the **Customize** menu choose **Units Setup**. In the **Units Setup** dialog box that appears, select **Metric** from the **Display Unit Scale** group. Next, select **Centimeters** from the drop-down list located below **Metric**, if already not selected. Click **OK**.

2. From the **File** menu, choose **Save** to open the **Save File As** dialog box. In the **File name** text box type **kitchen-cabinet-finish.max** and then click **Save** to save the file.

3ds Max 2021

Creating the Cabinet

Follow these steps:

1. In the **Create** panel, click **Geometry** and then in the **Object Type** rollout, click **Box**. Create a box in the **Top** viewport. Go to the **Modify** panel and then in the **Parameters** rollout, set **Length** to **38**, **Width** to **45**, and **Height** to **76**. Set the **Transform Type-In** boxes in the **Status Bar** to **0** to place the box at the origin [see Fig. E2].

2. Convert the **Box001** to an **Editable Poly** object. Select the top and bottom polygons of the box [see Fig. E3] and then click **Detach** from the **Modify** panel > **Edit Geometry** rollout. Click **OK** in the **Detach** dialog box to create a new object from the selected polygons with the name **Object001**.

3. Select **Object001** from the **Scene Explorer** and activate the **Polygon** sub-object level. Now, select the top and bottom polygons of **Object001**. Click **Settings** on the right of **Extrude** in the **Modify panel** > **Edit Polygons** rollout. In the **Extude**'s caddy, set **Height** to **5** and click **OK** [see Fig. E4]. Select the polygon, as shown in Fig. E5 and then move it by **3** units in the positive **X** direction [see Fig. E6].

4. Select the top polygon and then click **Settings** on the right of **Extrude** in the **Modify** panel > **Edit Polygons** rollout. In the **Extude**'s caddy, set **Height** to **5** and click **OK** [see Fig. E7].

5. Similarly, extrude the front polygon by **3** units [refer Fig. E8]. Select **Box001** from the **Scene Explorer** and then activate the **Edge** sub-object level. Select the edges, as shown in Fig. E9.

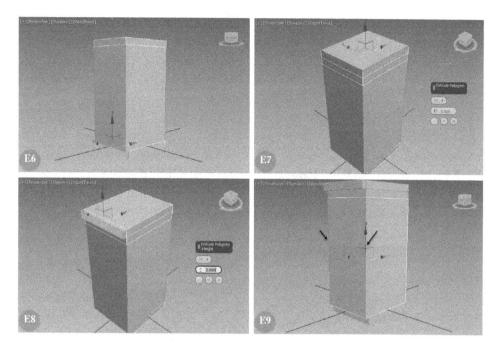

6. Click **Connect** in the **Modify** panel > **Edit Edges** rollout to connect the selected edges [see Fig. E10]. Select the polygons as shown in Fig. E11 and then click **Settings** on the right of **Inset** in the **Modify** panel > **Edit Polygons** rollout.

7. In the **Inset**'s caddy, set **Inset Type** to **By Polygon**, **Amount** to **2**, and then click **OK** [see Fig. E12]. Click **Settings** on the right of **Extrude** in the **Modify** panel > **Edit Polygons** rollout. In the **Extrude**'s caddy, set **Extrusion Type** to **By Polygon** and **Height** to **1.5** and click **OK** [see Fig. E13].

8. In the **Modify** panel > **Edit Geometry** rollout, click **Attach**. Click on **Object001** in a viewport to attach the two objects. Now, rename the resulting mesh as **cabinetGeo**. Activate the **Edge** sub-object level and then select the outside edges of the drawers [see Fig. E14].

9. In the **Modify** panel > **Edit Edges** rollout, click **Chamfer** > **Settings** to open the **Chamfer** caddy control. In the caddy control, change **Mitering** to **Quad**, **Edge Chamfer Amount** to **0.1**, **Connect Edge Segments** to **1**, **Edge Tension** to **1**, and then click **OK** [see Fig. E15].

Exercise 8: Creating a Book

In this exercise, you will create the model of a book [see Fig. E1]. Table E8 summarizes the exercise.

Table E8	
Skill level	Beginner
Time to complete	20 Minutes
Topics	• Specifying the Units for the Exercise • Creating the Book

Table E8	
Resources folder	**polygon-modeling**
Units	**US Standard – Decimal Inches**
Final file	**book-finish.max**

Specifying the Units for the Exercise

Follow these steps:

1. From the **Customize** menu choose **Units Setup**. In the **Units Setup** dialog box that appears, select **US Standard** from the **Display Unit Scale** group. Next, select **Decimal Inches** from the drop-down list located below **US Standard** and then click **OK** to accept the change.
2. From the **File** menu, choose **Save** to open the **Save File As** dialog box. In the **File name** text box type **book-finish.max** and then click **Save** to save the file.

Creating the Book

Follow these steps:

1. In the **Create** panel, click **Geometry**, and then in the **Object Type** rollout, click **Box**. Create a box in the **Top** viewport. Go to the **Modify** panel, and in the **Parameters** rollout, set **Length** to **7.44**, **Width** to **9.69**, and **Height** to **2**. Set the **Transform Type-In** boxes in the **Status Bar** to **0** to place the box at the origin. Now, rename the box as **bookGeo**.

2. **RMB** click on **bookGeo**. In the **transform** quadrant of the **Quad** menu that appears, choose **Convert To: Convert to Editable Poly**. Click **Edge** in the **Modify** panel > **Selection** rollout and then select the edge shown in Fig. E2. Click **Ring** to select the edge ring [see Fig. E3].

3. Click **Settings** on the right of **Connect** in the **Edit Edges** rollout. In the **Connect's** caddy, set **Slide** to **95** [see Fig. E4] and then click **OK** to connect the selected edges. Similarly, add four edge loops [**Segments: 4, Slide: 0**] to the part of the book that will make up the pages [see Fig. E5].

4. Click **Polygon** in the **Modify** panel **>** **Selection** rollout and then select the polygons shown in Fig. E6. Click **Settings** on the right of **Inset** in the **Edit Polygons** rollout. In the **Inset**'s caddy, set **Amount** to **0.08** [see Fig. E7] and then click **OK** to inset the polygons.

5. Click **Settings** on the right of **Extrude** in the **Edit Polygons** rollout. In the **Extrude**'s caddy, set **Group** to **Local Normal** and **Height** to **-0.129** [see Fig. E8] and then click **OK** to extrude the polygons. Click **Edge** in the **Modify** panel **>** **Selection** rollout and then select all outer edges of the cover shown in Fig. E9.

6. Click **Settings** on the right of **Chamfer** in the **Edit Edges** rollout. In the **Chamfer**'s caddy, set **Mitering** to **Quad**, **Edge Chamfer Amount** to **0.01**, and **Connect Edge**

Segments to **2**, **Edge Tension** to **0.5**[see Fig. E10] and then click **OK** to chamfer the edges. Click **Vertex** in the **Modify** panel > **Selection** rollout and then select the vertices in the **Left** viewport, as shown in Fig. E11.

7. Invoke the **Select and Move** tool from the **Main** toolbar and then adjust the vertices in the **Left** viewport to modify the shape of the book [see Fig. E12].

Quiz

Evaluate your skills to see how many questions you can answer correctly.

Multiple Choice
Answer the following questions:

1. Which of the following keys is used to add to the sub-object selection of a polygonal object?

   [A] Alt   [B] Ctrl
   [C] Alt+Ctrl   [D] Shift

2. Which the following keys is used to remove from the sub-object selection of a polygonal object?

   [A] Alt   [B] Ctrl
   [C] Alt+Ctrl   [D] Shift

3. Which the following keys is used to repeat the last command?

   [A] '   [B] .
   [C] >   [D] ;

4. Which of the following keys is used to enable polygon selection highlighting?

   [A] F3   [B] F2
   [C] F9   [D] F8

Fill in the Blanks
Fill in the blanks in each of the following statements:

1. The editable poly object is an editable object with five sub-object levels: _____, _____, _____, _____, and _____.

2. The editable poly object is similar to the edit mesh object with the only difference is that the edit mesh object comprises of _____ faces whereas the editable poly object comprises of polygons with any number of vertices.

3. When you convert an object to an editable poly object, you loose all of its creation parameters. If you want to retain the creation parameters, use the _____ modifier.

4. You can use the numeric keys from _____ to _____ to activate the **Vertex**, **Edge**, **Border**, **Polygon**, and **Element** sub-object levels, respectively. Press _____ to return to the Object level.

5. The _____ command allows you to attach other geometries to the selected poly object.

6. If a face is selected and you use the _____ key instead of the _____, key, 3ds Max can create holes in the poly mesh.

True or False
State whether each of the following is true or false:

1. You can lock a sub-object selection by pressing **Shift+Ctrl+N**.

2. If you are working with an editable object such as mesh, poly, patch, or spline, you can directly manipulate the selection using the transformations tools.

3. When you **Shift**+transform [move, scale, or rotate] a sub-object selection, the **Clone of Mesh** dialog box appears.

Practice Activities

Explore sub-objects levels: Create a standard primitive and then explore different ways of activating and selecting sub-object levels. Also, learn to lock and unlock the selections.

Clone sub-objects: Create a **Teapot** primitive, convert it to an editable poly object and then detach its lid using the **Shift**-transform technique. Rename the new object as **lid-cloned-geo**.

Convert sub-object selection: Explore and learn various methods of converting a sub-object selection to another type of sub-object selection.

Work with selection conversion: Create a **Sphere** primitive with **Radius** set to **40** and then convert it to an editable poly object. Next, make a polygon selection, as shown in Fig. A1. Convert this selection to the edge selection in a way so that all edges are selected that border the polygon selection [see Fig. A2].

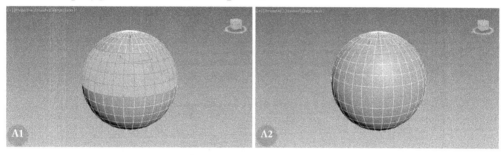

Work with the XForm Modifier: Create a **Sphere** primitive with **Radius** set to **40** and then convert it to an editable poly object. Next, apply the **Mesh Select** modifier and select the top half of the polygons [see Fig. A3]. Now, move these polygons along +z-axis to create the shape of a capsule [see Fig. A4].

Sub-object selection based on an angle: Create a **Torus Knot** primitive and then make polygon selection, as shown in Fig. A5, with a single click.

*Hint: Use the **By Angle** parameter in the Selection rollout to create the selection.*

Work with the Slice Plane feature: Create a **Cylinder** primitive and then set its **Radius** and **Height** to **45** and **140**, respectively. Now, using the **Slice Plane** feature, slice the cylinder, as shown in Fig. A6.

Copy-Paste Named Selection Sets: Create two **Teapot** primitives and rename them as **tpot-1** and **tpot-2**, respectively. Now, convert them to **Editable Poly**. Select **tpot-1** and make the **Polygon** mode active, select some of the polygons. Next, type the name as **tpot-1-selec** for the selection set in the **Named Selection Sets** drop-down list. Now, click **Copy** in the **Geometry** rollout; the **Copy Named Selection** dialog box appears. Select **tpot-1-selec** and then click **OK**. Now, paste the copied selection set onto **tpot-2**.

Chamfer Vertices: Create a **Plane** primitive and then set its **Length**, **Width**, **Length Segs**, **Width Segs** to **150**, **150**, **4**, and **4**, respectively. Convert it to editable poly and then weld the vertices [refer to Fig. A7] using the **Target Weld** feature. Next, create open chamfers, as shown in Fig. A8.

Attach splines: Create a **Box** and convert it to an editable poly object. Next, create a **Circle** primitive. Now, attach it to the box in a way so that both the objects become a single object, and **Circle** becomes the element of the new object.

Creating holes: Create a **Plane** primitive [see Fig. A9] and then create holes in it, as shown in Fig. A10.

Connect Vertices: Create a **Plane** primitive and then set its **Length**, **Width**, **Length Segs**, **Width Segs** to **150**, **150**, **4**, and **4**, respectively. Next, convert it to editable poly. Select the vertices, as shown in Fig. A11. Now, connect the vertices, as shown in Fig. A12. Next, remove the newly added edges.

Summary

The unit covered the following topics:

- Working with the polygon modeling tools
- Using the polygon modeling techniques
- Selecting polygon sub-objects
- Transforming sub-objects
- Soft selecting sub-objects

Multiple Choice

1. B, **2.** A, **3.** D, **4.** B

Fill in the Blanks

1. Vertex, Edge, Border, Polygon, Element, **2.** triangular, **3.** Edit Poly, **4.** 1, 5, 6, **5.** Attach, **6.** Delete, Backspace

True/False

1. T, **2.** T, **3.** F

- Working with **Graphite Modeling Tools**
- Selecting sub-objects
- Creating models using the tools available in the **Ribbon**

Unit 5: Graphite Modeling Tools

In the previous unit, I covered everything you need to know about modeling with polygons. You created geometric primitives and converted them into editable poly objects and then used the tools and commands available in the **Command** panel to create the models. 3ds Max provides another workflow for creating and editing polygons based on the **Ribbon** interface. If you have worked with any other Autodesk product such as products from the **Revit** family, you might be aware of the **Ribbon** interface. In this unit, I describe the tools available in the **Ribbon** interface and how you can use them to improve your modeling workflow.

The Ribbon

Graphite Modeling tools are available in the **Ribbon**. These tools offer a wide variety of features for editing polygons. The **Ribbon** comprises all standard **Editable Poly** tools and some additional tools for creating, selecting, and editing geometries. By default, **Ribbon** sits on top of the viewports in the collapsed state [see Fig. 1].

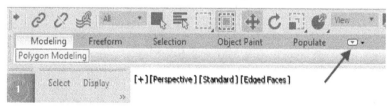

To expand the **Ribbon**, either double-click on the empty gray area of the **Ribbon** or click **Show Full Ribbon** [marked with an arrow in Fig. 1]. The **Ribbon** with the **Modeling** tab appears [see Fig. 2].

Tip: Toggling display of the Ribbon
*If **Ribbon** is not visible, click the **Show Ribbon** button on the **Main** toolbar or choose*
***Show UI** > **Show Ribbon** from the **Customize** menu.*

Tip: Docking Ribbon to the right
*You can doc the **Ribbon** on the left or right of the interface [see Fig. 3].*

Each tab in the **Ribbon** comprises various panels such as the **Polygon Modeling** panel in the **Modeling** tab [marked with an arrow in Fig. 4]. The display of the panel in the tab is context-sensitive. To view other panels in the tab, create a primitive in a viewport, and then convert it to **Editable Poly**.

When you click on the arrow on the right of the panel's name, the panel expands revealing the tools and commands available in that panel. Fig. 4 shows the expanded **Polygon Modeling** panel. Click on **Polygon Modeling** to collapse the panel [marked with an arrow in Fig. 4].

Table 1 summarizes the tabs available in the **Ribbon**.

Table 1: The tabs available in the **Ribbon**	
Tab	**Description**
Modeling	The tools in this tab are mainly used for polygon modeling. These tools are organized in different panels for easy access.
Freeform	This tab contains tools for creating and modifying geometry by painting on the surface of geometry. You can also specify settings for paintbrushes from this tab.

Table 1: The tabs available in the **Ribbon**

Tab	Description
Selection	The special tools in this tab allow you to make a sub-object selection uniquely. For example, you can select sub-objects from a concave or a convex area or select sub-objects that face the viewport.
Object Paint	The tools available in this tab allow you to freehand paint objects anywhere in the scene.
Populate	This tab provides tools for adding animated pedestrians and idlers in the scene.

 Tip: Tools help
*3ds Max provides extended tooltip for the tools available in the **Ribbon**. Position the mouse pointer on a tool; 3ds Max displays a smaller tooltip. If you place the mouse pointer on a tool for a little longer, 3ds Max expands the tooltip and sometimes you will also see an illustration in the tooltip. Fig. 5 shows an expanded tooltip when the mouse pointer was placed on the **Ring** tool.*

Modeling Tab

The **Modeling** tab contains the tools that you will use with the polygon models. These tools are organized into separate panels for easy access. Most of the tools in this tab are clones of the polygon editing tools found in the **Command** panel. The best way to understand these tools is to practice them. You will use these tools in the hands-on exercises of this unit.

Freeform Tab

The **Freeform** tab [see Fig. 6] provides tools for creating and modifying geometry by painting on the surface of the geometry. This tab contains three panels: **PolyDraw**, **Paint Deform**, and **Defaults**. These panels are discussed next.

PolyDraw Panel

The tools in this panel allow you to quickly sketch or edit a mesh in the main grid. You can also sketch on the surface of another object or on the object itself. This panel also provides tools for molding one object to the shape of another object. Before exploring the tools, let's understand the **Conform Options** panel which is always displayed when a conform brush tool is active.

Conform Options Panel

The options in this panel [see Fig. 7] let you specify the settings for modifying the tool's effects. When any conform brush tool other than the **Conform Brush** is active, the panel is named **Transform Conform Options**. Also, an additional toggle appears with the name **Offset Relative**.

Here's the quick rundown to the options available in the **Conform Options** panel.

Full Strength: Defines the size of the center area represented by a white circle in the brush [see Fig. 8]. The **Strength %** setting [see Fig. 7] is fully applied in this area. To adjust the brush size interactively, **Shift**+drag.

Falloff: Falloff is represented by the bigger black circle [see Fig. 8]. The **Strength** in this circle decreases from full strength to zero. To adjust the brush size interactively, **Ctrl**+drag.

Conform: It defines the rate at which the **Conform** brush deforms the painted object. The higher the values you specify for this option, the instant will be the conforming effect.

Mirror: When **Mirror** is active, the tool's effect is applied equally to both sides [see Fig. 9] across the mirror axis defined by the **Mirror Axis** parameter.

View/ Vertex Normals: These two options [see Fig. 10] control the direction in which the **Conform** brush moves the vertices. **View** pushes vertices away from the screen therefore it is dependent on the view angle of the scene. **Vertex Normals** pushes the vertices along their own normal toward the target.

Offset Relative: This brush is only available when you use one of the transform conform brushes. When on, it helps you in retaining the original shape of the object.

Strength %: This option defines the overall rate at which a brush deforms an object. To interactively change the value for this option, **Shift+Alt**+drag.

Use Selected Verts: When on, deform tools only affect the selected vertices. When off, it affects all vertices of the object.

Ignore Backfacing: When on, the tools affect vertices facing you.

Mirror Axis X/Y/Z: Allow you to choose the axis across which the conform action will be mirrored.

Freeze Axis X/Y/Z: When any **Freeze Axis** button is active, the tool is prevented from moving vertices on the corresponding axis of the object. To limit the effect to a particular axis, select **Freeze Axis** for the other two axes.

Freeze Selected Edges X/Y/Z: When any **Freeze Selected Edges** button is active, the tool is prevented from moving edges on the corresponding axis of the object. The un-selected edges move freely. These options apply to all sub-objects levels.

PolyDraw Panel - Drag and Conform Tools

The tools in this panel [see Fig. 11] produce different effects depending on which combination keys [**Ctrl, Alt**, and **Shift**] you press. Although, **PolyDraw** tools do not require you to select any sub-object level, however, it is recommended that you use these tools at the **Vertex** sub-object level for better results.

The **Min Distance** parameter allows you to specify a distance you need to drag the mouse before the next step in the tool is taken. There are two buttons available on the right of the **Min Distance** parameter: **in Pixels** and **in Units**. You can use these buttons to specify the minimum distance in pixels and world units, respectively.

The **Branch Taper** parameter allows you to specify the amount by which the branches taper as you draw them. On clicking the **New Object** button, 3ds Max creates a new empty editable object, activates the **Vertex** sub-object level, and keeps the current **PolyDraw** tool active. Now, you can use the **PolyDraw** tools to add geometry.

On clicking the **Solve Surface** button, 3ds Max attempts to create a workable mesh composed of mostly quads. You can use this tool to clean up the mesh after using tools such as **Draw Polygon Shapes**.

Drag: You can use the **Drag** tool to move sub-objects on a surface or grid. Table 2 summarizes the functions available with this tool.

Table 2: Functions of the **Drag** tool	
Function	**Description**
Normal	Without any modifier keys this tool moves vertices by dragging them.
Shift	Moves edges.
Ctrl+Drag	Moves polygons.
Shift+Ctrl+Drag	Moves edge loops.
Shift+Ctrl+Alt+Drag	Moves elements.

You can also use this tool to move the sub-objects in screen space [perpendicular to the current view selection]. Table 3 shows these functions.

Table 3: Functions of the **Drag** tool in the screen space

Function	Description
Alt+Drag	Moves vertices.
Alt+Shift+Drag	Moves edges.
Alt+Ctrl+Drag	Moves polygons.

 Conform Brush: The **Conform** brushes move the conform object's vertices towards the target to mold a conform object into the shape of the target object. You can use these brushes in a variety of modeling scenarios such as painting a road on hilly terrain or painting a mask on the face of a character.

To conform an object to the target object. Select the object that you want to conform. Activate the **Vertex** sub-object level for better control. Select **Draw On: Surface** from the **Draw On** drop-down list [🖉 Surface ▾] on the **PolyDraw** panel. Click **Pick** and then click the target object in a viewport. The name of the object appears on the **Pick** [Pick] button. Click **Conform**, adjust brush size and strength, and then drag the object toward the target using the **Conform** brush. The selected object takes the shape of the target object. In Fig. 12, I have conformed a **Plane** primitive to a **Sphere** primitive.

Apart from the basic **Conform** brush that is described above, 3ds Max also provides four transform based variants: **Move Conform Brush** 🖉, **Rotate Conform Brush** 🖉, **Scale Conform Brush** 🖉, and **Relax Conform Brush** 🖉. The **Relax Conform Brush** applies a relaxing effect to the vertices within a spherical volume.

PolyDraw Panel - Add Geometry and Optimize Tools

Step Build: This tool works at the **Object** level as well as the sub-objects level. You can use this tool to build a surface vertex by vertex or polygon by polygon. Table 4 summarizes the functions of this tool.

Table 4: Functions of the **Step Build** tool

Function	Description
Normal	Click to place vertices on the grid or surface.
Shift+Drag	Drag over the floating vertices to fill the gaps with quad polygons.
Ctrl+Click	Click on a polygon to delete it.
Alt+Click	Click on a vertex to remove it.
Ctrl+Alt+Click	Click on an edge to remove it.
Ctrl+Shift+Click	Click to place and select vertices. You can also select the existing vertices.
Shift+Alt	Move the mouse pointer [do not drag] over the vertices to select them.
Ctrl+Shift+Alt	Drag mouse pointer to move a vertex on a grid or surface.

⚠ *Caution: Vertex ticks*
*When the **Step Build** tool is active, vertex ticks are not always visible in the viewport. If you don't see the ticks at levels other than the **Vertex** level, change the display of the object to **By Object** in the object's display properties.*

 Extend Tool: You can use this tool with the open edges that are on the border of the surface that have only one polygon attached. Table 5 summarizes the functions of this tool.

Table 5: Functions of the **Extend** tool

Function	Description
Normal	Drag a border vertex to create a polygon.
Shift+Drag	Drag a border edge to create a polygon.
Ctrl+Shift+Drag	Drag an edge to extend its entire loop.
Ctrl+Alt+Drag	Drag between two edges to create a polygon.
Ctrl+Click	Click to delete a polygon and associated isolated vertices.
Ctrl+Shift+Alt+Drag	Drag a vertex to move it on the surface or grid.
Alt+Drag (Screen Space)	Drag a border to create a polygon.
Alt+Shift+Drag (Screen Space)	Drag a border edge to create a polygon.

 Optimize Tool: This tool is used to remove the details from the model by drawing on it. Table 6 shows the functions of this tool.

Table 6: Functions of the **Optimize** tool	
Function	**Description**
Normal	Click on the edges to collapse. It merges two vertices into one.
Shift+Drag	Drag from one vertex to another to weld them.
Ctrl+Drag	Drag between the vertices to connect them.
Alt+Click	Click to remove a vertex.
Shift+Ctrl+Click	Click to remove an edge loop.
Shift+Alt+Click	Click to remove a ring.
Ctrl+Alt+Click	Click on an edge to remove it.
Shift+Ctrl+Alt+Drag	Drag on a vertex to move it.

Draw On: The options in this drop-down list allow you to choose the entity type on which you want to draw. The **Grid** option creates geometry on the grid of the active viewport. This option works well with the orthographic views, however, you can also use it in the **Perspective** viewport. The **Surface** option allows you to draw on another object that you specify. The **Selection** option lets you create geometry on the selected object.

Pick: This button lets you pick an object to draw on. To pick object, select **Surface** from the **Draw On** drop-down list and then click **Pick**. Now, click on the object to draw on.

Offset: It specifies the distance that **PolyDraw** uses for creating the geometry.

PolyDraw Panel - Create Geometry Tools

Shapes: You can use this tool to draw polygons on a surface or grid. Click **Solve Surface** after creating the polygon to generate a workable mesh. The **Solve Surface** option will be displayed when you expand the **PolyDraw** panel [see Fig. 13].

When **Shapes** is active, you can delete a polygon by clicking on it with the **Ctrl** held down. To move a polygon, drag the mouse pointer with **Ctrl+Shift+Alt** held down.

Topology: This tool is used to create quad polygons by drawing lines in a viewport. As you draw the quads using this tool, 3ds Max fills them with a polygon. To draw the mesh, pick **Topology** and then draw lines in a viewport. When you are done with the lines, **RMB** click to complete the operation [see Fig. 14].

14

The drop-down list associated with **Topology** contains an option, **Auto Weld**. When **Auto Weld** is selected, 3ds Max automatically attaches the mesh to the selected object and weld their border vertices. If **Auto Weld** is off, **Topology** always creates a new mesh. The **Minimum Distance** parameter available in the expanded **PolyDraw** panel defines the resolution of the lines. The default value for this control is **10** which works well in most of the cases. When **Topology** is active, you can **Shift**+drag to continue a line from the closest endpoint. To delete a line, click on it with **Ctrl** held down.

Splines: This tool draws a spline on a surface or grid. The splines created using this tool are renderable. Select the desired option from the **Draw On** drop-down list and then draw to create splines. All splines are combined into a single [separate] object. When **Splines** is active, you can delete a spline by clicking on it with the **Ctrl** held down. You can also move a spline to the closest splines by dragging it with **Ctrl+Shift+Alt** held down.

Strips: This tool can be used to quickly layout the topology foundation for a mesh object. It paints strips of polygons that follow the mouse drag direction [see Fig. 15]. If you press **Shift** before starting the painting, 3ds Max paints from the closest existing edge. If you want to create polygon between two open edges, press **Alt** and then drag between the two open edges.

15

Surface: This tool paints a surface onto an object or grid. The size of the surface polygons is controlled by the **Minimum Distance** setting available in the expanded **PolyDraw** panel. The drop-down list associated with **Surface** has an option, **Quads**. When **Quads** is selected, the surface is made up of quads. When off, 3ds Max creates a surface with triangles. To start the surface from an existing border edge, hold **Shift** before you start the drawing. It ensures that overlapping polygons are not created. To delete a polygon, click on it with the **Shift** held down; the associated isolated vertices are also deleted.

Branches: This tool creates multi-segmented extrusions from polygons [see Fig. 16]. This tool works only on the selected object and **Draw On** settings does not affect it. The extent of tapering of the branches is controlled by the **Branch Taper** setting available in the expanded **PolyDraw** panel. To create branches, drag the mouse pointer on the selected object, 3ds Max creates branches from the polygons closest to the mouse pointer. Press **Shift** to draw branches from all selected polygons. If you are at the **Polygon** level, click with **Ctrl** held down to select a polygon. You can also select/de-select additional polygons with **Shilft+Alt** held down.

Paint Deform Panel

The tools in this panel [see Fig. 17] give you the ability to deform mesh geometry interactively in the viewport. These tools work similarly for at the **Object** level as well at the sub-object level and are independent of any sub-object selection. To exit any tool, either click its button or **RMB** click in a viewport. Let's explore various deformation tools available in 3ds Max.

 Shift/ Shift Rotate/ Shift Scale

These tools are used to move, rotate, or scale objects in the screen space [see Fig. 18]. These tools are like using standard transformation tools with soft selection. However, with these tools, no initial selection is required. You can revert to the previous state by using the **Revert** tool. However, this tool only works if you have used any other deform tool such as **Push/ Pull**.

Push/Pull

This tool drags the vertices outward [see the left image in Fig. 19]. To move vertices inward, drag with the **Alt** held down [see the right image in Fig. 19]. When this tool is active you can use:

- **Ctrl** to revert to the previously saved state.
- **Shift** to relax the mesh.
- **Ctrl+Shift** to resize the brush
- **Shift+Alt** to change the strength of the brush.

Note: The Paint Options panel
*When you use any deform tool except **Shift** tools, the floating **Paint Options** panel appears [see Fig. 20]. You can use the settings from this panel to control the behavior of the deform tools.*

Relax/Soften

This tool allows you to soften the corners [see Fig. 21]. With other brushes, you can soften a geometry with **Shift** held down.

Smudge

The **Smudge** tool is used to move the vertices [see Fig. 22]. It is somewhat similar to the **Shift** tool however it updates the effect continuously. Also, it does not use falloff.

Flatten

This tool lets you flatten the concave and convex areas.

Pinch/Spread

You can use this tool to move vertices together or spread them apart. To spread, drag with the **Alt** held down.

Noise

You can use this tool to add convex noise to a surface [see Fig. 23]. To create concave noise, drag with **Alt** held down.

Exaggerate

This tool makes the features of the surface more pronounced by moving the convex areas outward and concave areas inward.

Constrain to Spline

Apart from the **Shift** tools, all other tools can use a spline as a path for mesh deformation. Create a spline and place it near the surface you want to deform [see the left image in Fig. 24]. Click **Pick** available below **Constrain to Spline** and then click on the spline in a viewport.

Make sure **Constrain to Spline** is active then pick a deform tool such as **Noise**. Now, when you paint on the object, the deform gizmo can only be moved along the spline. Drag the mouse pointer to create the deformation [see the right image in Fig. 24].

Defaults Panel

You can use this panel to save and load brush settings. The **Load All Brush Settings** option opens a dialog box that you can use to load brush settings from an existing file. The **Save All Brush Settings** option opens a dialog box that you can use to store brush settings to a file. The **Set Current Settings as Default** option saves the current brush settings as default.

Selection Tab

The **Selection** tab provides a wide array of tools that allow you to make a sub-object selection such as you can select convex and concave areas, you can select the sub-object that face the camera, and so on. Let's explore the various panels available in the **Selection** tab.

Select Panel

The tools in this panel let you select the sub-object based on certain topologies. Table 7 summarizes the tools available in this panel.

Table 7: The tools available in the **Select** panel		
Tool	**Icon**	**Description**
Tops	⬜	This tool selects the top of the extruded polygon. The selection depends on the active sub-object level. When the **Vertex**, **Edge**, or **Polygon** sub-object level is active, the vertices, edge outlines, or tops of the extruded polygons are selected. Fig. 25 shows the top of the extruded polygons selected.
Open	◯	This tool selects all open sub-objects [see Fig. 26]. The final result depends on active sub-object.
Hard	▱	This tool is available at the **Edge** sub-object level. It selects all edges in a model whose faces do not share the same smoothing groups.
Non-Quads	⬠	This tool selects all non-quadrilateral polygons. This tool is available at **Polygon** sub-object level.
Patterns	▨	This tool allows you to grow the current selection based on the pattern you select from the **Pattern** drop-down list. The **Pattern 1** through **Pattern 8** options provide different selection patterns. Make a selection in the viewport and then experiment with various patterns. **Growlines** grows the selection with gaps of unselected lines [see Fig. 27]. **Checker** grows selection in form of a checkerboard pattern [see Fig. 28]. **Dots** grows the selection such that all sub-objects have a gap between them [see Fig. 29]. **One Ring** grows a single polygon ring around the initial selection [see Fig. 30].
By Vertex	-	When you click a vertex using this tool, all sub-objects that use the clicked vertex are selected.
By Angle	-	When on and if you select a polygon, the neighboring polygons are also selected based on the value you set in the spinner available on the right of **By Angle**.

Table 7: The tools available in the **Select** panel

Tool	Icon	Description
By Material ID	–	It opens the **Material ID** dialog box that you can use to set the material IDs. Also, you can select by ID and material name using this dialog box.
By Smoothing Group	–	It displays a dialog box that shows the current smoothing groups. To select polygon associated with a group, click the corresponding smoothing group.

Stored Selection Panel

The options in this panel let you quickly and easily store and retrieve selections. You can also apply some basic operations between the stored selections. Table 8 summarizes the tools available in this panel.

Tool	Icon	Description
Table 8: The tools available in the **Stored Selection** panel		
Copy Store 1/ Copy Store 2		You can use these two buffers to place the current sub-object selection. When a buffer contains a selection, the associated button turns blue.
Paste Store 1/ Paste Store 2		These two tools restore the stored selection, clearing the existing selection. If you want to retain the current selection, click on these buttons with the **Shift** held down.
Add 1+2		It adds the two buffers and applies the selection at the current sub-object level.
Subtract 1-2		It selects the non-overlapping area of **Store 1** and also clears both buffers.
Intersect		Selects the overlapping area of **Store 1** and **Store 2**.
Clear		Clears the stored selection.

Sets Panel

The tools in this panel give you the ability to copy and paste the named selection sets between objects. To use these tools, create named selection sets and then use the **Copy** {}ͭ and **Paste** {}ᵦ tools from this panel to copy/paste selection from the buffer.

By Surface Panel

The **Concave** ▣/**Convex** ▣ tools allow you to select sub-objects in the concave or convex area of the mesh [see Fig. 31]. The spinner located next to the drop-down list allows you to specify the degree of concavity or convexity.

By Normal Panel

The tools in this panel let you select sub-objects based on their normal directions on the world axes. To make a selection, choose an axis and then set the value for the **Angle** parameter.

You can invert the selection by clicking **Invert**. The selection is shown in Fig. 32 is created by setting **Angle** to **87** and choosing the **Z**-axis.

By Perspective Panel

The tools in this panel let you select sub-objects based on the extent they point toward the active view. To make a selection, define an angle using the **Angle** parameter and then click **Select** [see the left image in Fig. 33]. If you click **Outline**, 3ds Max selects the outermost sub-objects [see the right image in Fig. 33].

By Random Panel

The tools in this panel select sub-objects at random numbers or percentages. Also, you can grow or shrink the current selection randomly. To make a selection, click **Number #** or **Percent %** to enable random selection by number or percentage and then click **Select** to make the selection from the current settings. The **Select Within Current Selection** option in the **Select** drop-down list selects random sub-objects within the current selection [see Fig. 34]. **Random Grow** and **Random Shrink** grows or shrinks the selection randomly.

By Half Panel

These tools let you select half of the mesh on the specified axis based on the area or volume. To select, choose an axis and then click **Select** . To toggle the selection, click **Invert Axis** .

By Pivot Distance Panel

You can use this tool to select the sub-objects based on their distance from the pivot. The spinner in this panel defines the distance. In Fig. 35, the selection is defined by setting spinner to **99.2%.**

By View Panel

This feature allows you to select and grow the sub-objects selection based on the current view. You can specify the distance using the **Grow From Perspective View** parameter.

By Symmetry Panel

You can use this feature to mirror the current sub-object selection on the specified local axis. This feature works on a symmetrical model. The center of the object is defined by the location of the pivot of the object.

By Color Panel

The options in this panel let you select vertices by color or illumination value. These options are available at only **Vertex** sub-object level. To select vertices, choose **Color** or **Illumination** from the drop-down list. Then, use the color swatch to specify a color. Next, click **Select** to select the vertices.

By Numeric Panel

This feature allows you to select vertices by the number of connected edges or number of sides you specify. Fig. 36 shows the panel at the **Vertex** and **Polygon** levels, respectively. The selection displayed in Fig. 37 shows the selection made by specifying the number of **Sides** to **4** at the **Polygon** level.

Object Paint Tab

The tools available in this tab [see Fig. 38] allow you to paint objects freehand anywhere in the scene or on the target objects. You can paint multiple objects in a specific order or randomly. The objects that you add by painting are not combined with other objects. You can use the **Fill** tool to fill an edge selection with the objects.

To understand the concept, create few primitives in the viewport and then create a teapot [see the left image in Fig. 39]. Ensure teapot is selected in a viewport and then click **Paint With Selected Object(s)** from the **Paint Objects** panel. Make sure **Scene** is selected from the **Paint On** drop-down list. Set **Spacing** to **15** and then freehand paint on the objects in the scene [see the right image in Fig. 39]. **RMB** click to exit the paint mode.

Caution: Exiting the paint mode
*You can adjust stroke after painting, therefore, do not **RMB** click to exit the paint mode until you are satisfied with the result.*

You can use the features in the **Object Paint** tab to make creative scenes. You can also use them to populate the scenes with, for example, characters or trees. I would recommend that you practice these tools and then integrate them into your workflow to create creative artwork.

Hands-on Exercises

Exercise 1: Creating a Desk

In this exercise, you will the model of a desk [see Fig. E1].

Table E1 summarizes the exercise.

Table E1	
Skill level	Intermediate
Time to complete	1 Hour
Topics	• Specifying the Units for the Exercise • Creating the Desk
Resources folder	**graphite-tools**
Units	**Metric - Centimeters**
Final file	**desk-finish.max**

Specifying the Units for the Exercise

Follow these steps:

1. From the **Customize** menu choose **Units Setup**. In the **Units Setup** dialog box that appears, select the **Metric** option from the **Display Unit Scale** group. Next, select **Centimeters** from the drop-down list located below the **Metric** option, if already not selected. Click **OK** to accept the change.

2. From the **File** menu, choose **Save** to open the **Save File As** dialog box. In the **File name** text box type **desk-finish.max** and then click **Save** to save the file.

Creating the Desk
Follow these steps:

1. In the **Create** panel, activate **Geometry**, then in the **Object Type** rollout, click **Box**. Create a box in the **Top** viewport. In the **Modify** panel > **Parameters** rollout, set **Length** to **60**, **Width** to **150**, and **Height** to **2.5**. Invoke the **Move** tool from the **Main** toolbar.

2. Set the **Transform Type-In** boxes to **0** in the **Status Bar** to place the box at the origin. Create another box in the **Top** viewport. In the **Modify** panel > **Parameters** rollout, set **Length** to **60**, **Width** to **40**, and **Height** to **62**. Align the two boxes [see Fig. E2]. Create a copy of the box that you have just created and then align it [see Fig. E3].

 What next?
*Now, you will start using the tools and options available in the **Ribbon** to start shaping the desk. By default, the ribbon is minimized below the **Main** toolbar [see Fig. E4].*

3. Click **Show Full Ribbon** to display the full **Ribbon** [see Fig. E4]. You will notice that the tools in the **Polygon Modeling** panel are inactive because no polygon model exists in the scene [all objects are primitives at this stage]. To expand the **Polygon Modeling** panel and view all tools and options available in it, click **Polygon Modeling**. This action expands the panel and displays the tools available in it [see Fig. E5].

4. Select the top box. In the **Ribbon** > **Modeling** tab > **Polygon Modeling** panel, click **Convert to Poly** [refer to Fig. E6]. In the **Geometry (All)** panel, **Shift**-click on **Attach**. In the **Attach List** dialog box that appears, select **Box002** and **Box003** using **Ctrl** and then

click **Attach** to attach the selected boxes to the top box. Rename the unified geometry as **deskGeo**.

Tip: Opening settings of a tool
If you want to open settings for any tool available in the Ribbon, Shift-click on the tool.

Note: How materials of the objects are combined
*When you attach objects to a poly object, the materials of the objects are combined. If the objects being attached have no material, they inherit the material of the poly object. If the poly object that you are attaching to doesn't have a material, it inherits material of the objects being attached. In case, when both objects have materials, the resulting material is a new **Muti/Sub-object** material that includes the input materials.*

5. In the **Ribbon > Modeling** tab > **Polygon Modeling** panel, click **Edge**. Select the edge as shown in Fig. E7 and then in the **Ribbon > Modeling** tab > **Modify Selection** panel, click **Ring**. In the **Ribbon > Modeling** tab > **Loops** panel, click **Connect**. An edge loop appears.

6. Select the edges shown in Fig. E8 and then connect them as done before [see Fig. E9]. Hold **Ctrl** and double-click on the edge loop that you created earlier to select them [see Fig. E10]. In the **Ribbon > Modeling** tab > **Edges** panel, **Shift**-click on **Chamfer**. In the **Chamfer** caddy control, set **Edge Chamfer Amount** to **0.2** and **Connect Edge Segments** to **0**. Then, click **OK** [see Fig. E11].

7. In the **Ribbon > Modeling** tab > **Polygon Modeling** panel, click **Polygon**. Select the polygons [see Fig. E12]. Invoke the **Move** tool from the **Main** toolbar. In the **Perspective** viewport, press **Shift** and then move the selected polygon slightly [about 1.2 units] outward in the negative Y direction. Release **Shift**. In the **Clone Part of Mesh** dialog box that appears, select the **Clone To Object** option. Now, type **drawerGeo** in the text box next to **Clone To Object** and click **OK**.

8. Ensure the **drawerGeo** is selected. From the **Modifier** list > **Object-Space Modifiers** section, choose **Shell**. In the **Parameters** rollout, set **Outer Amount** to **1.5**. Align the **drawerGeo** with the **deskGeo** [see Fig. E13]. Similarly, detach the polygon shown in Fig. E14.

9. Name it as **drawerGeo1**, apply the **Shell** modifier, and then align it with **deskGeo** [see Fig. E15]. Hide the drawer geometries from the scene using the **Scene Explorer**. Now, you don't need the edges that you created earlier to create the drawer. Select those four edge loops and then press **Ctrl+Spacebar** to delete them and clean the model.

Tip: Removing Edges – Alternate Method

*In the **Ribbon** > **Modeling** tab > **Polygon Modeling** panel, click **Edge**. In the **Ribbon** > **Modeling** tab > **Edit** panel, click **Swift Loop** to make it active. Press **Ctrl+Shift** and then click on the edges on the drawers. This action will remove the edges.*

*The **SwiftLoop** tool allows you to interactively place edges. As you move the cursor over the object surface, a real-time preview is shown indicating that where the loop will be created when you click.*

Following are some different features of this tool:

- ■ ***Ctrl**-click to select an edge loop and activate the **Edge** sub-object level automatically.*
- ■ ***Alt**-drag a selected edge to slide the edge loop between its bounding loops.*
  ***Ctrl-Alt** drag is the same as the **Alt**-drag. However, it also straightens out the edge loop, if necessary.*
- ■ ***Ctrl-Shift** click on an edge loop to remove it.*
- ■ ***Shift**-click to insert a new loop and adjust it to the flow of the surrounding surface.*

10. Select **deskGeo** and activate the **Front** viewport. In the **Ribbon** > **Modeling** tab > **Polygon Modeling** panel, click **Edge**. In the **Ribbon** > **Modeling** tab > **Geometry (All)** panel, click **Slice Plane**. This action displays a slice plane gizmo in the viewport and opens the **Slice Mode** panel. Adjust the position of the plane as shown in Fig. E16 and then click **Slice** on **Slice Mode** panel to subdivide the geometry [see Fig. E17].

11. Similarly, add two more slices maintaining a gap of **2** units between them [see Fig. E18]. In the **Ribbon** > **Modeling** tab > **Polygon Modeling** panel, click **Polygon**. Select the polygons, refer to Fig. E19. In the **Ribbon** > **Modeling** tab > **Polygons** panel, **Shift**-click **Extrude**. In the **Extrude's** caddy, set **Height** to **4** and click **OK**.

12. Select the polygons shown in Fig. E20. In the **Ribbon** > **Modeling** tab > **Geometry (All)** panel, click on **Detach**. In the **Detach** dialog box that appears, set **Detach as** to **sliderGeo**. Also, select the **Detach as Clone** checkbox and then click **OK**. Select **sliderGeo** and move it slightly toward the negative Y-axis.

What just happened?

The **Detach** tool separates the selected sub-objects and associated polygons as a new object or element[s]. When you click **Detach**, the **Detach** dialog box appears. Type the name of the new object in the **Detach as** text box and click **OK** to create the new object with the specified name. The selection is removed from the original object. You can select **Detach To Element** to make the detached sub-object selection part of the original object but it becomes a new element. Select **Detach as Clone** to detach the selection as a copy of the original selection; the selection remains intact with the original object.

13. In the **Ribbon > Modeling** tab > **Polygon Modeling** panel, click **Polygon**. In the **Ribbon > Modeling** tab > **Polygons** panel, click **Bridge** to create a bridge between the selected polygons [see Fig. E21].

14. In the **Ribbon > Modeling** tab > **Polygon Modeling** panel, click **Border** and then select the border edges of **sliderGeo** [see Fig. E22]. In the **Ribbon > Modeling** tab > **Geometry (All)** panel, click on **Cap Poly** to cap the border edges.

15. Select **deskGeo** and then select the front polygon, refer to Fig. E23. Move it slightly toward the negative Y-axis [see Fig. E23].

16. Ensure the **drawerGeo** and **drawerGeo1** are visible in the scene. In the **Create** panel, activate **Geometry**, then in the **Extended Primitives** > **Object Type** rollout, click **ChamferCyl**.

17. Create a cylinder in the **Top** viewport. In the **Modify** panel > **Parameters** rollout, set **Height** to **6**, **Radius** to **1.5**, and **Fillet** to **0.074**. Now, set **Height Segs** to **2**, **Fillet Segs** to **3**, and **Sides** to **18**. Align it with **drawerGeo** [see Fig. E24].

18. Select the cylinder and press **Alt+Q** to isolate it. In the **Ribbon** > **Modeling** tab > **Polygon Modeling** panel, click **Convert to Poly**. In the **Ribbon** > **Modeling** tab > **Modeling** panel, click **Edge**. Select the edge loop shown in Fig. E25.

19. In the **Ribbon** > **Modeling** tab > **Edges** panel, **Shift**-click on **Chamfer**. In the **Chamfer's** caddy, set **Edge Chamfer Amount** to **0.1** and **Connect Edge Segments** to **0**. Then, click **OK** [see Fig. E26]. In the **Ribbon** > **Modeling** tab > **Polygon Modeling** panel, **Ctrl**-click **Polygon**. In the **Ribbon** > **Modeling** tab > **Modify Selection** panel, click **Shrink** to select the polygons created using the chamfer edge operation [see Fig. E27].

20. In the **Ribbon** > **Modeling** tab > **Polygons** panel, **Shift**-click **Inset**. In the **Inset** caddy control, set **Amount** to **0.02** and click **OK** [see Fig. E28].

21. In the **Ribbon > Modeling** tab > **Polygons** panel, **Shift**-click **Extrude**. In the **Extrude's** caddy, set **Extrusion Type** to **Local Normal** and **Height** to **-0.1**. Next, click **OK** [see Fig. E29]. Now, inset the selected polygon by **0.02** units.

22. Now, select the edges that you created using the **Inset** and **Extrude** operations [see Fig. E30] and then scale them down by to **70%** [see Fig. E31]. Switch to the **Object** mode. In the **Ribbon > Modeling** tab > **Edit** panel, click **NURMS** to smooth the object. Choose **End Isolate** from the **Tools** menu and then create two more copies of knob and align them [see Fig. E32].

What just happened?

*NURMS stands for **Non-Uniform Rational Mesh Smooth**. This tool allows you to smooth the objects using **NURMS** subdivision; the same method used by the **MeshSmooth** and **TurboSmooth** modifiers. When you click **NURMS**, the **NURMS** panel appears. The **Iterations** spinner in this panel specifies the number of iterations used to smooth the poly object.*

Caution: Calculation time

*Specify the number of iterations carefully. It increases the number of vertices and polygons in the object. As a result, the calculation time can increase as much as four times for each iteration. The value in the **Smoothness** spinner specifies how sharp a corner must be before polygons are added to smooth it.*

23. In the **Create** panel, activate **Geometry**, then on the **Extended Primitives** > **Object Type** rollout, click **ChamferBox**. Create a box in the **Top** viewport. In the **Modify** panel > **Parameters** rollout, set **Length** to **2**, **Width** to **26.4**, **Height** to **1.5**, and **Fillet** to **0.05**. Set **Width Segs** to **12**.

24. From the **Modifier** list > **Object-Space Modifiers** section, choose **Bend**. In the **Parameters** rollout, set **Angle** to **152** and **Bend Axis** to **X**. Now, align the handle with the **drawerGeo1** [see Fig. E33].

25. From the **Modifier** list > **Object-Space Modifiers** section, choose **Taper**. In the **Modify** panel > modifier stack display, expand **Taper** and click **Gizmo**. Invoke the **Scale** tool from the **Main** toolbar. Change the size of gizmo along the **x-axis** [see Fig. E34].

26. In the **Parameters** rollout, set **Amount** to **-1.1** and **Primary** to **Z**. Set **Effect** to **Y**. From the **Modifier** list > **Object-Space Modifiers** section, choose **TurboSmooth** to smooth the handle [see Fig. E35].

27. Convert **drawerGeo** and **drawerGeo1** to editable poly. Select **drawerGeo** and then in the **Ribbon** > **Modeling** tab > **Polygon Modeling** panel, click **Edge**. Press **Ctrl+A** to select all the edges of **drawerGeo**. In the **Ribbon** > **Modeling** tab > **Edges** panel, **Shift**-click **Chamfer**.

28. In the **Chamfer Edges** caddy control, set **Mitering** to **Quad**, **Edge Chamfer Amount** to **0.07**, and click **OK**. Similarly, chamfer all edges of **drawerGeo1**, **sliderGeo**, and **deskGeo**.

29. In the **Create** panel, activate **Geometry**, then on the **Extended Primitives > Object Type** rollout, click **ChamferBox**. Create a box in the **Top** viewport. In the **Modify** panel > **Parameters** rollout, set **Length** to **4**, **Width** to **4**, **Height** to **8**, and **Fillet** to **0.353**. Set **Fillet Segs** to **2**. Ensure the **Length Segs**, **Width Segs**, and **Height Segs** are set to **1** each.

30. Rename the box as **legGeo**. Next. align **legGeo** as shown in Fig. E36. Create seven more copies of **legGeo** and align them as shown in Fig. E37.

Exercise 2: Creating a USB Connector

In this exercise, you will create the model of a USB connector [see Fig. E1].

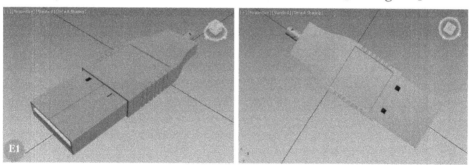

Table E2 summarizes the exercise.

Table E2	
Skill level	Intermediate
Time to complete	40 Minutes
Topics	• Specifying the Units for the Exercise • Creating the USB Connector
Resources folder	**graphite-tools**
Units	**Metric - Millimeters**
Final file	**usbconnector-finish.max**

Specifying the Units for the Exercise

Follow these steps:

1. From the **Customize** menu choose **Units Setup**. In the **Units Setup** dialog box that appears, select the **Metric** option from the **Display Unit Scale** group. Next, select **Millimeters** from the drop-down list located below the **Metric** option, if already not selected. Click **OK** to accept the change.

2. From the **File** menu, choose **Save** to open the **Save File As** dialog box. In the **File name** text box type **usbconnector-finish.max** and then click **Save** to save the file.

Creating the USB Connector

Follow these steps:

1. Create a box in the **Top** viewport. In the **Modify** panel > **Parameters** rollout, set **Length** to **15**, **Width** to **30**, **Height** to **5**, and **Width Segs** to **1**. Rename the box as **ucGeo**. Invoke the **Move** tool from the **Main** toolbar. Set the **Transform Type-In** boxes to **0** in the **Status Bar** to place the box at the origin.

2. In the **Ribbon > Modeling** tab > **Polygon Modeling** panel, click **Convert to Poly**. Activate the **Edge** sub-object level and then in the **Ribbon > Modeling** tab > **Edit** panel, click **SwiftLoop**. Create two loops [refer to Fig. E2]. Deactivate **SwiftLoop**.

3. Activate the **Vertex** sub-object level and then adjust the shape of the connector using the **Move** and **Scale** tools [see Fig. E3]. Activate the **Polygon** sub-object level and then select the front polygon. In the **Ribbon > Modeling** tab > **Polygons** panel, **Shift**-click **Inset**. In the **Inset** caddy control, set **Amount** to **0.5** and then click **OK** [see Fig. E4].

4. In the **Ribbon > Modeling** tab > **Polygons** panel, **Shift**-click **Extrude**. In the **Extrude Polygons** caddy control, set **Amount** to **-8** and then click **OK** [see Fig. E5]. Activate **Edge** sub-object level and then select the edge shown in Fig. E6.

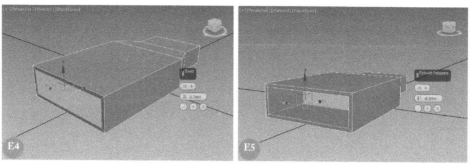

5. In the **Ribbon > Modeling** tab > **Modify Selection** panel, click **Ring**. In the **Ribbon > Modeling** tab > **Loops** panel, **Shift**-click **Connect**. In the **Connect Edges** caddy control, set **Segments** to **2** and **Pinch** to **62** [see Fig. E7]. Click **OK**. Similarly, create two more edge loops [see Fig. E8].

6. Activate the **Polygon** sub-object level and then select the polygon shown in Fig. E9. In the **Ribbon > Modeling** tab > **Polygons** panel, **Shift**-click **Inset**. In the **Inset** caddy control, set **Amount** to **0.5** and then click **OK**. In the **Ribbon > Modeling** tab > **Polygons** panel, **Shift**-click **Extrude**. In the **Extrude Polygons** caddy control, set **Amount** to **-0.3** and **then** click **OK** [see Fig. E10].

7. Activate the **Edge** sub-object level and then select the edge ring shown in Fig. E11. In the **Ribbon > Modeling** tab > **Loops** panel, **Shift**-click **Connect**. In the **Connect Edges** caddy control, set **Segments** to **14** and **Pinch** to **-25**. Click **OK** [see Fig. E12].

8. Activate **Polygon** sub-object level and then select every other polygon loop using the **Ctrl** and **Shift** [see Fig. E13].

9. Now, in the **Top** viewport, remove the polygons from the selection using **Alt** [see Fig. E14].

10. In the **Ribbon > Modeling** tab > **Polygons** panel, **Shift**-click **Inset**. In the **Inset** caddy control, set **Amount** to **0.1** and then click **OK**. In the **Ribbon > Modeling** tab > **Polygons** panel, **Shift**-click **Extrude**. In the **Extrude Polygons** caddy control, set **Extrusion Type** to **Local Normal** and **Amount** to **-0.2** and **then** click **OK** [see Fig. E15].

11. Activate **Edge** sub-object level and then on the **Ribbon > Modeling** tab > **Edit** panel, click **SwiftLoop**. Create edge loops around the sharp edges of the **ucGeo** [see Figs. E16 and E17].

12. Now, insert an edge loop shown in Fig. E18. In the **Ribbon > Modeling** tab > **Edges** panel, **Shift**-click **Chamfer**. In the **Chamfer** caddy, set **Edge Chamfer Amount** to **0.09** and **Connect Edge Segments** to **0.** Click **OK**.

13. Select the polygons created using the chamfer operation. In the **Ribbon > Modeling** tab > **Polygons** panel, **Shift**-click **Extrude**. In the **Extrude Polygons** caddy, set **Amount** to **-0.04** and then click **OK** [see Fig. E19].

14. Create more edge loops using the **SwiftLoop** tool [see Fig. E20]. Similarly, add edge loops in the front of the connector [see Fig. 21]. From the **Object-Space Modifiers** section of the **Modifier** list, select **MeshSmooth**. In the **Subdivision Amount** rollout, change **Iterations** to **3** [see Fig. E22].

15. Create a box in the **Top** viewport. In the **Modify** panel > **Parameters** rollout, set **Length** to **14**, **Width** to **20**, **Height** to **4**, and **Width Segs** to **1**. Rename the cylinder as **cGeo**. In the **Ribbon > Modeling** tab > **Polygon Modeling** panel, click **Convert to Poly.**

16. Activate the **Polygon** sub-object level and then select the front polygon. In the **Ribbon >**
Modeling tab > **Polygons** panel, **Shift**-click **Inset**. In the **Inset** caddy control, set **Amount**
to **0.5** and then click **OK** [see Fig. E23]. In the **Ribbon > Modeling** tab > **Polygons**
panel, **Shift**-click **Extrude**. In the **Extrude Polygons** caddy control, set **Amount** to **-6**
and then click **OK** [see Fig. E24].

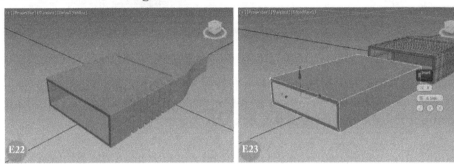

17. Activate the **Edge** sub-object level and then select the ring shown in Fig. E25. In the
Ribbon > Modeling tab > **Loops** panel, **Shift**-click **Connect**. In the **Connect Edges**
caddy control, set **Segments** to **2** and **Pinch** to **-85**. Click **OK**.

18. Select the newly created polygons and in the **Ribbon > Modeling** tab > **Polygons** panel,
Shift-click **Extrude**. In the **Extrude Polygons** caddy control, set **Amount** to **-0.2**, **Type**
to **Local Normal**, and then click **OK** [see Fig. E26].

19. Activate the **Edge** sub-object level. Insert edge loops using **SwiftLoop** as shown in
Fig. E27. Activate the **Polygon** sub-object level. Select the polygons shown in Fig. E28
and delete them using **Delete**.

20. Activate the **Edge** sub-object level and select the outer edges shown in Fig. E29. In the **Ribbon > Modeling** tab > **Edges** panel, **Shift**-click **Chamfer**. In the **Chamfer** caddy control, set **Mitering** to **Quad**, **Edge Chamfer Amount** to **0.06**, and **Connect Edge Segments** to **1**. Click **OK**.

21. Select the edges that make up the holes and then on the **Ribbon > Modeling** tab > **Edges** panel, **Shift**-click **Extrude**. In the **Extrude Edges** caddy control, set **Height** to **-0.1**, **Width** to **0**, and then click **OK**. Place the metal connector inside its case. If you find that the metal connector is large in size, you can adjust the shape by moving the vertices [see Fig. E30].

22. Now, create a new box primitive and then place inside the metal connector as shown in Fig. E31.

23. Create a cylinder in the **Top** viewport. In the **Modify** panel > **Parameters** rollout, set **Radius** to **2**, **Height** to **4.3**, and **Height Segments** to **5**. Align it with the USB connector.

24. In the **Ribbon > Modeling** tab > **Polygon Modeling** panel, click **Convert to Poly**. Activate **Polygon** sub-object level and then select the polygons shown in Fig. E32.

25. In the **Ribbon > Modeling** tab > **Polygons** panel, **Shift**-click **Inset**. In the **Inset** caddy control, set **Amount** to **0.2** and then click **OK**. In the **Ribbon > Modeling** tab > **Polygons** panel, **Shift**-click **Extrude**. In the **Extrude Polygons** caddy control, set **Amount** to **-0.5** and **then** click **OK** [see Fig. E33].

Exercise 3: Creating a Flash Drive

In this exercise, you will the model a flash drive [see Fig. E1].

Table E3 summarizes the exercise.

Table E3	
Skill level	Intermediate
Time to complete	1 Hour
Topics	• Specifying the Units for the Exercise • Creating the Flash Drive
Resources folder	**graphite-tools**
Units	**Metric - Millimeters**
Final file	**flash-drive-finish.max**

Specifying the Units for the Exercise

Follow these steps:

1. From the **Customize** menu choose **Units Setup**. In the **Units Setup** dialog box that appears, select the **Metric** option from the **Display Unit Scale** group. Next, select **Millimeters** from the drop-down list located below the **Metric** option, if already not selected. Click **OK** to accept the change.

2. From the **File** menu, choose **Save** to open the **Save File As** dialog box. In the **File name** text box type **flash-drive-finish.max** and then click **Save** to save the file.

Creating the Flash Drive
Follow these steps:

1. Create a cylinder in the **Top** viewport. In the **Modify** panel > **Parameters** rollout, set **Radius** to **7.5**, **Height** to **7**, **Height Segments** to **1**, and **Sides** to **32**. Rename the cylinder as **usbGeo**. Invoke the **Move** tool from the **Main** toolbar. Set the **Transform Type-In** boxes to **0** on the **Status Bar** to place the cylinder at the origin. In the **Ribbon > Modeling** tab > **Polygon Modeling** panel, click **Convert to Poly.** Activate the **Vertex** sub-object level and then select the vertices in the **Front** viewport [see Fig. E2].

2. In the **Top** viewport, move the selected vertices towards right along the x-axis about **25** units [see Fig. E3].

3. In the **Ribbon > Modeling** tab > **Geometry (All)** panel, click **Slice Plane**. This action will display a slice plane gizmo in the viewport and opens the **Slice Mode** panel. Adjust the position of the plane, as shown in Fig. E4, and then click **Slice** on **Slice Mode** panel to subdivide the geometry. In the **Ribbon > Modeling** tab > **Geometry (All)** panel, click **Slice Plane** to deactivate the slice plane feature.

4. Activate **Edge** sub-object level and then in the **Front** viewport, drag a selection window to select the edges [see Fig. E5].

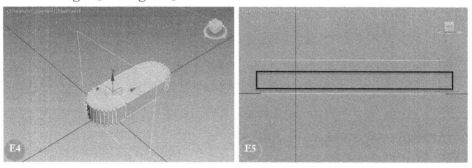

5. Press **Ctrl+I** to invert the selection. Remove the edges from the selection that you created using **Slice Plane**. In the **Ribbon > Modeling** tab > **Edges** panel, **Shift**-click **Chamfer**. In the **Chamfer** caddy control, set **Edge Chamfer Amount** to **0.8** and **Connect Edge Segments** to **7** [see Fig. E6]. Click **OK**. Activate **Polygon** sub-object level and then select polygons [see Fig. E7].

6. In the **Ribbon > Modeling** tab > **Geometry (All)** panel, click **Detach**. In the **Detach** dialog box that appears, type **capGeo** in the **Detach as** text box and then make sure that the **Detach to Element** and **Detach As Clone** checkboxes are clear. Now, click **OK**. Move the cap slightly towards left and then apply a **Shell** modifier to it. In the **Parameters** rollout, set **Inner Amount** to **0.4** and **Outer Amount** to **0**.

7. Activate the **Border** sub-object level for **usbGeo** and then make the border selection [see Fig. E8]. In the **Ribbon > Modeling** tab > **Geometry (All)** panel, click **Cap Poly** to create a polygon.

8. Activate the **Polygon** sub-object level and then select the newly created polygon. In the **Ribbon > Modeling** tab > **Polygons** panel, click **Shift**-click **Inset**. In the **Inset** caddy control, set **Amount** to **0.5** and then click **OK**. In the **Ribbon > Modeling** tab > **Polygons** panel, **Shift**-click **Extrude**. In the **Extrude Polygons** caddy control, set **Amount** to **0.8** and then click **OK** [see Fig. E9].

9. Activate the **Edge** sub-object level and then select the edge loops shown in Fig. E10. In the **Ribbon > Modeling** tab > **Edges** panel, **Shift**-click **Chamfer**. In the **Chamfer** caddy control, set **Mitering** to **Uniform**, **Edge Chamfer Amount** to **0.05** and **Connect Edge Segments** to **4**. Click **OK** [see Fig. E11].

10. Activate the **Polygon** sub-object level and then select the top polygon of the **usbGeo** [see Fig. E12]. In the **Ribbon > Modeling** tab > **Polygons** panel, **Shift**-click **Inset**. In the **Inset** caddy control, set **Amount** to -**0.3** and **then** click **OK** [see Fig. E13].

11. In the **Ribbon > Modeling** tab > **Polygons** panel, **Shift**-click **Extrude**. In the **Extrude Polygons** caddy control, set **Amount** to -**0.4** and **then** click **OK** [see Fig. E14].

12. Activate the **Edge** sub-object level and then select the loop shown in Fig. E15. In the **Ribbon > Modeling** tab > **Edges** panel, **Shift**-click **Chamfer**. In the **Chamfer** caddy control, set **Mitering** to **Uniform**, **Edge Chamfer Amount** to **0.4** and **Connect Edge Segments** to **3.** Click **OK** [see Fig. E16]. Now, create the USB connector as done in the previous exercise [see Fig. E17].

E16 E17

Quiz

Evaluate your skills to see how many questions you can answer correctly.

Multiple Choice
Answer the following questions:

1. Which the following panels is used to quickly sketch or edit a mesh on the grid or a surface?

   [A] PolyDraw   [B] SketchDraw
   [C] ObjectPaint   [D] None of the above

2. Which of the following keys is used to interactively change the conform brush's strength?

   [A] Ctrl+drag   [B] Alt+Drag
   [C] Shift+drag   [D] Ctrl+Shift+Drag

3. Which of the following tools is used to quickly layout the topology foundation for a mesh object?

   [A] Splines   [B] Stripes
   [C] Surface   [D] Branches

Fill in the Blanks
Fill in the blanks in each of the following statements:

1. The Graphite Modeling tools are available in the _____.

2. This _____ tool is used to remove the details from the model by drawing on it.

True or False

State whether each of the following is true or false:

1. When the **Step Build** tool is active, vertex ticks are not always visible in the viewport.

2. The options in the **Stored Selection Panel** let you quickly and easily store and retrieve selections.

Summary

The unit covered the following topics:

- Working with the **Graphite Modeling Tools**
- Selecting sub-objects
- Creating models using the tools available in the **Ribbon**

Multiple Choice
1. A, **2.** A, 3.B

Fill in the Blanks
1. Ribbon, **2.** Optimize

True/False
1. T, **2.** T

- Generate planar and 3d surfaces
- Paths and shapes for the loft components
- Generate extrusions
- Generate revolved surfaces
- Define motion path for animations

Unit 6: Spine Modeling

A shape in 3ds Max is an object consists of one or more lines. These lines which can be 2D or 3D, are used to create components for other objects. 3ds Max provides two types of shape objects: **Splines** and **NURBS** curves. Most of the default shapes in 3ds Max are splines.

3ds Max provides thirteen basic spline objects, five extended spline objects, and two types of NURBS curves. You can use these objects in the following ways:

- Generate planar and 3d surfaces
- Paths and shapes for the loft components
- Generate extrusions
- Generate revolved surfaces
- Define motion path for animations

Apart from what mentioned above, you can also render the shape as is. When rendering is enabled for the shapes, 3ds Max renders them using a circular or rectangular cross-section.

You can convert a basic spline or an extended spline to an editable spline object. This object offers a variety of parameters to create less regular and complex shapes. It allows you to edit the shape at the sub-object level. However, when you convert a spline to an **Editable Spline** object, you lose the parametric nature of the spline and cannot adjust the creation parameters. The **Editable Spline** object will be discussed later in this unit. You can use the **Edit Spline** modifier to retain the parametric nature of a primitive spline. This modifier matches all the capabilities of the **Editable Spline** object with some exceptions given next:

- The **Rendering** and **Interpolation** rollouts are not available when you are using the **Edit Spline** modifier.
- Direct vertex animation capabilities are not available.

It is recommended that you use the base **Editable Spline** object to edit the splines rather than store the changes in an **Edit Spline** modifier. The **Editable Spline** object is more reliable and efficient than the **Edit Spline** modifier.

Spline and Extended Splines Primitives

You can access the shape creation tools from the **Create** panel. Go to the **Create** panel and then click **Shapes**.

A drop-down list appears below the **Shapes** button with the entries: **Splines**, **NURBS Curves**, **Compound Shape**, **CFD**, **Max Creation Graph**, and **Extended Splines** [see Fig. 1].

Table 1 summarizes the available tools. You can also access these tools from the **Create** menu.

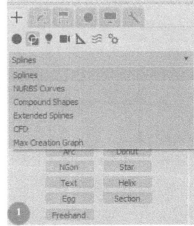

Table 1: The shapes tools available in 3ds Max	
Splines	**Line, Rectangle, Circle, Ellipse, Arc, Donut, NGon, Star, Text, Helix, Egg, Section**, and **Freehand**
NURBS Curves	**Point Curve** and **CV Curve**
Extended Splines	**WRectangle, Channel, Angle, Tee**, and **Wide Flange**

Spline Primitives

In this section, I will explain the basic spline primitives. Let's start with the **Line** spline.

Line Spline

A **Line** spline is a free-form spline that is made up of multiple segments. To create a line, go to the **Create** panel, click **Shapes**, and then click **Line** in the **Object Type** rollout. Notice that various rollouts appear in the **Create** panel. Choose the creation method from the **Creation Method** rollout. Click or drag in the viewport to create the first vertex [if you click, a **Corner** vertex is created otherwise a **Bezier** vertex will be created]. Now, click or drag to create additional points. To finish the creation method, do one of the following: either **RMB** click to create an open spline [see Fig. 2] or click on the first vertex and then choose **Yes** from the **Spline** message box that appears [see Fig. 3].

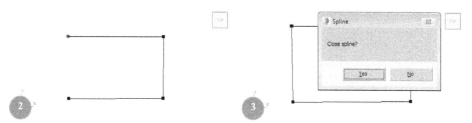

Tip: Constraining new points
Press and hold **Shift** *while creating splines to constrain new points to **90** degrees angle increments. Make sure that you are using the default initial type settings.*

Tip: Constraining new points to a custom angle increment
You can also constrain new points to a custom angle increment value. Select **Grids And Snaps** *>* **Grid And Snap Settings** *from the* **Tools** *menu. In the* **Grid and Snap Settings** *dialog box that appears, choose the* **Options** *panel and then set a value for the* **Angle** *spinner. Close the dialog box. Now, click* **Angle Snap Toggle** *in the* **Main** *toolbar. Press and hold* **Ctrl** *while creating new points to constrain them to the value you specified for the* **Angle** *spinner.*

Tip: Panning and orbiting while creating splines
If a spline requires two or more steps for its creation [such as **Line** *or* **Donut**]*, you can pan and orbit the viewport between the creation steps.*

Note: Editable Spline object
3ds Max automatically converts a **Line** *spline to an editable spline object because it has no dimensions parameters. No need to convert it to an* **Editable Spline** *object or apply an* **Edit Spline** *modifier on it.*

Now, let's take a look at the various aspects/parameters associated with the **Line** spline. Many of them are common to most of the spline objects.

Combining Shapes While Creating Them

3ds Max allows you to combine shapes to create compound shapes. You can use this feature to create complex shapes. To create a compound shape, in the **Create** panel, clear the checkbox preceding the **Start New Shape** button and then begin creating shapes. Each spline that you create, added to the compound spline.

You can check whether all splines are part of a compound shape or not. Go to the **Modify** panel and then click **Editable Spline** in the modifier stack. You will notice that all splines are selected in the viewport [see Fig. 4].

Caution: Parametric nature of splines
You cannot change the creation parameters of a compound shape. For example, if you first create a circle, and then add a rectangle to create a compound shape, you cannot switch back and change the creation parameters of the circle.

Creation Method Rollout

The controls in this rollout allow you to specify what type of vertex that will be created when you click or drag vertices in the viewport. The creation method options for the **Line** spline are different from other spline primitives.

Table 2 summarizes the parameters available in the **Creation Method** rollout.

Table 2: Parameters in the **Creation Method** rollout of the **Line** spline	
[Group]/ Parameter	**Description**
[Initial Type Group]	The parameters in this group set the type of vertex created when you click [not drag] a vertex location.
Corner	**Corner** creates sharp points and the spline created is linear to either side of the point.
Smooth	**Smooth** creates a smooth curve through the vertex that you can adjust manually. The curvature of the spline segment is controlled by the spacing of the vertices. Fig. 5 shows the splines created using the **Corner** and **Smooth** initial type options, respectively.
[Drag Type Group]	The parameters in this group define the type of vertex created when you drag a vertex location.
Corner, Smooth	The **Corner** and **Smooth** parameters work as discussed above.

Table 2: Parameters in the **Creation Method** rollout of the **Line** spline	
[Group]/ Parameter	**Description**
Bezier	The **Bezier** parameter produces a smooth adjustable curve. The amount of curvature and direction of the curve is controlled by dragging the mouse at each vertex. You can manually change the smoothness or curvature by manipulating the vertex handles [refer right-most spline in Fig. 6].

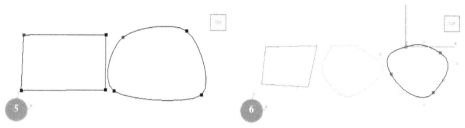

Keyboard Entry Rollout

You can use the **Keyboard Entry** rollout to precisely place vertices of a spline. To add a vertex, enter its coordinates in the **X**, **Y**, and **Z** spinners and then click **Add Point** to add a new point. The subsequent points you insert will be added to the existing line until you click **Close** or **Finish**. **Close** closes the shape whereas **Finish** completes the line without closing it.

Rendering Rollout

The options in this rollout let you toggle the shape renderability in the viewports as well as in the rendered output. You can also use the options to generate the mapping coordinates and convert the mesh to an editable mesh or editable poly object. Table 3 summarizes the parameters available in the **Rendering** rollout.

Table 3: Parameters in the **Rendering** rollout of the **Line** spline	
Parameter	**Description**
Enable In Renderer	Select the **Enable In Renderer** checkbox to render the shape as a 3D mesh using the **Radial** or **Rectangular** parameters set for the renderer. When the **Enable In Renderer** checkbox is selected, you have two options for controlling the size of the mesh: **Radial** and **Rectangular**. **Radial** renders the shape with a circular cross-section whereas **Rectangular** displays the mesh of the spline as a rectangle. Fig. 7 shows the spline shape with the circular cross-section on rendering [**Thickness=2**, **Sides=12**]. Fig. 8 shows the mesh with the rectangular cross-section [**Length=6**, **Width=2**].

Table 3: Parameters in the **Rendering** rollout of the **Line** spline

Parameter	Description
Enable In Viewport, Use Viewport Settings	Select the **Enable In Viewport** checkbox to display the shape in the viewport as a 3D mesh with the circular or rectangular cross-section [see Figs. 9 and 10]. Select **Use Viewport Settings** to display the mesh using the **Viewport** settings. When on, **Viewport** is activated and then you can use the **Viewport** settings to control the appearance of the mesh of the spline in the viewport.
Generate Mapping Coords	Select **Generate Mapping Coords** to apply mapping coordinates to the spline mesh. 3ds Max generates coordinates in the **U** and **V** directions. The **U** coordinate wraps around the spline whereas the **V** coordinate is mapped along the length of the spline.
Real-World Map Size	The **Real-World Map Size** checkbox will only be available if you select **Generate Mapping Coords**. This parameter allows you to specify the actual width and height of a 2D texture map in the material editor.
Auto Smooth	**Auto Smooth** is turned on by default. The spline is automatically smoothed using the threshold value defined by the **Threshold** spinner available below **Auto Smooth**. This value is an angle measured in degrees.

Radial and Rectangular Options: Now, let's have a look at the various parameters available for the radial and rectangular cross-sections. Table 4 summarizes these parameters.

Table 4: Various parameters available for the radial and rectangular cross-sections	
Parameter	**Description**
Thickness	Controls the diameter of the rendered spline mesh. Fig. 11 shows the splines rendered with the **Thickness** value set to **0.5** and **1**, respectively.
Sides	Controls the number of sides [or facets] of the mesh. Fig. 12 shows the splines rendered with the **Sides** value set to **4** and **62**, respectively.
Angle	Controls the orientation of the rendered cross-section. Fig. 13 shows the splines rendered with the **Angle** value set to **0** and **60**, respectively.
Length	Controls the size of the cross-section along the local Y-axis.
Width	Controls the size of the cross-section along the local X-axis.
Aspect	Controls the aspect ratio of width to length. If the **Lock** button next to the spinner is active, adjusting length or width automatically adjusts the other to maintain the aspect ratio.

Interpolation Rollout

The parameters on this rollout allow you to adjust the smoothness of a curve. Each spline segment is made up of divisions called steps. Higher the number of steps, smoother the curve will be. By default, **Optimize** is turned on. When on, 3ds Max removes the steps that are not necessary. For example, 3ds Max will not add steps on the straight lines when **Optimize** is selected. When **Adaptive** is selected, the **Steps** parameter becomes inactive. It sets the number of steps for each spline to produce a smooth looking result. Fig. 14 shows the wireframe view of the spline mesh created using the **Optimize** and **Adaptive** options, respectively.

Note: *Adaptive*
*When **Adaptive** is selected, the straight segments get zero steps.*

Rectangle Spline

It creates square or rectangular splines [see Fig. 15]. If you want to create a square spline, press and hold **Ctrl** while dragging in a viewport. To create a rectangular spline, first, select a creation method and then drag the mouse pointer in a viewport to create a rectangle. Table 5 summarizes the parameters available in the **Parameters** rollout of the **Rectangular** spline:

Table 5: Parameters in the **Parameters** rollout of the **Rectangular** spline	
Parameters	**Description**
Length, Width	The **Length** and **Width** parameters specify the size of the rectangle along the **Y** and **X** axes, respectively.
Corner Radius	The **Corner Radius** parameter allows you to create rounded corners. See the right-most spline in Fig. 15.

Circle Spline

It allows you to create close circular splines made up of four vertices [see Fig. 16]. To create a circular spline, first, select the creation method and then drag the mouse pointer in a viewport to draw a circle. Table 6 summarizes the parameters available in the **Parameters** rollout of the **Circle** spline.

Table 6: Parameter in the **Parameters** rollout of the **Circle** spline	
Parameter	**Description**
Radius	The **Radius** parameter specifies the center to edge distance of the circle.

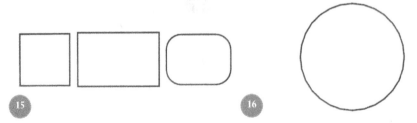

15   16

Ellipse Spline

You can use it to create circular or elliptical splines [see Fig. 17]. If you want to create a circular spline, press and hold **Ctrl** while dragging in the viewport. To create an elliptical spline, first, select the creation method and then drag the mouse pointer in the viewport to draw the ellipse. Table 7 summarizes the parameters available in the **Parameters** rollout of the **Ellipse** spline:

Table 7: Parameters in the **Parameters** rollout of the **Ellipse** spline	
Parameters	**Description**
Length, Width	The **Length** and **Width** controls specify the size of the ellipse along the local **Y** and **Z** axes, respectively.
Outline, Thickness	The **Outline** checkbox lets you create an elliptical outline, see the middle spline in Fig. 17. The **Thickness** parameter lets you specify the thickness of the outline.

Arc Spline

You can use the **Arc** spline to create open and closed partial circles made up of four vertices [see Fig. 18].

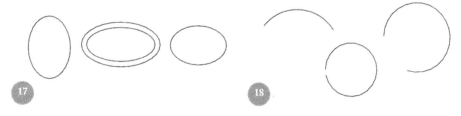

17 18

Creation Method Rollout

The **Arc** spline provides two methods for creating arcs: **End-End-Middle** and **Center-End-End**. To create an arc using the **End-End-Middle** method, make sure **End-End-Middle** is selected in the **Creation Method** rollout and then drag in the viewport to define the two ends of the arc. Now, release the mouse button. Next, move the mouse pointer up or down to specify the third point between the two endpoints.

To create an arc using the **Center-End-End** method, make sure **Center-End-End** is selected in the **Creation Method** rollout and then click to set the radial center of the arc. Drag the mouse pointer and click to specify the start point of the arc. Now, move the mouse and click to specify the other end of the arc. Table 8 summarizes the parameters available in the **Parameters** rollout of the **Arc** spline.

Table 8: Parameters in the **Parameters** rollout of the **Arc** spline	
Parameter	**Description**
Radius	**Radius** specifies the radius of the arc.
From, To	**From** specifies the location of the start point which is measured as an angle from the local positive Y-axis. **To** specifies the location of the endpoint which is measured as an angle from the local positive X-axis.
Pie Slice	When **Pie Slice** is on, it creates straight segments from the endpoints to the radial center which results in closed spline [see Fig. 19].
Reverse	When **Reverse** is on, the direction of the **Arc** spline is reversed.

Donut Spline

It creates the donut-like shape of two concentric circles [see Fig. 20]. To create a **Donut** spline, first, select a creation method. Drag the mouse pointer and then release the mouse button to define the first circle of the donut. Move the mouse pointer and then click to define the second concentric donut circle.

19   20

Table 9 summarizes the parameters available in the **Parameters** rollout of the **Donut** spline:

Table 9: Controls in the **Parameters** rollout of the **Donut** spline	
Parameters	**Description**
Radius 1, Radius 2	The **Radius 1** and **Radius 2** parameters specify the radius of the first and second circles, respectively.

NGon Spline

It creates flat-sided splines with N number of sides and vertices [see Fig. 21]. To create an **NGon** spline, select a creation method, and then drag the mouse pointer in a viewport. Release the mouse button to create the spline. Table 10 summarizes the parameters available in the **Parameters** rollout of the **NGon** spline.

Table 10: Controls in the **Parameters** rollout of the **NGon** spline	
Parameters	**Description**
Radius, Inscribed, Circumscribed	The **Radius** parameter specifies the distance from the radial center to the edge of the NGon. If **Inscribed** is on [default], the distance is measured from the radial center to the corners. If **Circumscribed** is on, the distance is measured from the radial center to the side centers.
Sides	**Sides** specifies the number of sides which ranges from **3** to **100**.
Corner Radius	**Corner Radius** controls rounding applied to the corners of the NGon.
Circular	When **Circular** is on, 3ds Max creates a circular NGon which is equivalent to a circular spline but it may contain more than four vertices. The **Circle** spline creates a circular object with four control vertices.

Star Spline

It creates closed star-shaped splines with any number of points [see Fig. 22]. To create a **Star** spline, drag the mouse pointer and then release the mouse button to define the first radius. Move the mouse pointer and then click to define the second radius. The second radius can be less, equal, or greater than the first radius depending on how you moved the mouse pointer.

21   22

Table 11 summarizes the parameters available in the **Parameters** rollout of the **Star** spline.

Table 11: Parameters in the **Parameters** rollout of the **Star** spline	
Parameters	**Description**
Radius 1, Radius 2	The **Radius 1** and **Radius 2** parameters specify the first set of vertices [created with the first drag] and the second set of vertices, respectively.
Points	**Points** controls the number of points on the star. **Distortion** allows you to produce a sawtooth effect. This effect is generated by rotating **Radius 2** vertices about the center of the star.
Fillet Radius 1, Fillet Radius 2	**Fillet Radius 1** and **Fillet Radius 2** let you smooth the first and second sets of vertices, respectively. The rounding is created by producing two **Bezier** vertices per point.

Text Spline

It creates splines in the shape of the text [see Fig. 23]. The text can be created using any **Windows** font [both **TrueType** and **OpenType**] installed on your system as well using the **Type 1 PostScript** font installed in the **Fonts** folder of the 3ds Max installation folder.

To create text, enter the text in the **Text** text box and then either click in a viewport to place the text or drag the mouse pointer to place the text and then release the mouse button. Table 12 summarizes the parameters available in the **Parameters** rollout of the **Text** spline.

Parameter	Description
Table 12: Parameters in the **Parameters** rollout of the **Text** spline	
Parameter	Description
Text Parameters	From this rollout, you can choose the font, font size, text alignment, kerning [distance between letters], and leading [distance between lines] for the text that you enter in the **Text** text box. The **Text** text box does not support word-wrap however you can paste multiple lines from the clipboard.

Helix Spline

It creates spiral-like shapes [see Fig. 24]. To create a **Helix** spline, click and drag the mouse pointer to set the starting point as well as its starting radius [**Center** creation method] or diameter [**Edge** creation method]. Now, move the mouse pointer vertically and then click to define the height. Move the mouse pointer and then click to define the end radius. Table 13 summarizes the parameters available in the **Parameters** rollout of the **Helix** spline.

Parameters	Description
Table 13: Parameters in the **Parameters** rollout of the **Helix** spline	
Parameters	Description
Radius 1, Radius 2	The **Radius 1** and **Radius 2** parameters specify the radius of helix start and end, respectively. **Height** controls the height of the helix.
Turns	**Turns** specifies the number of turns in the helix.
Bias	**Bias** forces the turns in the helix to accumulate at the one end of the helix. Fig. 25 shows the rendered helix with **Bias** set to **-1**, **0.2**, and **1**, respectively.
CC and CCW	**CC** and **CCW** specify whether helix should turn clockwise or counterclockwise.

Egg Spline

It creates an egg-shaped spline [see Fig. 26]. To create an **Egg** spline, drag the mouse pointer vertically to define the initial dimension of the egg. Now, drag horizontally to change the orientation [angle] of the egg. Release the mouse button to complete the creation process. Table 14 summarizes the parameters available in the **Parameters** rollout of the **Egg** spline.

Table 14: Parameters in the **Parameters** rollout of the **Egg** spline

Parameter	Description
Length, Width	The **Length** and **Width** parameters specify the length and width of the egg along its long and short axes, respectively.
Outline, Thickness	When **Outline** is on, **Thickness** sets the distance between the main shape of the egg and its outline.
Angle	**Angle** specifies the angle of rotation around the shape's local Z axis. When **Angle** is equal to **0**, the narrow end of the egg is at the top.

Section Spline

The **Section** spline is a special type of spline that lets you generate splines based on a cross-sectional slice through a geometry. To create a **Section** shape, click **Section** from the **Object Type** rollout and then drag a section plane in the viewport. Now, place and orient the plane in the viewport using transformation tools [see Fig. 27]. Notice a yellow line is displayed where the section intersects the mesh. Now, on the **Section Parameters** rollout, click **Create Shape**. In the **Name Section Shape** dialog box that appears, type the name for the spline and then click **OK**. Now, select the shape in the **Scene Explorer** and then move it away using the **Move** tool [see Fig. 28]. Table 15 summarizes the parameters available in the **Section Parameters** rollout of the **Section** spline.

Table 15: Parameters in the **Section Parameters** rollout of the **Section** spline

[Group]/ Parameter	Description
Create Shape	When you click this button, a shape is created based on the currently displayed intersection lines. The shape generated is an editable spline.
[Update]	The parameters in this group specify when the intersection line is updated.
When Section Moves	It updates the intersection line when you move or resize the section shape.
When Section Selected	It updates the intersection line when you select the section shape. Click **Update Section** to update the intersection.
Manually	It updates the intersection line only when you click **Update Section**.
[Section Events]	These parameters let you specify the extents of the cross-section.
Infinite	When on, the selected plane is infinite in all directions [see Fig. 29].
Section Boundary	When on, the cross-section is generated only for those objects that are within or touched by the boundary of the section shape [see Fig. 30].
Off	No cross-section is displayed or generated.
Color Swatch	You can use it to change the display color of the intersection.

Section Size Rollout

The **Length** and **Width** parameters in the **Section Size** rollout control the size of the section rectangle.

Freehand Spline

You can use the **Freehand** spline to create hand-drawn splines directly in the viewport. You can use a mouse or any other pointing device to draw the spline. You can also draw it on the selected objects in the viewport; it will automatically follow the contours. Table 16 summarizes the parameters available in the **Freehand Spline** rollout of the **Freehand** spline.

Table 16: Parameters in the **Freehand Spline** rollout of the **Freehand** spline

[Group]/ Parameter	Description
Show Knots	When on, the knots are displayed on the spline [see the right image in Fig. 31].
[Create Group]	
Granularity	Defines the number of cursor position samples taken before a knot is created.
Threshold	Defines how far the cursor must move before a knot is created. The higher the value you specify, the more the distance between the knots will be.
Constrain	When on, you can constrain the spline to the selected objects. To constrain the spline, select the objects in the viewport and then select **Constrain**. Selected objects will appear in the list box. You can pick additional objects using the **Pick Object** button. To clear the list, click **Clear**. Now, drag on the selected objects to constrain the spline [see Fig. 32].
[Options Group]	
Curved, Straight	You can use these settings to define whether the segments between the knots are curved or straight.
Closed	Select this checkbox to close the spline.
Normals	When on, 3ds Max shows the resulting normals of the constrained spline in the viewport [see the right image in Fig. 32].
Offset	You can use **Offset** to control the distance between the spline and the surface of the constraining object.
[Statistics Group]	
# of Splines	Displays the number of splines in the shape.
Orig Knots	Displays the number of knots automatically created while drawing the spline.
New Knots	Displays the new number of knots.

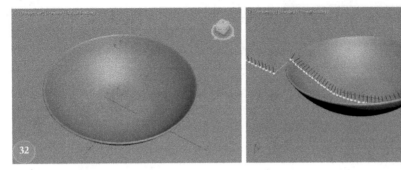

Extended Spline Primitives

In this section, I will explain extended spline primitives. Let's start with the **WRectangle** spline.

WRectangle Spline

The **WRectangle** spline [walled rectangle] lets you create a closed shape from two concentric rectangles. Each rectangle is made up of four vertices [see Fig. 33]. To create a **WRectangle** spline, drag the mouse pointer in a viewport and then release the mouse button to define the outer rectangle. Move the mouse pointer and then click to define the inner rectangle.

Table 17 summarizes the parameters available in the **Parameters** rollout of the **WRectangle** spline.

Table 17: Parameters in the **Parameters** rollout of the **WRectangle** spline	
Parameters	**Description**
Length, Width	These parameters define the length and width of the **WRectangle** section, respectively.
Thickness	Controls the thickness of the **WRectangle** section.
Sync Corner Fillets	When on, the value specified for **Corner Radius 1** is used for both the interior and exterior corners.
Corner Radius 1	When **Sync Corner Fillets** is off, it controls the radius of the exterior corners.
Corner Radius 2	This parameter is only available when **Sync Corner Fillets** is off. It controls the radius of the interior corners.

Channel Spline

It creates a closed C shaped spline [see Fig. 34]. To create a **Channel** spline, drag the mouse pointer in a viewport and then release the mouse button to define the outer perimeter. Move the mouse pointer and then click to define the thickness of the walls of the channel. Table 18 summarizes the parameters available in the **Parameters** rollout of the **Channel** spline.

Table 18: Parameters in the **Parameters** rollout of the **Channel** spline	
Parameter	**Description**
Length, Width	These parameters define the length and width of the channel section, respectively.
Thickness	Controls the thickness of the channel section.
Sync Corner Fillets	When on, the value specified for **Corner Radius 1** is used for both the interior and exterior corners.
Corner Radius 1	When **Sync Corner Fillets** is off, it controls the radius of the exterior corners.
Corner Radius 2	This parameter is only available when **Sync Corner Fillets** is off. It controls the radius of the interior corners.

Angle Spline

It creates a closed L shaped spline [see Fig. 35]. To create an **Angle** spline, drag the mouse pointer in a viewport and then release the mouse button to define the initial size of the angle. Move the mouse pointer and then click to define the thickness of the walls of the angle. Table 19 summarizes the parameters available in the **Parameters** rollout of the **WRectangle** spline.

34   35

Table 19: Parameters in the **Parameters** rollout of the **Angle** spline	
Parameter	**Description**
Length, Width	These parameters define the height and width of the vertical and horizontal legs, respectively.
Thickness	Controls the thickness of the legs of the angle.
Sync Corner Fillets	When on, the value specified for **Corner Radius 1** controls the radius for both the vertical and horizontal legs.

Table 19: Parameters in the **Parameters** rollout of the **Angle** spline	
Parameter	**Description**
Corner Radius 1	When **Sync Corner Fillets** is off, it controls the exterior radius between the vertical and horizontal legs of the spline.
Corner Radius 2	This parameter is only available when **Sync Corner Fillets** is off. It controls the interior radius between the vertical and horizontal legs of the spline.
Edge Radii	Controls the interior radius at the outermost edges of the vertical and horizontal legs.

Tee Spline

It creates a closed T shaped spline [see Fig. 36]. To create a **Tee** spline, drag the mouse pointer in a viewport and then release the mouse button to define the initial size of the tee. Move the mouse pointer and then click to define the thickness of the walls of the tee. Table 20 summarizes the parameters available in the **Parameters** rollout of the **Tee** spline.

Table 20: Parameters in the **Parameters** rollout of the **Tee** spline	
Parameter	**Description**
Length, Width	These parameters define the height and width of the vertical web and flange crossing, respectively.
Thickness	Controls the thickness of the web and flange.
Corner Radius	Controls the radius of the two interior corners between the vertical web and horizontal flange.

Wide Flange Spline

It creates a closed I shaped spline [see Fig. 37]. To create a **Wide Flange** spline, drag the mouse pointer in a viewport and then release the mouse button to define the initial size of the wide flange. Move the mouse pointer and then click to define the thickness of the walls of the wide flange. Table 21 summarizes the parameters available in the **Parameters** rollout of the **Wide Flange** spline.

36   37

Table 21: Parameters in the **Parameters** rollout of the **Wide Flange** spline	
Parameter	**Description**
Length, Width	These controls define the height and width of the vertical web and horizontal flange crossing, respectively.
Thickness	Controls the thickness of the wide flanges.
Corner Radius	Controls the radius of the two interior corners between the vertical web and horizontal flanges.

Editing Splines

You can convert a spline object to an editable spline object. The editable spline object allows you to create complex shapes using the three sub-object levels that this object provides: **Vertex**, **Spline**, and **Segment**. The vertices define points and curve tangents. The segments connect vertices. The splines are made up of one or more connected segments.

You can convert a spline object into an **Editable Spline** object by using one of the following methods:

1. Select a spline in a viewport and then go to the **Modify** panel. Next, **RMB** click on the spline entry in the stack display and then choose **Editable Spline** from the popup menu displayed [see Fig. 38].
2. Select a spline in a viewport and then **RMB** click. Choose **Transform** [in the **transform** quadrant] **> Convert To: > Convert to Editable Spline** [see Fig. 39].
3. Select a spline in a viewport and then apply the **Edit Spline** modifier to it.
4. Import a **.shp** file to the scene.
5. Merge a shape from a 3ds Max file.

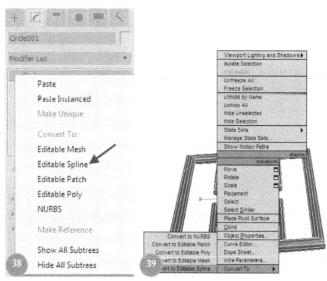

Selecting Sub-objects

You can select sub-objects using one of the following ways:

1. Expand the spline object's hierarchy in the stack display and then choose a sub-object level [see Fig. 40].
2. Click a selection button from the **Selection** rollout [see Fig. 40].
3. **RMB** click on a spline object in a viewport and then choose the sub-object level from the **tools1** quadrant of the **Quad** menu displayed [see Fig. 41].
4. Choose a selection or transform tool and then click on the sub-objects in a viewport using the standard selection techniques.

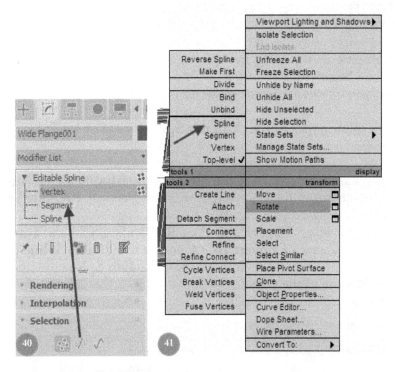

Note: Cloning sub-objects
*You can clone the sub-objects by first selecting them and then press and hold **Shift** while transforming them.*

Note: Adding and removing from the selection
*To select a segment, vertex, or spline, click it. To add to the sub-object selection, press and hold **Ctrl** and click. You can also drag a selection region to select a group of sub-objects. To subtract from the sub-object selection, press and hold **Alt** and click. You can also drag a selection region to deselect a group of sub-objects.*

Vertex Level

Vertices define points and curve tangents for a spline object. To select a vertex type, select vertex or vertices and then **RMB** click. Now, choose the required level from the **tools1** quadrant of the **Quad** menu [see Fig. 42]. Table 22 shows the list of vertex types available in 3ds Max.

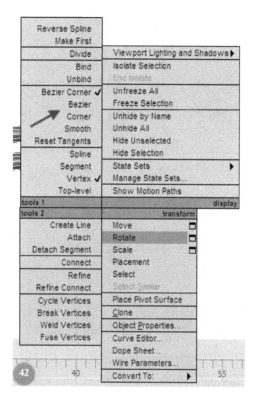

Table 22: The vertex types

Type	Description
Corner	Creates non-adjustable vertices that generate sharp corners [see Fig. 43].
Bezier	Creates adjustable vertices with locked continuous tangent handles that produce a smooth curve. The curvature is determined by the direction and magnitude of the tangent handles [see Fig. 44]. You can adjust the tangent handles using the **Move** and **Rotate** tools.
Bezier Corner	Creates adjustable vertices with discontinuous tangent handles that produces a sharp corner [see Fig. 45]. The curvature is determined by the direction and magnitude of the tangent handles. You can adjust the tangent handles using the **Move** and **Rotate** tools.

Table 22: The vertex types	
Type	**Description**
Smooth	Creates non-adjustable vertices that generate smooth continuous curves. The curvature is determined by the spacing between the adjacent vertices [see Fig. 46].

Tip: Resetting tangents

Tip: Resetting tangents
*To reset the tangent position, **RMB** click on the vertex or vertices and then choose **Reset Tangents** from the **tools1** quadrant of the **Quad** menu.*

Tip: Vertex types in the Quad menu
*If you are at the **Vertex** sub-object level, the vertex types are always displayed in the **Quad** menu. The mouse pointer doesn't have to be exactly over the vertices.*

Selection Rollout

The parameters in this rollout allow you to select sub-object levels of a spline, work with named selection sets and tangent handles, and display settings. Also, you can see information about the selected entities in this rollout.

At the top of the rollout, there are three buttons: **Vertex**, **Segment**, and **Spline**. These buttons let you select sub-object levels of a spline. The **Copy** and **Paste** buttons in the **Named Selections** rollout allow you to place the selection into the copy buffer and paste the selection from the copy buffer, respectively.

Generally, you can transform bezier handles of a single vertex in the viewport even if multiple vertices are selected. If you want to simultaneously transform bezier handles of multiple vertices, select the **Lock Handles** checkbox. When **Alike** is on, as you drag the handle of an incoming or outgoing vector, all incoming and outgoing handles move simultaneously [except the broken tangents]. If you select the **All** option, any handle you move will affect all other handles regardless of whether they are broken or not.

Tip: Breaking tangents
*To break a tangent and move its handles independently, click on the tangent with **Shift** held down.*

Caution: Breaking Tangents
*To break a tangent, the **Alike** must be turned on.*

When the **Area Selection** checkbox is selected, you can define a radius in the associated spinner. When you click a vertex, all vertices that fall within the specified radius of the clicked vertex will be selected. When the **Segment End** checkbox is selected, you can select a vertex by clicking on a point on the segment close to the vertex. You can add to the selection using **Ctrl**. The **Select By** button allows you to select vertices on the selected spline or segment. You need to first select a spline or segment using the **Spline** or **Segment** sub-object level and then you need to switch to the **Vertex** sub-object level. Click **Select By** to open the **Select By** dialog box. Now, click the desired button on the dialog box to select the vertices.

The **Show Vertex Numbers** checkbox toggles the display of vertex numbers in the viewport. The numbers are displayed next to the selected spline's vertices. If you select **Selected Only**, the vertex number only appears for the selected vertices.

Geometry Rollout
Now, let's explore the options available for editing the editable spline object at sub-object levels. These options are listed in the **Geometry** rollout.

New Vertex Type Group
The parameters in this group let you choose the type of tangency for vertices that are created when you clone segments or splines using the **Shift** key.

Caution: Scope
*These parameters have no effect on the tangency of the vertices created using tools such as **Create Line**, **Refine**, and so on. **Linear** sets linear tangency for the new vertices. **Smooth** sets smooth tangency. When on, the new overlapping vertices will be welded together. **Bezier Corner** sets the **Bezier** corner tangency.*

Note: Editable spline – object level
*The following parameters are also available at the editable spline object level: **New Vertex Type** group, **Create Line**, **Attach**, **Attach Mult.**, **Cross Section**, **Automatic Welding**, and **Insert**. This level is the one that is active when no sub-object level is selected.*

To use the **Connect Copy** feature, create a **Circle** spline, and then convert it to an editable spline. Activate the **Segment** sub-object level and then select the segments, as shown in the left image of Fig. 45. Select the **Connect** checkbox in the **Connect Copy** group. Now, invoke the **Scale** tool and then scale the segments outward with **Shift** held down. 3ds Max connects the newly created vertices with the original vertices [see the right image in Fig. 47].

Create Line

Create Line adds more lines to the existing selected spline. The lines are separate splines but are part of the selected spline. To add another spline to the selected spline, select the existing spline, and then create the new spline in the same way as you create the line spline.

Break

Break allows you to split a spline at the selected vertex or vertices. To split a spline, select one or more vertices and then click **Break**. Two overlapping vertices will be created at the break-point. Use the **Move** tool to separate the vertices [see Fig. 48].

Attach

Attach attaches another spline object from the scene to the selected spline to create a compound shape. To attach a spline, select the spline and then click **Attach**. Now, hover the mouse pointer on the target spline. When the shape of the mouse pointer changes, click on the target spline to attach it to the selected spline. When you attach shapes, the materials assigned to the two objects are combined. Here's how:

- If the target object does not have a material assigned, it inherits the material from the selected object.
- If the selected object does not have a material assigned, it inherits the material from the target object.

- If both objects have materials, the **Attach Options** dialog box appears [see Fig. 49]. Select the desired options from the dialog box and then click **OK**. The resulting material will be a **Multi-Subobject** material.

 Caution: Target shape's creation parameters
The target shape loses all its creation parameters. If there is any modifier stack attached to the target shape, it will be collapsed.

Attach Multiple

Attach Multiple lets you attach multiple shapes to a selected spline in a single operation. To understand this feature, select a spline object and then click **Attach Multiple**. Now, select the shapes in the **Attach Multiple** dialog box that appears [see Fig. 50] and click **OK** to attach the selected shapes.

 Note: Reorienting attached splines
*When **Reorient** is on, the attached splines are reoriented so that the local coordinate system of the attached splines is aligned with the selected spline.*

Cross Section

Cross Section allows you to create a spline cage out of cross-sectional shapes. To create a spline cage, make sure that all splines are attached. Click **Cross Section** and then click on

3ds Max 2021

the first spline, then second, and so on. **RMB** click to complete the process and create a cage [see Fig. 51].

Tip: Keeping vertices together
*If you want to edit the spline cage, select **Area Selection** in the **Selection** rollout before selecting the vertices otherwise you would not be able to keep their position together.*

Refine

Refine adds vertices to the spline object without changing the curvature of the spline. To add vertices, click **Refine** and then hover the mouse pointer on the segments in a viewport. The shape of the mouse pointer changes on the eligible segments. Now, click to add a vertex. When you are done, click **Refine** again or press **RMB**.

If you click on an existing vertex, 3ds Max displays the **Refine & Connect** dialog box asking if you want to refine the vertex or connect to the vertex. If you choose **Connect Only**, a new vertex will not be created instead the clicked vertex will be connected to the existing vertex.

Caution: Connecting vertices
*You must select **Connect** before clicking **Refine**.*

The type of vertex created during the **Refine** operation is dependent on the bordering vertices of the segment:

- If bordering vertices are smooth, a vertex of a **Smooth** type is created.
- If bordering vertices are of **Corner** type, a vertex of a **Corner** type is created.
- If either of the bordering vertices is of a **Corner** or a **Bezier Corner** type, a vertex of **Bezier Corner** type is created.
- If the bordering vertices do not fit in the above-mentioned criterion, a vertex of **Bezier** type is created.

Connect: It creates a new spline sub-object by connecting the two vertices.

To understand the functioning of **Connect**, create two straight lines in a viewport, and attach them [see Fig. 52]. Select the **Vertex** sub-object level. Select **Connect**. Notice that there are some options that get activated in the **Refine** group. Now, click **Refine** and then click on the first segment. Now, click on the second segment [see Fig. 53], **RMB** click to create to connect two vertices [see Fig. 54].

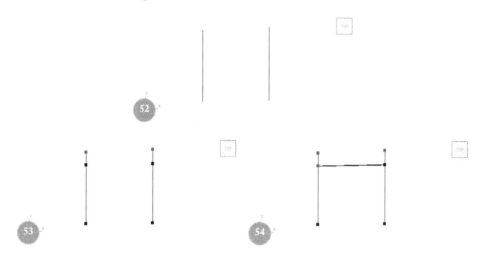

When **Linear** is on, the **Refine** operation creates straight lines using the vertices of the **Corner** type. When off, the created vertices are of **Smooth** type. **Closed** allows you to create closed splines by connecting the first and last vertices [see Fig. 55, numbers show clicking order].

When **Bind first** is on, it sets the first vertex created to be bound to the center of the selected segment [see Fig. 56]. **Bind last** sets the last vertex created to be bound to the center of the selected segment.

> *Note: Bound vertices*
> *Binding vertices helps in connecting splines when building a spline network for use with the **Surface** modifier. To distinguish the bound vertices from the standard vertices, 3ds Max makes them black. You cannot transform a bound vertex directly. However, you can move it by shifting the connected vertices. You can also change the type of the bound vertices from the **tools1** quadrant of the **Quad** menu.*

Automatic Welding

When on, the end vertex is welded automatically, if you move or place the vertex and the vertex fall within a distance specified using **Threshold Dist**.

Note: Automatic welding
This feature is available at the object as well as at all the sub-object levels.

Weld

Weld welds two end vertices or two adjacent vertices into a single vertex. To weld vertices, move the vertices close to each other and click **Weld**. If the vertices fall within a threshold defined by the spinner next to **Weld**, the selected vertices are welded to a single vertex [see Fig. 57].

57

Connect

Connect connects two end vertices. To connect the vertices, click **Connect** and then drag the mouse pointer from one end vertex to another end vertex. It creates a linear segment by ignoring the tangent values of the end vertices. To connect the end-points, click **Connect** and hover the cursor over one of the end vertices. When the shape of the cursor changes, drag mouse pointer to the other end vertex to make the connection.

Insert

Insert lets you add one or more vertices creating additional segments in a spline. Click **Insert** and then click on the spline to attach the mouse pointer to the spline. Now, click to place the vertex; the spline gets attached to the mouse pointer. Now, continue clicking to create more vertices. **RMB** click to complete the operation. You are still in the insert mode, you can continue adding vertices on another segment or you can **RMB** click to exit. A single click creates a corner vertex whereas dragging the mouse pointer creates a bezier vertex.

Make First

It allows you to define which vertex in a spline is the first vertex. The first vertex in a spline is indicated by a small box around it. To make a vertex first vertex, select the vertex, and then click **Make First**. If you are editing an open spline, the first vertex should be end point that is already not the first vertex. On closed spline, you can make any vertex first vertex. The first vertex has special significance in many operations in 3ds Max. Table 23 summarizes the importance of the first vertex.

Table 23: First vertex use	
Use	**Description**
Loft Path	Indicates the start of the path [Level 0].
Loft Shape	Controls the initial skin alignment.
Path Constraint	Indicates the start of the path [indicates 0% on the location of the path].
Trajectory	Indicates the first position key.

Fuse

Fuse lets you move all selected vertices to their averaged center. To fuse the vertices, select them [first attach all splines] and then click **Fuse** to move the vertices to the same location [see Fig. 58]. Note that the **Fuse** operation does not weld the vertices, it simply moves them to the same location.

Cycle

Cycle allows you to select a specific vertex from the group of coincident vertices [vertices that shares the same location]. To select a specific vertex, select one or more vertices that share the same location, and then click **Cycle** repeatedly until you select the vertex you are looking for. To lean the functioning of this feature, fuse two or three splines and then use **Cycle** to select the coincident vertices. Check the info about the selected vertex at the bottom of the **Selection** rollout.

CrossInsert

CrossInsert adds vertices at the intersection of two splines that are part of the same spline object. To add a vertex, click **CrossInsert** and then click at the intersection of the two splines. If the distance between the splines is within the threshold defined by the spinner next to **CrossInsert**, the vertices are added [they are not welded] to both splines [see Fig. 59].

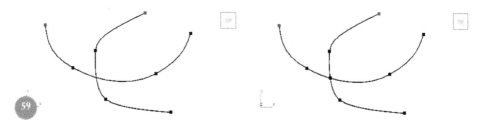

Fillet

Fillet lets you create the rounded corners by adding new control vertices. You can create rounded corners by dragging the mouse pointer in a viewport or by entering precise values in the spinner on the right of **Fillet**. To fillet the vertices, click **Fillet** and then drag the vertices in a viewport to add rounded corners [see Fig. 60]. As you drag with **Fillet**, the spinner on its right shows the fillet amount. You can continue dragging to add a fillet to other vertices. To finish the operation, **RMB** click.

Chamfer

Chamfer chops off the selected vertices by creating segments connecting new vertices [see Fig. 61]. Like **Fillet**, you can chamfer edges interactively or by entering precise values.

> *Note: Fillet/Chamfer functions*
> *Unlike the **Fillet/Chamfer** modifiers, you can apply these functions to any type of vertex. These modifiers only work with the **Corner** and **Bezier Corner** vertices.*

Tangent

The parameters available in this group let you copy-paste vertex handles from one vertex to another. To copy a tangent, select a vertex, and then click **Copy**. Click on a tangent to copy tangent to the clipboard. Now, select another vertex, click **Paste**, and then click on the tangent of the vertex to paste the tangent [see Fig. 62]. When **Paste Length** is on, the length of the handle is also copied.

Hide
It allows you to hide the selected vertices and connected segments.

Unhide All
Unhide All allows you to unhide all hidden objects.

Bind/Unbind
Bind lets you create bound vertices. To create a bound vertex, click **Bind** and then drag from any end vertex to any segment except the one connected to the vertex, a dashed line connects the vertex and the current mouse position. When the mouse is over an eligible segment, the pointer changes to a **Connect** symbol. When you release the mouse button, the vertex jumps to the center of the segment and bound to it. **Unbind** lets you disconnect the bind vertices.

Delete
Allows you to delete the selected vertices as well as one attached segment per deleted vertex.

Show selected segs
Lets you display the selected segments in red color at the **Vertex** sub-object level [see Fig. 63]. When off, the segments displayed in red only at **Segment** sub-object level.

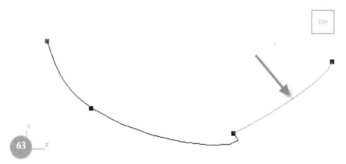

Segment Level
A segment is a part of the spline between two vertices of the spline. You can select one or more segments by activating the **Segment** sub-object level. Once selected, you can transform them using the transformation tools.

Most of the parameters available for segments are similar to those discussed in the **Vertex Level** group. The other parameters available at the segment sub-object level are discussed next.

Geometry Rollout
Divide
Divide subdivides the selected segment(s) by adding a number of vertices that are specified by using the spinner available on the right of this parameter. To subdivide a segment, select segment or segments of the spline. Now, specify the number of vertices and then click **Divide** [see Fig. 64]. The distance between the vertices is dependent on the curvature of the segment.

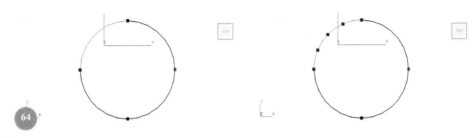

Delete

Deletes the selected segments from the spline [see Fig. 65].

Detach

It lets you detach/copy selected segments from the spline. To detach a segment or segments, select them and then click **Detach**. In the **Detach** dialog box that appears, type name in the **Detach as** text box and then click **OK**. The segment will be detached from the spline and new shape will be created [see Fig. 66].

There are some other parameters that can be used with the detach operation. Table 24 summarizes these options.

Table 24: The **Detach** options	
Parameter	**Description**
Same Shp	When on, **Reorient** gets deactivated. The detached segment remains part of the same spline. If **Copy** is also on, the detached segment is copied at the same location.
Reorient	When on, the detached segment copies the transformation values of the spline's creation local coordinate system.
Copy	Copies the selected segment without detaching it from the spline.

Surface Properties Rollout

The parameters in this rollout allow you to apply different material IDs to spline segments. The material appears on the renderable shapes. To assign a material ID to a segment or segments, select them and then enter the **ID** in the **Set ID** spinner. **Select ID** lets you select the segments corresponding to the material ID set in the spinner on the right of **Select ID**. The drop-down list below **Select ID** shows the name of the sub-materials if you have applied **Multi-Subobject** material to the object. If you have applied a material other than the **Multi-Subobject** material, this drop-down list will be inactive.

When **Clear Selection** is on, selecting a new ID or material name deselects the previously selected segments or splines.

Changing Segment Properties

You can switch between the **Curve** or the **Line** type for the selected segments. To change the type, select segments and then **RMB** click. Now, choose **Line** or **Curve** from the **tools1** quadrant of the **Quad** menu [see Fig. 67]. Fig. 68 shows a segment converted from the **Curve** type to the **Line** type.

Spline Level

The **Spline** sub-object level allows you to select a single spline or multiple splines in a single object. Once selected, you can transform them using the transformation tools. Most of the parameters available for segments are similar to those discussed in the **Vertex Level** and **Segment Level** sections. The other parameters available at the **Spline** sub-object level are discussed next.

Geometry Rollout
Connect Copy Group

Connect Copy works when you make a clone of the spline using **Shift**. You must select **Connect** before the cloning operation. When on, 3ds Max creates a new spline sub-object that connects the vertices of the original and cloned objects [see Fig. 69]. **Threshold** defines the distance that the soft selection uses during the **Connect Copy** operation.

Outline

Outline makes a copy of the spline. The copy offsets in all directions specified by the spinner on the right of **Outline**. You can also create an outline interactively by using the mouse. To create an outline, select one or more splines and then click **Outline**. Now, drag a spline to create the outline [see Fig. 70]. When **Center** is on, the original spline and its outline move away from an invisible center line by the distance specified by dragging operation or by the value specified for the spinner on the right of **Outline**.

Caution: Selecting splines
If there is one spline is in the scene, it is automatically selected for the outlining process. However, if you are using the spinner to add an outline, you must select it first.

Note: Open spline
If you are outlining an open spline, the outlining process creates a single closed spline [see Fig. 71].

Boolean

Boolean combines two splines. It alters the first spline you select and deletes the other one. There are three types of **Boolean** operations available. Table 25 summarizes those operations.

Table 25: The boolean operations	
Operation	**Description**
Union	Combines two overlapping splines into a single spline. The overlapping portion is removed.
Subtraction	Subtracts the overlapping portion of the second spline from the first spline.
Intersection	Leaves the overlapping portions of the two splines.

To boolean splines, make sure both splines are part of a single spline object [use **Attach** to attach them]. Select a spline and then click **Union**, **Subtraction**, or **Intersection**. Now, click **Boolean**. Hover the mouse pointer on the second spline and then click when the shape of the cursor changes to complete the operation [see Fig. 72].

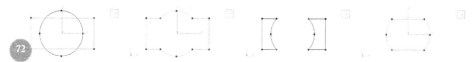

Mirror

Mirror allows you to mirror splines horizontally, vertically, and diagonally. To mirror a spline, ensure it is selected and then click **Mirror Horizontally**, **Mirror Vertically**, or **Mirror Both**. Next, click **Mirror** to complete the operation [see Fig. 73].

If **Copy** is on, 3ds Max creates a mirror copy of the spline [see Fig. 74].

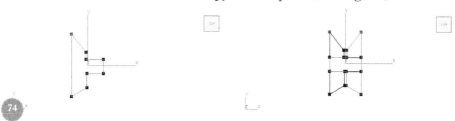

When **About Pivot** is on, 3ds Max mirrors the spline along with its geometric center otherwise mirrors along with the spline object's pivot point [see Fig. 75].

75

Trim

Trim allows you to clear the overlapping segments in a shape. The two splines must overlap each other and they should be part of the same spline object. To trim a spline, select the spline that will be used to trim the target spline. Click **Trim** and hover the cursor over the spline that you want to trim and then click when the shape of the cursor changes [see Fig. 76].

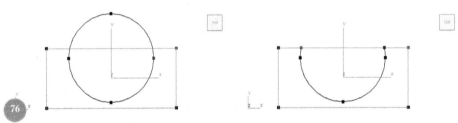

76

Extend

Extend allows you to extend an open spline. To extend spline, you need a segment that can extend to an intersecting segment of the spline. **Extend** does not work if the intersection is not possible. To understand the **Extend** feature, create a circle and a line [see the left image in Fig. 77]. Convert the circle to an editable spline object and then attach it with the line. Select the **Spline** sub-object mode, click **Extend**. Now, click on each end of the line to extend it to the circle [see the right image in Fig. 77]. When the **Infinite Bounds** checkbox is selected, 3ds Max treats open splines as infinite in length.

77

Explode

Explode breaks the segments of a selected spline and convert segments into separate splines or objects. There are two options available for the explode operation: **Splines** and **Objects**.

If you choose **Objects**, the **Explode** dialog box appears. Type a name in the **Object Name** text box and click **OK**. Each successive object will use a name appended with an incremental three-digit number. For example, if you type name as **myShape** and click **OK**. The name of other objects will be: **myShape001**, **myShape002**, **myShape003**, and so on.

> *Note: Explode and Detach*
> **Explode** *is* **Detach** *on steroids.*

Changing the Spline Type

You can change the spline type from **Curve** to **Line** and visa-versa. To change type, select the spline and **RMB** click. Choose **Line** or **Curve** from the **tools1** quadrant of the **Quad** menu. The right image in Fig. 78 shows the spline object converted from the **Curve** type into the **Line** type.

> *Note: Checking self-intersecting splines*
> *You can use the* **Shape Check** *utility to check self-intersecting splines and NURBS curves. The self-intersecting shapes may produce unpredictable results when used in the loft, extrude, or lathe operations. To check the intersection point, go to the* **Utilities** *panel and then click on* **More** *to open* **Utilities** *dialog box. Select* **Shape Check** *from the* **Utilities** *list and click* **OK**. *The* **Shape Check** *rollout appears in the* **Utilities** *panel. Click* **Pick Object** *and then click the spline or NURBS curve in a viewport. The red squares appear on the intersection points [see Fig. 79].*

Hands-on Exercises

Exercise 1: Creating Bowling Pin and Ball

In this exercise, you will create the model of a bowling pin and a ball [see Fig. E1]. Table E1 summarizes the exercise.

Table E1	
Skill level	Beginner
Time to complete	20 Minutes
Topics	• Specifying the Units for the Exercise • Setting the Blueprint • Creating the Bowling Pin • Creating the Ball
Resources folder	**spline-modeling**
Units	**Generic Units**
Final file	**pin-finish.max**

Specifying the Units for the Exercise

Follow these steps:

1. From the **Customize** menu choose **Units Setup**. In the **Units Setup** dialog box that appears, select **Generic Units** from the **Units Setup** dialog box. Click **OK** to accept the changes made.

2. From the **File** menu, choose **Save** to open the **Save File As** dialog box. In the **File name** text box type **pin-ball-finish.max** and then click **Save** to save the file.

Setting the Blueprint
Follow these steps:

1. Switch to the **Create** panel, click **Geometry**, then click **Plane**. In the **Front** viewport, create a plane. In the **Modify** panel > **Parameters** rollout, change **Length** to **100** and **Width** to **75**.

2. Invoke the **Move** tool from the **Main** toolbar. Set the **Transform Type-In** boxes to **0** in the **Status Bar** to place the box at the origin. Also, clear the **Real-World Map Size** checkbox, if not already clear. In the **Front** viewport, change the display mode to **Default Shading** [see Fig. E2].

3. Click **Material Editor** in the **Main** toolbar; the **Slate Material Editor** appears. Drag the **Physical Material** from the **Slate Material Editor** > **Material/Map Browser** > **Materials** rollout > **General** rollout to **View1** tab and then apply it to the plane.

4. Use the **pin-reference.jpeg** for the **Base Color** map using the **Bitmap** node and then set **Transparency** weight to **0.8** for the material [see Fig. E3].

5. **RMB** click on the material node and then select **Show Shaded Material in the Viewport** option (if not already selected) to display the image on the plane in the viewport.

6. Select the **Bitmap** node and then in the **Parameter Editor** > **Coordinates** rollout, make sure **Use Real-World Scale** is off and **U Tiling** and **V Tiling** are set to **1** each. Change **V Offset** to **-0.043** [see Figs. E4 and E5].

7. **RMB** click on the plane and then choose **Object Properties** from the **Quad** menu. Select the **Freeze** checkbox from the **Interactivity** area and clear the **Show Frozen in Gray** checkbox from the **Display Properties** area. Click **OK**.

What just happened?
Here, I've frozen the object. Once you freeze the object, you won't be able to accidentally select or move it and it would be easy for you to trace the logo using splines.

Creating the Bowling Pin

Follow these steps:

1. In the **Create** panel, click **Shapes**, and then click **Line**. Using the **Line** tool, create a half profile of the pin and then move the spline to the right [see Fig. E6]. In the **Modify** panel > **Selection** rollout, click **Vertex** to activate the vertex sub-object level.

2. Select all vertices except the first and last vertex and then **RMB** click; choose **Smooth** from the **Quad** menu > **tools 1** quadrant [see Fig. E7].

3. In the **Modify** panel > **Selection** rollout, click **Segment** to activate the segment sub-object level. Select the segment, as shown in Fig. E8. **RMB** click; choose **Line** from the **Quad** menu > **tools 1** quadrant. Now, align the bottom two points [see Fig. E9].

4. Move the line back on the profile and adjust the shape using the **Move** tool. Make sure that the start and end vertices are at the same **X** position [see Fig. E10].

5. From the **Object-Space Modifiers** section of the **Modifier** list, select **Lathe**. In the **Modify** panel > **Parameters** rollout > **Align** group, click **Min**. Now, select the **Weld Core** checkbox and change **Segments** to **32** [see Fig. E11]. Now, unfreeze and hide the plane using the **Scene Explorer**. Place the pin at the origin [see Fig. E12].

Creating the Ball

Follow these steps:

1. In the **Create** panel, click **Geometry**, and then in the **Object Type** rollout, click **Sphere**. In the **Perspective** viewport, create a sphere. Switch to the **Modify** panel and on the **Parameters** rollout, change **Radius** to **35** and **Segments** to **45**.

2. In the **Create** panel, click **Geometry**, and then in the **Object Type** rollout, click **Sphere**. Select the **AutoGrid** checkbox and then create **3** spheres on the surface of the sphere you just created [see Fig. E13]. Change the radius of all small spheres to **5**.

3. Change the coordinate system to **Local** and then invoke the **Scale** tool. Now, scale the spheres about **350** units along the z-axis [see Fig. E14].

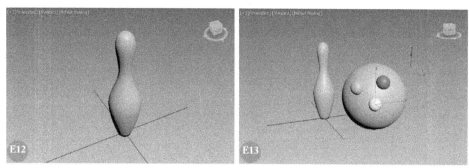

4. Select the bigger sphere. In the **Create** panel, click **Geometry**, and then choose **Compound Objects** from the drop-down list located below **Geometry**. Click **ProBoolean** and then make sure that **Subtraction** is selected in the **Parameters** rollout > **Operation** group. Click **Start Picking** and then click on small spheres one by one to create holes [see Fig. E15]. Click the **Start Picking** button again to finish the operation.

Exercise 2: Creating the Apple Logo

In this exercise, you will create a 3D Apple logo [see Fig. E1].

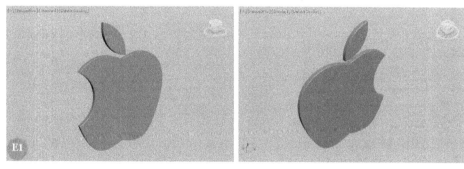

Table E2 summarizes the exercise.

Table E2	
Skill level	Basic
Time to complete	30 Minutes

Table E2	
Topics	• Getting Started • Creating the Logo
Resources folder	**spline-modeling**
Units	**Generic Units**
Final file	**logo-finish.max**

Getting Started

Follow these steps:

1. From the **Customize** menu choose **Units Setup**. In the **Units Setup** dialog box that appears, select the **Generic Units** option from the **Display Unit Scale** group.

2. Switch to the **Create** panel, click **Geometry**, then click **Plane**. In the **Front** viewport, create a plane. In the **Modify** panel > **Parameters** rollout, change **Length** to **180** and **Width** to **150**.

3. Invoke the **Move** tool from the **Main** toolbar. Set the **Transform Type-In** boxes to **0** in the **Status Bar** to place the box at the origin. Also, clear the **Real-World Map Size** checkbox, if not already clear. In the **Front** viewport, change the display mode to **Default Shading**. Also, press **G** to turn off the grid.

4. Click **Material Editor** in the **Main** toolbar; the **Slate Material Editor** appears. Drag the **Physical Material** from the **Slate Material Editor** > **Material/Map Browser** > **Materials** rollout > **General** rollout to **View1** tab and then apply it to the plane.

5. Use the **apple-logo.jpg** for the **Base Color** map using the **Bitmap** node and then set **Transparency** weight to **0.8** for the material.

6. **RMB** click on the material node and then select **Show Shaded Material in the Viewport** option (if not already selected) to display the image on the plane in the viewport.

7. Select the **Bitmap** node and then in the **Parameter Editor** > **Coordinates** rollout, make sure **Use Real-World Scale** is off and **U Tiling** and **V Tiling** are set to **1** each.

8. **RMB** click on the plane and then choose **Object Properties** from the **Quad** menu. Select the **Freeze** checkbox from the **Interactivity** area and clear the **Show Frozen in Gray** checkbox from the **Display Properties** area. Click **OK** [see Fig. E2].

Creating the Logo
Follow these steps:

1. Go to the **Create** panel, click **Shapes**, and then click **Line**. In the **Front** viewport, create a shape [see Fig. E3]. Ensure the line is selected and then activate the **Vertex** mode from the **Modify** panel. Select all vertices except the first and last vertex and then **RMB** click; choose **Smooth** from the **Quad** menu > **tools 1** quadrant. Now, adjust the shape of the line according to the background image [see Fig. E4]. Make sure the X position of the two end vertices is the same.

2. Activate the **Spline** level and select the spline in the viewport. Now, in the **Modify** panel > **Geometry** rollout, select the **Copy** checkbox below **Mirror** and then click **Mirror**. Press **S** to activate the **Snap** toggle and then snap the copied spline with the original spline [see Fig. E5].

3. Weld the end vertices that you just snapped [see Fig. E6]. If required, adjust the shape of the spline to fit the contours of the logo. Go to the **Create** panel, click **Shapes**, and then click **Circle**. Select **Edge** from the **Creation Method** rollout. Create a circle [see Fig. E7].

4. Select the profile curve of the logo and then in the **Create** panel, select **Shapes**, and then select **Compound Shapes** from the drop-down list. Next, click **ShpBoolean**. In the **Boolean Parameters** rollout, click **Add Operands** and then select the **Circle** in the viewport. In the **Operands Parameters** rollout, click **Subtract** to subtract circle from the profile curve [see Fig. E8]. Create two circles for the upper part of the logo [see Fig. E9].

5. Create a **ShpBoolean** object and connect the two circles with it. In the **Operands Parameters** rollout, click **Intersect** to create the shape of the leaf [see Fig. E10].

6. Convert the compound shape to editable spline and then attach them. Now, to make the unified spline smooth, in the **Modify** panel > **Interpolation** rollout, set **Steps** to **32**. Unfreeze and hide the plane object using the **Scene Explorer**.

7. From the **Modifier** list > **Object-Space Modifiers** section, choose **Bevel**. In the **Bevel Values** rollout, select the **Level 2** and **Level 3** checkboxes. Now, set **Start Outline** to **-0.5**, **Level 1 Height** to **0.5**, **Level 1 Outline** to **0.5**, **Level 2 Height** to **5**, **Level 2 Outline** to **0**, **Level 3 Height** to **0.5**, and **Level 3 Outline** to **-0.5**.

Exercise 3: Creating a Corkscrew

In this exercise, you will the model of a corkscrew using the **Helix** Spline and the **Loft** compound object [see Fig. E1].

Table E3 summarizes the exercise.

Table E3	
Skill level	Beginner
Time to complete	15 Minutes
Topics	• Specifying the Units for the Exercise • Creating the Corkscrew
Resources folder	**spline-modeling**
Units	**Generic Units**
Final file	**corkscrew-finish.max**

Specifying the Units for the Exercise

From the **Customize** menu choose **Units Setup**. In the **Units Setup** dialog box that appears, select the **Generic Units** option from the **Display Unit Scale** group.

Creating the Corkscrew

Follow these steps:

1. Go to the **Create** panel, click **Shapes**, then click **Helix**. In the **Top** viewport, create a shape. In the **Modify** panel > **Parameters** rollout, set **Radius 1** to **8**, **Radius 2** to **8**, **Height** to **120**, and **Turns** to **5.5**. In the **Front** viewport, rotate it by **90** degrees around Y-axis [see Fig. E2].

2. **RMB** click on the helix and then choose **Convert To: > Convert to Editable Spline** from the **transform** quadrant of the **Quad** menu. In the **Modify** panel > **Selection** rollout, click **Vertex** and then move the **first yellow** vertex toward left about **60** units in the **Front** viewport [see Fig. E3].

3. Apply the **Normalize Spline** modifier to the helix. In the **Modify** panel > **Parameters** rollout, set **Seg Length** to **5**. **RMB** click on the helix and then choose **Convert To: > Convert to Editable Spline** from the **transform** quadrant of the **Quad** menu.

> **?** *What just happened?*
> *You might have noticed that there were lots of vertices on the helix when I converted it into an editable spline. To reduce the number of vertices, I have applied the **Normalize Spline** modifier to the helix spline. This modifier adds new control points at regular intervals.*

4. Go to the **Create** panel, click **Shapes**, then click **Circle**. In the **Left** viewport, create a circle. In the **Modify** panel > **Parameters** rollout, set **Radius** to **2.5**. Select helix in a viewport. Go to the **Create** panel, click **Geometry** > **Compound Objects**, then click **Loft**. In the **Creation Method** rollout, click **Get Shape** and then click the circle in a viewport to loft the circle along the helix [see Fig. E4].

5. In the **Modify** panel > **Skin Parameters** rollout > **Options** group, set **Shape Steps** to **1** and **Path Steps** to **2**. In the **Modify** panel > **Deformations** rollout, click **Scale**. In the **Scale Deformation** dialog box that appears, click **Insert Corner Point** and then add a point below the **80** mark [see Fig. E5]. Now, click **Move Control Point** and move the endpoint downward [see Fig. E6] to scale the end area of the corkscrew [see Fig. E7]. Close the **Scale Deformation** dialog box.

6. Go to the **Create** panel, click **Geometry > Standard Primitives**, then click the **Cylinder** button. In the **Front** viewport, create a cylinder. In the **Modify** panel > **Parameters** rollout, set **Radius** to **4.857**, **Height** to **43.771**, **Height Segments** to **6**, and **Sides** to **18**. Now, align the cylinder with the corkscrew [see Fig. E8].

7. Convert the cylinder into an editable poly object and then activate the **Edge** mode. Select the edges, as shown in Fig. E9. In the **Modify** panel > **Edit Edges** rollout, click the **Connect > Settings** button to open the **Connect Edges** caddy. Set **Segments** to **2**, **Pinch** to **-18**, and then click **OK** to connect the edges [see Fig. E10].

8. Select polygon loops, as shown in Fig. E11. Click the **Inset > Settings** button to open the **Inset** caddy. Set **Type** to **Group**, **Amount** to **0.31**, and then click **OK** [see Fig. E12].

9. Click the **Extrude > Settings** button to open the **Extrude Polygons** caddy. Set **Type** to **Local Normals**, **Height** to **-0.1**, and then click **Apply and Continue**. Now, set **Amount**

to **-0.2** and then click **OK** [see Fig. E13]. Now, select the polygon loops, as shown in Fig. E14.

10. First, extrude them by **0.4** units and then inset by **0.3** units [see Fig. E15]. Select the edge loops, as shown in Fig. E16 and then scale them down by **25%** using the **Select and Uniform Scale** tool [see Fig. E17].

11. Now, select the border edges at both ends of the cylinder and then chamfer them [see Fig. E18]. Now, apply the **TurboSmooth** modifier to the cylinder.

Exercise 4: Creating a Model of a Glass and Liquid

In this exercise, you will create model of a glass filled with liquid [see Fig. E1]. Table E4 summarizes the exercise.

Table E4	
Skill level	Intermediate
Time to complete	1 Hour
Topics	• Specifying the Units for the Exercise • Setting the Blueprint • Creating the Glass • Creating the Liquid
Resources folder	**spline-modeling**
Units	**Generic Units**
Final file	**glass-liquid-finish.max**

Specifying the Units for the Exercise

From the **Customize** menu choose **Units Setup**. In the **Units Setup** dialog box that appears, select the **Generic Units** option from the **Display Unit Scale** group.

Setting the Blueprint
Follow these steps:

1. Switch to the **Create** panel, click **Geometry**, then click **Plane**. In the **Front** viewport, create a plane. In the **Modify** panel > **Parameters** rollout, change **Length** to **100** and **Width** to **75**.

2. Invoke the **Move** tool from the **Main** toolbar. Set the **Transform Type-In** boxes to **0** in the **Status Bar** to place the box at the origin. Also, clear the **Real-World Map Size** checkbox in **Plane** > **Modify** panel > **Parameters** rollout, if not already clear. In the **Front** viewport, change the display mode to **Default Shading**.

3. Click **Material Editor** in the **Main** toolbar; the **Slate Material Editor** appears. Drag the **Physical Material** from the **Slate Material Editor** > **Material/Map Browser** > **Materials** rollout > **General** rollout to **View1** tab and then apply it to the plane.

4. Use the **glassRef.png** for the **Base Color** map using the **Bitmap** node and then set **Transparency** weight to **0.8** for the material.

5. **RMB** click on the material node and then select **Show Shaded Material in the Viewport** option (if not already selected) to display the image on the plane in the viewport.

6. Select the **Bitmap** node and then in the **Parameter Editor** > **Coordinates** rollout, make sure **Use Real-World Scale** is off and **U Tiling** and **V Tiling** are set to **1** each.

7. **RMB** click on the plane and then choose **Object Properties** from the **Quad** menu. Select the **Freeze** checkbox from the **Interactivity** area and clear the **Show Frozen in Gray** checkbox from the **Display Properties** area. Click **OK** [see Fig. E2].

Creating The Glass
Follow these steps:

1. Go to the **Create** panel, click **Shapes**, then click **Line**. In the **Front** viewport, create a shape [see Fig. E3].

2. In the **Modify** panel > **Selection** rollout, click **Vertex**. In the **Modify** panel > **Geometry** rollout, click **Fillet**. Click and drag over the vertices to get the shape [see Fig. E4]. Make sure the **X** coordinate value for the selected vertices, shown in Fig. E5, is the same.

3. Make sure the profile of the curve is selected and then apply the **Lathe** modifier to it. In the **Modify** panel > **Parameters** rollout, click **Min** in the **Align** group. Set **Segments** to **32**. Now, select **Weld Core** [see Fig. E6]. Unfreeze and hide the plane and then rename the geometry as **glassGeo**. Place **glassGeo** at the origin.

Creating The Liquid
Follow these steps:

1. Select **glassGeo** and then on the **Ribbon > Polygon Modeling** panel, click **Convert to Poly.** Activate the **Edge** sub-object level and then on the **Ribbon > Edit** panel, click **SwiftLoop**. Insert an edge loop as shown in Fig. E7. Click **SwiftLoop** again to deactivate it. Activate **Polygon** sub-object level and then select the inner polygons shown in Fig. E8.

2. **Shift**-drag the selected polygons to the right. In the **Clone Part of Mesh** dialog box that appears, select **Clone to Object** and then type **liquidGeo** as the name of the clone, and then click **OK** [see Fig. E9]. Make sure all polygons of **liquidGeo** are selected and then click **Flip** on the **Modify** panel > **Edit Polygons** rollout to flip the normals.

What just happened?

*When you created **liquidGeo** using the **Shift**-drag method, you would have noticed that the outer area of the geometry is appearing dark. It happens because of the wrong orientation of the surface normals. By flipping the polygons, normals are properly oriented now.*

3. Select **liquidGeo** and then activate **Border** sub-object level. Now, select the border [see Fig. E10]. In the **Ribbon > Geometry (All)** panel, click **CapPoly**. Now, activate **Polygon** sub-object level and then select the cap polygon. In the **Ribbon > Polygons** panel, **Shift**-click **Inset** . In the **Inset** caddy control, set **Amount** to **5** and then click **OK** [see Fig. E11].

4. In the **Ribbon > Polygon Modeling** panel, **Ctrl**-click **Vertex**. In the **Ribbon > Vertices** panel, **Shift**-click **Weld**. In the **Weld Vertices** caddy, set **Weld Threshold** to **15** and then click **OK** [see Fig. E12] to weld the vertices. Activate the **Edge** sub-object level and then select the edge loop shown in Fig. E13.

5. In the **Ribbon > Edges** panel, **Shift**-click **Chamfer**. In the **Chamfer** caddy control, set **Edge Chamfer Amount** to **0.09** and **Connect Edge Segments** to **2** [see Fig. E14]. Click **OK**. Align the **glassGeo** and **liquidGeo** using the **Align** tool [see Fig. E15].

Exercise 5: Creating a Jug

In this exercise, you will create the model of a jug using spline and polygon modeling techniques [see Fig. E1]. Table E5 summarizes the exercise.

Table E5	
Skill Level	Intermediate
Time to Complete	30 Minutes
Topics	• Getting Ready • Creating Shape of the Jug Using Line and NGon Spline Primitive • Creating the Handle of the Jug Using Extrude Along Spline Feature • Refining the Model
Units	**Generic Units**
Resources folder	**spline-modeling**
Final file	**jug-finish.max**

Getting Ready

From the **Customize** menu choose **Units Setup**. In the **Units Setup** dialog box that appears, select the **Generic Units** option from the **Display Unit Scale** group.

Creating Shape of the Jug Using Line and NGon Spline Primitive

Follow these steps:

1. Activate the **Front** viewport. Go to the **Create** panel, click **Shapes**, and then ensure that **Splines** is selected in the drop-down list below the **Shapes** button. In the **Object Type** rollout, click **Line**. Expand the **Keyboard Entry** rollout, and then click **Add Point** to add a point at the origin. Now, set **Y** to 30 and then click **Add Point**. This action creates a line in the **Front** viewport [see Fig. E2]. This line will serve as a path for the **Loft** tool. Click **Select Object** in the Main toolbar to deactivate the line tool.

2. In the **Object Type** rollout, click **NGon** and then create an **NGon** in the **Front** viewport. In the **Modify** panel > **Parameters** rollout, set **Radius** to **7**, and **Sides** to **26**. Select the **Circular** checkbox. Create four more copies of the **NGon**. The total number of **NGons** will be **5** [see Fig. E3]. Change the radius of the three right-most **NGons** to **4** [see Fig. E4].

> **?** *Why NGon is used instead of Circle?*
> *You can also use the **Circle** primitive to create the shapes for the jug but by default, a **Circle** spline object just has four vertices. The **NGon** primitive we have used has 26 sides. As a result, a smooth surface will be created when we will loft the shapes along the path.*

3. The last **NGon** will be the spout of the jug. Select it and then convert into the **Editable Spline** object. Activate the **Vertex** sub-object level and then select the top four vertices as shown in Fig. E5.

4. **RMB** click on the vertices and then choose **Corner** from the **tool1** quadrant of the **Quad** menu. Now, select the middle two vertices and move them using the **Select and**

Move tool [see Fig. E6]. Ensure the vertices are still selected and them **RMB** click. In the **tool1** quadrant of the **Quad** menu, choose **Smooth** to make the shape of the spout [see Fig. E7]. If you want, you can fillet the other two corner vertices to create a smooth curve. Deactivate the **Vertex** sub-object level.

5. Select the **Line** in the **Front** viewport. Go to the **Create** panel, click **Geometry**, and then select **Compound Objects** in the drop-down list below the **Geometry** button. In the **Object Type** rollout, click **Loft**. In the **Path Parameters** rollout, ensure **Path** to set to **0** and click **Get Shape** button on the **Creation Method** rollout. Now, click on the first **NGon** that you have created. Set **Path** to **1** and then click **Get Shape**. Now, click on the second **NGon** in the **Front** viewport.

6. Similarly, pick the other three **NGons** with **Path** value set to **82**, **85**, and **100**, respectively. This action creates the shape of the jug in the viewport [see Fig. E8].

7. In the **Modify** panel, clear **Cap End** checkbox in the **Skin Parameters > Capping** group. In the **Options** group, set **Shape Steps** to **0** and **Path Steps** to **3**. Select the **Linear Interpolation** checkbox. Now, delete all spline objects from the scene.

8. Add a **Shell** modifier to the stack and then set **Outer Amount** to **0.559** in the **Modify** panel **> Parameters** rollout [see Fig. E9].

Creating the Handle of the Jug Using Extrude Along Spline Feature

Follow these steps:

1. Convert the model to an **Editable Poly** object. Select all polygons and then in the **Modify** panel > **Polygon : Smoothing Groups** rollout, click **Auto Smooth**. Now, select the edges as shown in Fig. E10. In the **Ribbon > Loops** panel, click **Connect** with the **Shift** held down, the **Connect Edges** caddy appears in the viewport. Set **Segments** to **4** [see Fig. E11] and click **OK**.

2. In the **Left** viewport, using the **Arc** tool, create a shape, as shown in Fig. E12. Now, select the vertices shown Fig. E13 and then click **Connect** from the **Modify** panel > **Edit Vertices** rollout to connect the vertices. Similarly, connect the other vertices diagonally [see Fig. E14].

3. Select the center vertex and click **Chamfer > Settings** button on the **Modify** panel > **Edit Vertices** rollout. In the **Chamfer** caddy control, set **Amount** to **1.059**, and **Vertex Chamfer Segments** to **0**. Then, click **OK** [see Fig. E15].

4. Select the edges, as shown in Fig. E16. In the **Ribbon > Loops** panel, click **Connect** with the **Shift** held down, the **Connect Edges** caddy appears in the viewport. Set **Segments** to **3** [see Fig. E17] and click **OK**. Similarly, connect other edges [see Fig. E18].

5. Select the vertices, as shown in Fig. E19 and then apply the **Spherify** modifier to round the shape [see Fig. E20]. Convert geometry to editable poly to bake the **Spherify** modifier. Select all polygons and then in the **Modify** panel > **Polygon : Smoothing Groups** rollout, click **Auto Smooth** [see Fig. E21].

6. Similarly, create the round shape for the other part of the handle [see Fig. E22]. Convert geometry to editable poly. Select the polygon, as shown in Fig. E23 and then on the **Ribbon > Polygons** panel, click **Extrude on Spline** with the **Shift** held down, the **Extrude Along Spline** caddy control appears.

7. Click **Pick Spline** and then click on the curve in a viewport to extrude the selected polygon along the spline. In the **Extrude Along Spline** caddy, set the values as shown in Fig. E24 and then click **OK**.

8. Select the polygons shown in Fig. E25 and then bridge them [see Fig. E26]. In the **Ribbon > Edit** panel, click **NURMS** to display a smooth model in the viewport. [see Fig. 27].

Quiz

Evaluate your skills to see how many questions you can answer correctly.

Multiple Choice
Answer the following questions:

1. Which of the following keys is used to constrain new points to 90 degrees angle increments while creating splines?

   [A] Shift   [B] Alt
   [C] Ctrl   [D] Shift+Alt

2. Which of the following is used to create splines in the shape of the text?

   [A] Text Object   [B] Text spline
   [C] Text   [D] All of the above

3. Which of the following keys is used to break a tangent and move its handles independently?

   [A] Alt   [B] Shift
   [C] Ctrl   [D] Shift+Alt

Fill in the Blanks
Fill in the blanks in each of the following statements:

1. 3ds Max provides two types of shape objects _____ and _____ curves.

2. You can use the _____ modifier to retain the parametric nature of a primitive spline.

3. The _____ and _____ rollouts are not available when you are use the **Edit Spline** modifier.

4. A _____ spline is a free-form spline that is made up of multiple segments.

5. The _____ spline is used to create spiral-like shapes.

6. The _____ spline is a special type of spline that lets you generate splines based on a cross-sectional slice through geometry objects.

7. To reset the tangent position, **RMB** click on the vertex or vertices and then choose _____ from the upper left quadrant of the **Quad** menu.

True or False
State whether each of the following is true or false:

1. 3ds Max allows you to combine shapes to create compound shapes.

2. You cannot change the creation parameters of a compound shape.

3. You cannot clone the sub-objects by first selecting them and then pressing and holding **Shift** while transforming them.

4. The **Fuse** tool lets you move all selected vertices to their averaged center.

5. The **Fillet** tool lets you create linear corners by adding new control vertices.

Practice Activities

Create a wine glass: Create the model of a wine glass [see the left image in Fig. A1] using the **Line** primitive.

*Create a shape [see the right image in Fig. A1] and then use the **Lathe** modifier to create the glass.*

Create a glass rack: Create the model of a glass rack using the **Rectangle** spline, the **ChamferCyl** primitive, and the **Extrude** modifier [see the left image in Fig. A2].

*Create a **Rectangle** spline, convert it to an editable spline, give it some outline, and then apply the **Extrude** modifier [see the right image in Fig. A2].*

Spin a spider web: Using the spline modeling tools, spin a spider web, as shown in Fig. A3.

*Use a **Circle** for the perimeter of the web and then use the **Editable Spline > Create Line** tool to spin the web.*

Summary
The unit covered the following topics:

- Generate planar and 3d surfaces
- Paths and shapes for the loft components
- Generate extrusions
- Generate revolved surfaces
- Define motion path for animations

Answer to Quiz
Multiple Choice
1. A, **2.** B, **3.** B

Fill in the Blanks
1, Splines, NURBS, **2.** Edit Spline, **3.** Rendering, Interpolation, **4.** Line, **5.** Helix, **6.** Section, **7.** Reset Tangents

True/False
1. T, **2.** T, **3.** F, **4.** T, **5.** F

- Using modifiers
- Stack display
- Object-Space modifiers vs World-Space modifiers
- How transform affects modifiers

Unit 7: Modifiers

Modifiers in 3ds Max allow you to sculpt or edit the objects without changing its base structure. For example, if you apply a **Taper** modifier to a cylinder, you will still be able to change its parametric properties such as **Radius** and **Height**. Modifiers can change the geometry of the objects as well as their properties. In other words, modifiers add more parameters to the objects.

Following are some points that you should remember about modifiers:

- When you apply modifiers to the objects, they are stored in a stack and displayed as a stack in the **Modify** panel. You can change the order of the modifiers in the stack to change their effect. You can also collapse the stack to make the changes permanent.
- You can apply any number of modifiers to an object.
- When you delete a modifier, its effect on the object also vanishes.
- You can copy modifiers from one object to another.
- The order of the modifier in the stack determines the final effect. Each modifier in the stack affects the modifiers that are applied after it.
- You can apply modifiers to sub-object levels.
- You can toggle the effect of the modifiers from the stack display.

Object Space Modifiers Vs World Space Modifiers

Some modifiers that 3ds Max offers operate in the world-space. These modifiers use the world-space coordinates and are applied to the object after all object-space modifiers and transforms have been applied. You can apply the world-space modifiers like any other object-space modifier. A world-space modifier is indicated by either an asterisk or the text **WSM**.

On the other hand, the object-space modifiers affect the geometry of the object in local space. They use the object's local coordinate system. The local coordinate system relates specifically to the selected object. Each object has its own local center and coordinate system. The local center and the coordinate system defines the object's local space. Unlike the world coordinate system, the directions of the object's axes [X, Y, and Z] depends on the current transform of the object.

Transform

Transformations [move, rotate, and scale] are the most basic manipulations of 3d objects. Unlike most of the modifiers, transforms are independent of the internal structure of an object. The transformation values are stored in a matrix called the **Transformation Matrix**. This matrix is applied to the entire object. The matrix is applied after all object-space modifiers have been applied but before the word-space modifiers.

Data Flow

Once you create an object and apply a modifier to it, 3ds Max evaluates the flow as per the table given below:

Order	Category	Modifiers/Transform/ Properties	Illustration
Table 1: The data flow			
1	Creation Parameters	Cylinder	
2	Object Modifiers	Bend, Taper	
3	Transforms	Rotate, Position, and Scale	
4	Space Warps	Ripple	

Table 1: The data flow			
Order	Category	Modifiers/Transform/ Properties	Illustration
5	Object Properties	Checker Material	

Using Modifiers

You can access modifiers from the **Modifiers** menu, the **Modifier** list from the **Modify** panel, and the applicable **Modifier Set** menu. To keep all modifiers organized, they are grouped in the **Modifiers** menu. The following table summarizes the options available in the **Modifiers** menu.

Table 2: The **Modifiers** menu overview	
Menu Item	**Sub-menu Items**
Selection Modifier	FFD Select, Mesh Select, Patch Select, Poly Select, Select By Channel, Spline Select, and Volume Select
Patch/Spline Editing	Cross Section, Delete Patch, Delete Spline, Edit Patch, Edit Spline, Fillet/Chamfer, Lathe, Normalize Spline, Renderable Spline Modifier, Surface, Sweep, Trim/Extend, Optimize Spline, Spline Mirror, and Spline Relax
Mesh Editing	Cap Holes, Chamfer, Delete Mesh, Edit Mesh, Edit Normals, Edit Poly, Extrude, Face Extrude, MultiRes, Normal Modifier, Optimize, ProOptimizer, Quadify Mesh, Smooth, STL Check, Symmetry, Tessellate, Vertex Paint, Vertex Weld, and Weighted Normals
Conversion	Turn to Mesh, Turn to Patch, and Turn to Pol
Animation	Attribute Holder, Flex, Linked XForm, Melt, Morpher, Patch Deform, Patch Deform (WSM), Path Deform, Spline Influence, Spline Morph, Spline Overlap, Path Deform (WSM), Skin, Skin Morph, Skin Wrap, Skin Wrap Patch, SpineIk Control, Surf Deform, and Surf Deform (WSM)
Cloth	Cloth, Garment Maker, and Welder
Hair and Fur	Hair and Fur (WSM)
UV Coordinates	Camera Map, Camera Map (WSM), MapScaler (WSM), Projection, Unwrap UVW, UVW Map, UVW Mapping Add, UVW Mapping Clear, and UVW XForm

Table 2: The **Modifiers** menu overview	
Menu Item	**Sub-menu Items**
Cache Tools	Point Cache and Point Cache (WSM)
Subdivision Surfaces	Crease, CreaseSet, HSDS Modifier, MeshSmooth, OpenSubdiv, and TurboSmooth
Free Form Deformers	FFD 2x2x2, FFD 3x3x3, FFD 4x4x4, FFD Box, and FFD Cylinder
Parametric Deformers	Affect Region, Bend, Data Channel, Displace, Lattice, Mirror, Noise, Physique, Push, Preserve, Relax, Ripple, Shell, Slice, Skew, Stretch, Spherify, Squeeze, Twist, Taper, Substitute, XForm, and Wave
Surface	Disp Approx, Displace Mesh (WSM), Material, and Material By Element
NURBS Editing	Displace Approx, Surf Deform, and Surface Select
Radiosity	Subdivide and Subdivide (WSM)
Cameras	Camera Correction

Using the Modify Panel

To apply a modifier to an object, select the object in the scene, and then go to the **Modify** panel. The name of the selected object appears on the top of the **Modify** panel. Apply a modifier to the object by using one of the following methods:

- Choose a modifier from the **Modifier** list available in the **Modify** panel. You can either use the mouse to click on the **Modifier** or use the keyboard. For example, if you are looking for the **Mirror** modifier, type **mi**, the modifiers whose name starts with **mi** [in this case the **Mirror** modifier only] appear in the **Modifier** list. Now, you can click on the **Modifier** or press **Enter** to apply it.
- Choose a modifier from the **Modifiers** menu.
- If the **Modifier** buttons are available in the **Modify** panel, click one of the buttons.

 Tip: Dragging a modifier to an object
*To drag a modifier form one object to another object in the scene, select an object that already has a modifier. To copy a modifier without instancing it, drag the modifier name from the stack display to the target object in the scene. If you want to create an instance, **Ctrl**-drag the modifier's name.*

 Tip: Modifier instances
*When you create an instance of a modifier, its name appears in italics in the **Modify** panel indicating that the modifier is instanced.*

Using the Configure Modifier Sets Dialog box

When you click on the **Configure Modifier Sets** button in the **Modify** panel [below modifier stack], a menu is displayed. Choose **Show Buttons** from the menu to display the modifier buttons below the **Modifier** list. The buttons associated with the currently selected set will be displayed in the **Modify** panel. You can select various sets from the menu. Fig. 1 shows the buttons associated with the **Selection Modifiers** set.

When you choose the **Configure Modifier Sets** option from the menu, the **Configure Modifier Sets** dialog box appears [see Fig. 2]. This dialog box lets you create custom modifiers and button sets for the **Modify** panel. To create a new set, specify the number of desired buttons using the **Total Buttons** option and then drag a modifier from the modifier list to a button.

You can also add a modifier by first highlighting the button and then double-clicking a modifier in the **Modifier** list. When you assign a modifier by double-clicking on its name, the highlight moves to the next button in the **Modifiers** group. Now, enter the name of the new set in the **Sets** edit field and then click **Save** to save the set. Click **OK** from the **Configure Modifier Sets** dialog box to exit it. Similarly, you can modify an existing set.

Using the Modifier Stack

The modifier stack [also referred to as just stack] is a list of modifiers that you apply to an object. The stack is evaluated from bottom to top. The first entry in the stack [from bottom] is always the object. The object-space modifiers appear above the object type. The world-space modifiers and space warps bound to the object are placed at the top.

You can use the stack in one of the following ways:

- Find a particular object and adjust its parameters using rollouts.
- Change the order of the modifiers.
- Deactivate the effect of the modifier in the stack, viewport, or both.
- Select components [such as **Gizmo** or **Center**] of a modifier.
- Delete modifiers.

The buttons at the bottom of the stack allow you to manage the stack. Table 3 summarizes the functioning of these buttons.

Table 3: The buttons found below the modifier stack		
Name	**Icon**	**Description**
Pin Stack		It locks the stack and all parameters in the **Modify** panel to the selected object stack.
Show end result on/off toggle		When active, it shows the effect of the entire stack on the selected object. When inactive, it shows the result up to the currently highlighted modifier.
Make unique		It makes an instanced object unique.
Remove modifier from the stack		It deletes the current modifier from the stack.
Configure Modifier Sets		When this button is clicked, a menu is displayed that allows you to configure the modifier button sets.

Tip: Copying and pasting modifiers
*You can copy and paste modifiers between the objects. If you **RMB** click on a modifier; a popup menu appears. You can use the **Cut**, **Copy**, **Paste**, and **Paste Instanced** options from the menu to edit the stack.*

Caution: World-space modifiers
*While copy-pasting the modifiers, ensure that you select the world-space and object-space modifiers separately. The **Cut**, **Copy**, and **Paste** options are disabled in the menu if you select both types of modifiers.*

Caution: Word-space modifiers
If you paste a word-space modifier in a section of object-space modifiers, the paste occurs at the top of the world-space section.

Collapsing the Stack

You can collapse the modifier stack of an editable object to merge the cumulative effect of the collapsed modifiers. You can collapse the modifier stack in one of the following situations:
- You have finished the model and you want to keep it as is.
- You want to discard animation tracks.
- You want to save the memory by simplifying the model.

In most of the cases, collapsing the entire modifier stack or part of the stack saves memory. However, some modifiers such as **Bevel** when collapsed increases the file size as well as the memory used.

Caution: Parametric nature of the objects
Once you collapse the modifier stack, you lose access to the parametric creation parameters of the object.

Tip: Preserving the original copy
Before you collapse a stack, choose ***Save As > Save Selected*** *from the* ***File*** *menu to preserve a copy of the original parametric object.*

3ds Max provides two options to collapse the stack: **Collapse To** and **Collapse All**. You can access these options by **RMB** clicking on the stack. The **Collapse To** option collapses the stack up to and including the chosen modifier to an editable object. You can still adjust the modifiers above the chosen modifier. The resultant object type depends on the uppermost modifier and the type of geometry it outputs. For example, if the uppermost modifier is **Edit Poly**, the resultant object will be an **Editable Poly** object. If no such modifier exists in the stack, the resultant object is an editable mesh. The **Collapse All** option collapses the entire stack. It does not affect any world-space bindings.

Exploring Modifiers

As already discussed, 3ds Max offers two types of modifiers: word-space modifiers and object-space modifiers. Let's explore these modifiers.

Word-Space Modifiers

The word-space modifiers act as object-specific space warps. They use world-space rather than object-space. When you apply a world-space modifier to an object, it appears at the top of the modifier stack. The world-space modifiers are discussed next.

Hair and Fur (WSM)

This modifier is the engine of the **Hair and Fur** feature in 3ds Max. You can apply this modifier to either a mesh object or a spline object. If you apply it to splines, the hair grows between the splines. When you select an object on which you have applied this modifier, hair is displayed in the viewport. You cannot select the fur itself in the viewport. However, you can select hair guides using the **Guides** sub-object level.

Note: Hair in the viewports
*The hair only renders in the **Perspective** or **Camera** viewport. If you try to render an orthographic viewport, 3ds Max presents a warning that says that the hair will not appear in the render.*

Camera Map (WSM)

This modifier is similar to the **Camera Map** modifier. It is used to apply the **UVW** mapping coordinates to the object based on a specified camera. It causes the object to blend with the background if you apply the same map to the object as you apply to the scene environment.

Displace Mesh (WSM)

This modifier allows you to see the effect of the **Displacement** mapping on editable mesh objects in the viewports. Also, you can see the effect of the **Displacement** mapping if you have applied a **Disp Approx** modifier to an object. This is useful when you want to visualize the effect of **Displacement** mapping in the viewports especially when you have animated the **Displacement** map or when you want to create an editable mesh from the displaced geometry in the scene.

Note: The Disp Approx modifier
If you are applying displacement to an editable mesh object, you don't need to apply this modifier to see the displacement effect in the viewport.

If you have changed parameters of the map [the **Noise** map in this case], click **Update Mesh** on the **Displacement Approx** rollout to update the mesh in the viewports. When **Subdivision Displacement** is on [you need to select the **Custom Settings** checkbox first, this modifier uses the settings that you specify in the **Subdivision Method** group of the rollout. You can also use the presets available in the **Subdivision Presets** group of the rollout. If **Subdivision Displacement** is off, this modifier applies the map by moving the vertices just as the **Displace** modifier does.

MapScalar (WSM)

This modifier is used to maintain the scale of a map that is applied to the object. In other words, it lets you resize the geometry without changing the scale of the map.

Patch Deform (WSM)
This modifier allows you to deform an object based on the contours of a patch object.

Point Cache (WSM)
This modifier allows you to store the modifier and sub-object animation to a disk file in your HDD. This file records changes in the vertex positions. When animation is played back, this file is used instead of the modifier keyframes. This modifier is useful when computation for vertex animation slows down the system and playback. This modifier is also useful in cloth animations.

Subdivide (WSM)
This modifier is similar to the object-space **Subdivide** modifier. However, in the world-space version, the size limit is on for the mesh after it is transformed into world-space coordinates.

Surface Mapper (WSM)
This modifier takes a map assigned to the **NURBS** surface and then projects it onto the modified objects. It is useful in applying a single map to a group of surface sub-objects within the same **NURBS** model.

SurfDeform (WSM)
The functioning of this modifier is the same as of the **PathDeform (WSM)** modifier, except that it uses a **NURBS Point** or a **CV** surface instead of a curve.

PathDeform (WSM)
The **PathDeform** modifier deforms an object based on a shape, a spline, or a NURBS curve. This modifier works the same as the object-space **PathDeform** modifier. Create a line and a cone in the scene [see Fig. 3]. Apply the **PathDeform (WSM)** modifier to the cone. In the **Modify** panel > **Parameters** rollout, click on the **Pick Path** button, and then click the line in the viewport. Now, click **Move to Path** button to snap the cone to the line [see Fig. 4].

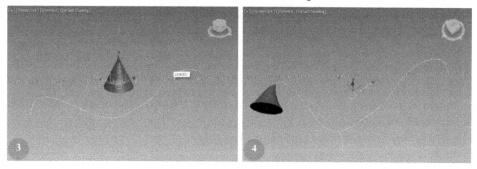

Adjust the **Stretch** spinner to stretch the cone along the line [see Fig. 5]. Adjust the **Height Segments** spinner of the cone object to smooth the stretch. You can also use the radius parameters to adjust the shape [see Fig. 6]. Now, if you want to create a growing vine-like animation, you can animate the **Stretch** parameter. Also, refer to **pathdeform-wsm.max**.

Object-Space Modifiers

The object-space modifiers affect the geometry in the local space. These modifiers are discussed next:

Affect Region

This modifier is a surface modeling tool. It works well at the **Vertex** sub-object level. You can use it to create a bubble or indentation on the surface. When you add this modifier to the stack, it assigns an arrow-like gizmo to the object that you can use in the viewport to alter the geometry. The parameters in the **Parameters** rollout allow you to numerically control the shape of the deformation [see Fig. 7]. Also, refer to **affect-region-osm.max**.

Attribute Holder

This modifier allows you to hold custom attributes for the objects in the **Modify** panel. It is an empty modifier to which you can add the custom attributes. It is a stripped-down version of the **Parameter Collector** dialog box. It can collect only the custom attributes and appears in the **Modify** panel instead of a floating dialog box.

Create a **Cylinder** primitive in the scene with the **Radius** and **Height** parameters set to **10** and **100**, respectively. Add the **Bend** modifier to the stack followed by the **Attribute Holder** modifier. Ensure that the **Attribute Holder** modifier is highlighted in the stack. Choose

Parameter Editor from the **Animation** menu to open the **Parameter Editor** dialog box.

In this dialog box, set **Add to Type** to **Selected Object's Current Modifier**, **Parameter Type** to **Float**, **UI Type** to **Slider**, and **Name** to **Cylinder Height** [see Fig. 8]. Click **Add** from the **Attribute** Rollout, the **Cylinder Height** parameter appears in the **Modify Panel > Custom Attributes** rollout [see Fig. 9].

Set **Add to Type** to **Selected Object's Current Modifier**, **Parameter Type** to **Integer**, **UI Type** to **Spinner**, and **Name** to **Cylinder H Segments**. In the **Integer UI Options** rollout, set **Range > From** and **Range > To** to **1** and **60**, respectively. Click **Add** on the **Attribute** rollout of the **Parameter Editor** dialog box.

Similarly, add two more float spinners with the name **Bend Angle**, and **Bend Direction**, respectively [see Fig. 10]. Close the **Parameter Editor** dialog box.

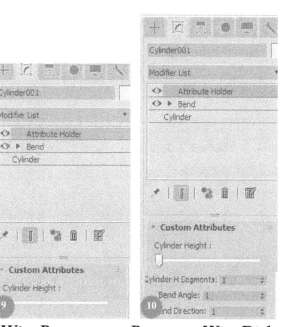

Choose **Animation > Wire Parameters > Parameter Wire Dialog** from the menubar to open the **Parameter Wiring** dialog box. In the left pane of the dialog box, choose **Objects > Cylinder001 > Modified Object > Cylinder (Object) > Height**. In the right pane, choose **Objects > Cylinder001 > Modified Object > Attribute Holder > Custom_Attributes > Cylinder Height**. Now, click **Two-way connection** followed by **Connect** to create a connection between the selected attributes [see Fig. 11].

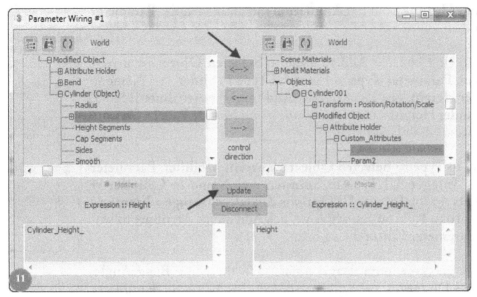

The label on the **Connect** button changes to **Update**. Similarly, connect the **Cylinder (Object) > Height Segments, Bend > Angle**, and **Bend > Direction** parameters from the left pane to **Cylinder H Segs, Bend Angle**, and **Bend Direction**, respectively, parameters of the right pane [see Fig. 12]. Close the **Parameter Wiring** dialog box.

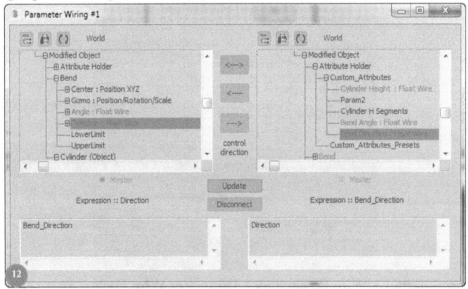

Now, experiment with the parameters available in the **Modify** panel > **Custom Attributes** rollout of the **Attribute Holder** modifier [see Fig. 13]. Also, refer to **attribute-holder-osm. max**.

Bend

You can use this modifier to create a uniform 360-degree bend on a geometry about a single axis. You can limit bend to a section of the geometry as well as you can control the bend angle and direction.

To bend an object, add the **Bend** modifier to the stack. In the **Parameters** rollout of the modifier, set **Angle** and **Direction** in the **Bend** group to specify the angle to bend from the vertical plane and direction of the bend relative to the horizontal plane, respectively. Specify the axis to be bent from the **Bend Axis** group. To limit the bending effect to a particular area of the object, select the **Limit Effect** checkbox and then specify the limit using the **Upper Limit** and **Lower Limit** parameters [see Fig. 14].

This modifier offers two sub-objects. You can change the effect of the modifier using the **Gizmo** sub-object by transforming or animating it [see Fig. 15]. You can translate or animate the **Center** sub-object to change the shape of the **Gizmo** resulting in the change of the bending effect [see Fig. 16].

Bevel

This modifier allows you to extrude spline shapes into 3D objects and then applies a flat or round bevel on the edges. You can control the beveling from the **Bevel Values** rollout of the modifier. Create a **Text** spline and then add a **Bevel** modifier to the stack. Adjust the parameters in the **Parameters** and **Bevel Values** rollouts of the modifier [see Fig. 17]. Also, refer to **bevel-osm.max**.

Bevel Profile

This modifier is another version of the **Bevel** modifier but it extrudes a shape using a path or profile [beveling profile]. Create a shape and profile curve and then apply the **Bevel Profile** modifier to the shape's stack. Create a **Text** object and a **Helix** object. Select the **Text** object and then add **Bevel Profile** to the stack. In the **Modify** panel > **Parameters** rollout > **Bevel Profile** group, select the **Classic** option. Now, in the **Classic** rollout, click **Pick Profile** and then click the **Helix** object in a viewport to create the bevel [see Fig. 18]. Also, refer to **bevel-profile-osm.max**.

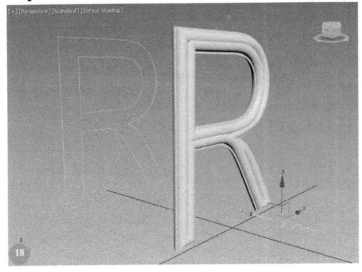

*There is another method that you can use to bevel a shape using a profile, it's called **Improved** method. To use this method, select the **Improved** option from the **Parameters** rollout > **Bevel Profile** group and then open the **Bevel Profile Editor** by clicking on the **Bevel Profile Editor** button. Now, create a profile for the bevel using this editor. You can also use bevel presets from the drop-down list available in the **Improved** rollout. Refer to **bevel-profile-osm-2.max**.*

Camera Map

This modifier is the object-space version of the **Camera Map (WSM)** modifier. It assigns the planar mapping coordinates based on the current frame and a specified camera. This behavior is different from the **Camera Map (WSM)** modifier which updates the coordinates at every frame.

Cap Holes

This modifier build faces on the holes in a mesh. This modifier works well with the planar holes, however, it does a reasonable job when applied to non-planar holes [see Fig. 19].

Cross Section

This modifier creates a skin across multiple various-shaped splines by connecting the vertices of the 3D splines. The result is another spline object to which you can apply the **Surface** modifier to create a patch surface. These two modifiers sometimes also referred to as **Surface Tools**.

Create an **Arc** object in the scene and convert it to **Editable** spline. Now, create three more copies of the **Arc** object and change their shapes using the **Scale** tool [see the left image in Fig. 20]. Attach all splines to form a single spline object. Add the **Cross Section** modifier to form a combined spline [see the middle image in Fig. 20]. Now, add the **Surface** modifier to the stack to create skin [see the right image in Fig. 20]. To change the shape, edit the combined spline at the sub-objects level. Also, refer to **cross-section-osm.max**.

The output of the **Surface** modifier is a patch surface. Therefore, you can add the **Edit Patch** modifier to the stack and edit the surface using the patch edit parameters.

Data Channel
The **Data Channel** modifier is used to automate complex modeling operations. You can feed mesh data through a series of parameters to create a variety of effects that dynamically update in the viewport.

Delete Mesh
This modifier allows you to parametrically delete sub-object selection based on faces, vertices, edges, and objects. Create a **Teapot** object and then add the **Poly Select** modifier to the stack. Select the polygons as shown in the left image of Fig. 21. Add a **Delete Mesh** modifier to delete the selected faces [see the right image in Fig. 21].

Delete Patch
It provides parametric deletion based on the patch sub-object selection. The possible choices are vertices, edges, patches, and elements.

Delete Spline
It provides parametric deletion based on the **Spline** sub-object selection. The possible choices are vertices, segments, and splines. Create a **Line** object. Add the **Spline Select** modifier to the stack and then select a segment. Now, add the **Delete Spline** modifier to the stack to delete the selected segment [see Fig. 22].

Displace Approx
See the **Displace Mesh Modifier (WSM)**.

Displace

This modifier pushes the object's geometry to reshape it using a map or bitmap texture. This modifier allows you to apply the effect using two methods:

- Apply the effect directly onto the object using the **Strength** and **Decay** values.
- Apply the effect using the grayscale values of a bitmap image.

You can use this modifier to simulate magnetic push like effect by animating its gizmos. The four gizmos provided by this modifier are: **Planar**, **Cylindrical**, **Spherical**, and **Shrink Wrap**. These gizmos are used to distribute the force specified by the **Strength** and **Decay** values. Create a **Plane** primitive with **30** length and width segments. Add a **Displace** modifier to the stack and then set **Strength** to **-100** and **Decay** to **-0.66** in the **Parameters** rollout of the modifier. Choose **Spherical** from the **Map** group of the rollout and then select the **Gizmo** sub-object from the stack. Now, use the **Move** tool to see the effect of this modifier [see the left image in Fig. 23]. Also, refer to **displace-osm-1 .max**.

You can also use a bitmap or map to produce this effect. Click **None** associated with the **Map** parameter in the **Image** group to open **Material/Map Browser**. Double-click on a **Noise** map to select this map. Select **Planar** from the **Map** group and then set **Strength** to **38**; the effect of the modifier is displayed in the viewport [see the right image in Fig. 23]. Also, refer to **displace-osm-2 .max**.

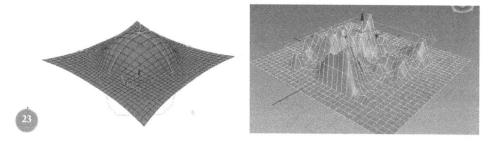

To change the parameters of the **Noise** map, drag the **Map** button to the material editor. Choose **Instance** from the dialog box displayed. Now, double-click on the map node to view its properties. Change the properties as per your requirement.

Edit Mesh

The **Edit Mesh** modifier has all the capabilities of the **Editable Mesh** object except that you cannot animate sub-objects.

Edit Normals

You can use this modifier to procedurally and interactively change the vertex normals of an object. This modifier is specifically used when you intend to output the meshes for the game and 3D rendering engines that support specified normals. The orientation of the vertex normals affects how light is reflected by the neighboring surfaces. By default in 3ds Max, rules of real-world physics are followed in which the angle of reflection is equal to the angle of incidence. However, using this modifier, you can set the angle of reflection as required.

Edit Patch

The **Edit Patch** modifier has all the capabilities of the **Editable Patch** object except that you cannot animate sub-objects.

Edit Poly

The **Edit Poly** modifier has all the capabilities of the **Editable Poly** object except **Vertex Color** information, **Subdivision Surface** rollout, **Weight** and **Crease** settings, and **Subdivision Displacement** rollout. This modifier lets you animate sub-object transforms and parameters.

Edit Spline

The **Edit Spline** modifier has all the capabilities of the **Editable Spline** object. The **Rendering** and **Interpolation** rollouts are not available for this modifier. Also, you cannot create direct vertex animation using this modifier.

Extrude

This modifier allows you to add depth to a shape object. It also makes the shape object parametric. Create a **Rectangle** shape object and convert it to an editable spline. Create an outline and apply the **Extrude** modifier to the spline object. In the **Parameters** rollout, specify a value for the **Amount** parameter to set the depth of extrusion [see Fig. 24]. Specify a value for the **Segments** parameter to set the segments that will be created for the extruded object.

You can use the **Cap Start** and **Cap End** parameters to generate a flat surface over the start and end of the extruded object [see Fig. 24]. The parameters in the **Output** group let you choose the output mesh type when the stack is collapsed. The available options are **Patch**, **Mesh**, and **NURBS**.

Face Extrude

This modifier extrudes the faces along their normals [see Fig. 25]. There are many differences between the **Face Extrude** function and the **Face Extrude** modifier. The one big difference is that all parameters of this modifier are animatable.

FFD

FFD stands for **Free-Form** deformation. You can use these modifiers in a variety of ways. You can use it to create a bulge in a mesh, animate dancing cars, and so on. When you apply an **FFD** modifier such as **FFD 2x2x2**, **FFD 3x3x3**, or **FFD 4x4x4**, it surrounds the selected geometry with a lattice. You can transform the lattice and use its control points to adjust the shape of the geometry [see Fig. 26].

Each modifier provides a different lattice resolution [**2x2x2**, **3x3x3**, and **4x4x4**]. For example, a **4x4x4** resolution produces a lattice with four control points across each of its dimensions resulting in **12** points in each side of the lattice.

There are three sub-objects available with this modifier. At the **Control Points** sub-object level, you can select the control points of the lattice and then change the shape of the underlying geometry by transforming them. At the **Lattice** sub-object level, you can transform the lattice box separately from the geometry. At **Set Volume** level, the color of the lattice control points turns green. You can select and manipulate the points without affecting the underlying geometry. You should use this level to set the initial state of the lattice.

> ✎ *Note: The FFD(box) and FFD(cyl) modifiers*
> *You can use the **FFD(box)** and **FFD(cyl)** modifiers to create box-shaped or cylinder-shaped FFD lattices. These modifiers are also available as space warps.*

Fillet/Chamfer

This modifier lets you fillet or chamfer corner vertices between linear segments of the shape objects. This modifier rounds corners where the segments meet by adding new control vertices. It also bevels the corners. This modifier works on the splines at the sub-object level. It does not work between two independent shape objects.

Create a **Star** shape object in the scene, convert it to an editable spline, and add the **Fillet/ Chamfer** modifier to the stack. Now, at the **Vertex** sub-object level of the modifier, select the vertices that you want to affect and then specify the desired settings in the **Edit Vertex** rollout to generate different shapes [see Fig. 27].

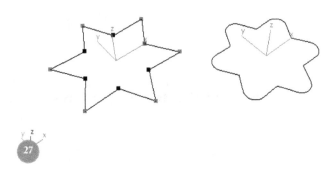

Flex

This modifier creates virtual springs between vertices of an object thus simulating a soft body dynamics behavior. You can control the stiffness and stretch of the springs. You can also control the sway of the springs that is how much the spring angle changes in relation to the movement of the springs. This modifier works with NURBS, patches, polygon and mesh objects, shapes, FFD space warps, and any plug-in-based object types that can be deformed.

HSDS

HSDS stands for **Hierarchical SubDivision Surfaces**. This modifier implements the Hierarchical SubDivision Surfaces. You can use this modifier as a finishing tool for subdivision surfaces.

Lathe

You can use the **Lathe** modifier to rotate a shape or NURBS curve about a specified axis. Create a **Shape** object [see the left image in Fig. 28] and add the **Lathe** modifier to the stack. In the **Parameters** rollout of the modifier, ensure that **Degrees** is set to **360** to create a full 360 degrees lathe. Specify the segments for the lathe object using the **Segments** parameter. Click **Y** in the **Direction** group to set the Y-axis as the axis of revolution relative to the pivot point of the object. Click **Min** from the **Align** group to align the axis of revolution to the minimum extent of the shape. The right image in Fig. 28 shows the full lathe object.

You can select the **Weld Core** checkbox to weld vertices that lie on the axis of revolution. This modifier also presents the **Axis** sub-object. At this level, you can transform and animate the axis of revolution.

Lattice

This modifier allows you to create a renderable structure from a geometry. It can be thought of as an alternative method to create a wireframe effect. It gives you options to create joints, struts, or both. Fig. 29 shows a sphere with joints, struts, and both join and struts, respectively.

Linked XForm

This modifier links the transform of any object or sub-object selection to another object. The other object is called the control object. The transforms of the control object are passed onto the object or sub-object selection.

Create a **Sphere** and a **Cone** primitive in the scene. The cone will be the control object. Now, select sphere and add **Linked XForm** modifier to the stack. In the **Parameters** rollout, click **Pick Control Object** and then click on the cone in a viewport. Now, when you transform [move, scale, or rotate] the cone, the sphere will also receive the transforms. Refer to **linked-xform-osm.max**.

Delete the modifier from the stack and convert the sphere to **Editable Poly**. At the **Vertex** sub-object level, select some vertices [see the left image in Fig. 30]. Link **Cone** to vertices as discussed above. Now, when you move the cone, the selected vertices will also receive the transform. Refer to **linked-xform-osm-2.max**.

MapScalar
See the **MapScalar Modifier (WSM)** modifier.

Material
This modifier allows you to animate or change the assignment of the existing material IDs on an object.

MaterialByElement
This modifier allows you to apply different material IDs to objects containing multiple elements. You can apply IDs at random or you can use a formula. Select **Random Distribution** from the **Parameters** rollout to assign the material IDs to different elements at random. The **ID Count** parameter lets you assign the minimum number of materials IDs. Select **List Frequency** to define a percentage of each [up to eight] of the material IDs.

Melt
This modifier allows you to create a realistic melting effect on all types of objects, including editable patches and NURBS objects. It also works on the sub-object selections passed up the stack. Create a cylinder with enough sub-divisions and then apply the **Melt** modifier to it. In the **Melt** group of the **Parameters** rollout, specify the strength of the melt using the **Amount** parameter. The **% of Melt** parameter in the **Spread** group lets you specify the spread of the melt [see Fig. 31].

The parameters in the **Solidity** group determine the center of the melted object. There are several presets available in this group that you can use to specify the solidity of the object. If you want to specify a custom solidity, select **Custom** from this group. This modifier has two sub-objects, **Gizmo** and **Center**. You can transform and animate these two sub-objects to change the effect of the melt.

Mesh Select
This modifier provides a superset of the selection functions available in the **Edit Mesh** modifier. It allows you to pass the sub-object selection up the stack to another subsequent modifier.

MeshSmooth

This modifier allows you to smooth the geometry by subdividing it. You can use this modifier to produce a **Non-Uniform Rational MeshSmooth** object, **NURMS** in short. A **NURMS** object is similar to the **NURBS** object in which you set different weights for vertices [see Fig. 32]. You can farther alter the geometry by modifying the edge weight.

You can choose the desired method from the **Subdivision Method** drop-down list of the **Subdivision Method** rollout. The available methods are: **NURMS**, **Classic**, and **Quad Output**. The **Iterations** parameter in the **Subdivision Amount** rollout lets you specify the number of times you want to subdivide the mesh.

Mirror

This modifier allows you to parametrically mirror an object or a sub-object selection [see Fig. 33]. Apply this modifier to the stack and then select the axis or axis pair from the **Mirror Axis** group of the **Parameters** rollout. If you want to create a copy of the object, select the **Copy** checkbox, and then specify the offset distance using the **Offset** parameter.

Tip: Modeling a character
When you have created one side of a character and you want to mirror the other side, use the ***Symmetry*** *modifier instead of the* ***Mirror*** *modifier as the* ***Symmetry*** *modifier allows you to weld the seam which results in a better-looking model.*

Morpher

You can use this modifier to change the shape of the mesh, patch, or **NURBS** model. Morphing is generally used for lip-syncing and facial expressions. This modifier also allows you to morph splines and world-space **FFDs**. Also, you can morph from one shape to another using this modifier.

MultiRes

This modifier reduces the number of polygons in a mesh to improve the rendering time [see Fig. 34]. You can also reduce the number of vertices and polygons using the **Optimize** modifier. However, this modifier has certain advantages over the **Optimize** modifier such as it is faster and lets you specify the exact percentage for reduction. You can also specify the vertex count for reductions.

To reduce the polygons, apply this modifier to the stack. In the **Generation Parameters** group of the **MultiRes Parameters** rollout, click **Generate** to initialize the modifier. In the **Resolution** group, specify a value for the **Vert Percent** or **Vert Count** to reduce the polygons.

Noise

This modifier alters the position of the vertices of an object along with any combination of three axes [see Fig. 35]. You can use it to create random variations in the shape of the object. You can also animate the change in the shape of the mesh. Add the modifier to the stack and then in the **Strength** group of the **Parameters** rollout, set the strength using the **X, Y,** and **Z** parameters. Select the **Fractal** checkbox from the **Noise** group to produce a fractal-like effect [see Fig. 36]. When you select this checkbox, the **Roughness** and **Iterations** parameters appear in the rollout. You can use these parameters to determine the extent of the fractal variation and the number of iteration used by the modifier, respectively.

Normal

This modifier allows you to unify or flip the normals of an object without first converting it to an **Edit Mesh** modifier. Select the **Unify Normals** checkbox in the **Parameters** rollout to unify the normals so that they all point in the same direction, usually outward. Select the **Flip Normals** checkbox to reverse the direction of all surface normals.

Normalize Spline

You can use this modifier to add new control points at a regular interval in a spline [see Fig. 37]. This is useful in normalizing the spline that you will use with the motion paths. The **Set Length** parameter in the **Parameters** rollout allows you set the length of the spline segments. 3ds Max uses this control to set the vertices at the regular intervals.

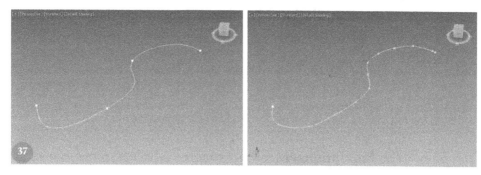

Optimize
See the **MultiRes Modifier**.

Patch Select
This modifier provides a superset of selection functions available in the **Edit Patch** modifier.

Patch Deform
See the **PatchDeform Modifier (WSM)** modifier.

PathDeform
See the **PathDeform Modifier (WSM)** modifier.

Point Cache
See the **Point Cache Modifier (WSM)** modifier.

Poly Select
This modifier provides a superset of selection functions available in the **Edit Poly** modifier.

Preserve
When you push and pull vertices to model a surface, the edges of the mesh get stretched which results in an irregular geometry. This modifier allows you to retain [as much as possible] the original length of the edge thus producing a cleaner mesh.

Projection
This modifier is generally used for producing normal bump maps. Apply this modifier to the low-resolution object and then pick a high-resolution object as the source of the projected normals.

Projection Holder
This modifier appears when the **Project Mapping** feature of the **Projection** modifier is used.

It contains data generated by the **Project Mapping** feature such as the **UVW** mapping data.

ProOptimizer

This modifier allows you to interactively reduce the number of vertices in a model while preserving the original appearance/features of the model such as material, mapping, and vertex color information. When this modifier is used, the memory requirement for a model is reduced. You can optimize a model using one of the following two methods:

- You can use the **ProOptimizer** modifier to interactively optimize the model.
- You can use the **Batch ProOptimizer** utility to optimize multiple scenes at one go. When you use this utility, you can optimize the meshes before you import them to save time.

Push

This modifier allows you to push the selected vertices inward or outward along the average vertex normals to create inflation like effect [see Fig. 38].

Quadify Mesh

You can use this modifier to convert object structure to quadrilateral polygons using the relative size that you specify. This modifier helps you to create a mesh with a rounded model with the help of the **Smooth** modifier.

Relax

This modifier allows you to reduce the surface tension by moving the vertices closer to or away from their neighbors. This results in a smooth object, however, the model appears a little smaller than the un-relaxed model.

> *Note: Neighboring vertex*
> *A neighboring vertex is a vertex that shares a visible edge with the current vertex.*

Renderable Spline

This modifier makes a spline object renderable without needing to convert it to an **Editable Spline** object. It also allows you to apply the same rendering properties to multiple splines. This modifier is useful when you link an AutoCAD drawing.

Ripple

You can use this modifier to create a ripple effect on the geometry [see Fig. 39]. You can use its **Gizmo** sub-object to change the ripple effect.

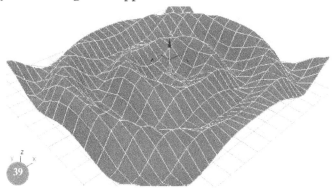

> Note: The Ripple space warp
> *The **Ripple** space warp has the same features as the **Ripple** modifier. However, you can apply the **Ripple** space warp to a large number of objects.*

Select By Channel

This modifier is used with the **Channel Info** utility. When you save a vertex selection into a sub-component using the **Channel Info** utility, you can use this modifier to quickly access the selection.

Shell

This modifier allows you to give thickness to an object by creating an extra set of faces in the opposite direction of the existing faces [see Fig. 40]. You can specify the offset distances using the **Inner Amount** and **Outer Amount** parameters available in the **Parameters** rollout.

Skew

This modifier can be used to create a uniform offset in an object's geometry [see Fig. 41]. You can control the direction of the skew on any of the three axes. You can also limit the skew effect by selecting the **Limit Effect** checkbox and then using the **Upper Limit** and **Lower Limit** parameters.

Skin Modifier

This modifier is a skeleton deformation tool that allows you to deform one object with another object. You can deform the **Mesh**, **Patch**, and **NURBS** objects using the bones, splines, and other objects.

Skin Morph

This modifier allows you to use a bone's rotation to drive the deformation of the mesh object. This modifier is used with other modifiers such as **Skin** and **Physique**.

Skin Wrap

You can use this modifier to deform an object with another object. Although, you can use this modifier in a variety of ways its primary use is to animate a high-resolution object mesh with the help of a low-resolution mesh.

Skin Wrap Patch

This modifier allows you to deform a mesh object with the help of a patch object. Each point on the patch object influences a surrounding volume of points on the mesh object.

Slice

You can use this modifier to slice through selected objects or sub-objects using a cutting plane. Its functioning is similar to that of the **Slice** function of the **Editable Mesh** object. However, it does not require to be an **Editable Poly** or **Editable Mesh** object. You can also animate the position and rotation of the slicing plane.

Smooth

You can smooth a faceted geometry using this modifier. It eliminates the faceting by grouping the faces into smoothing groups. It smoothens the faces based on the angle of adjacent faces.

Spherify

This modifier distorts an object into a spherical shape [see Fig. 42]. The end result is dependent on the topology of the object.

Spline IK Control

The basic use of this modifier is to prepare a spline or **NURBS** curve for use with the **Spline IK Solver**. When this modifier is applied to a spline object, you can transform its vertices without needing to access the **Vertex** sub-object level. It places knots [control points] at each vertex and then you can manipulate the knots to change the shape of the spline.

Spline Influence Modifier

This modifier creates a soft selection of the spline knots. The selection is shown in the viewport as a color gradient ranging from red to blue. The red color represents completely selected knots whereas the blue color represents the un-selected knots.

Spline Mirror Modifier

Similar to the **Symmetry** modifier, this modifier duplicates a spline along a specified axis. Available normals are also duplicated.

Spline Morph Modifier

You can use this modifier to morph between splines using either a progressive or blended method.

Spline Overlap Modifier

This modifier allows you to detect self-overlapping splines and adjusts the displacement of the intersection elements.

Spline Relax Modifier

This modifier relaxes knot positions and/or handles resulting in the smooth out splines.

Spline Select

This modifier is a superset of the selection functions found in the **Edit Spline** modifier. It passes a sub-object selection up the stack to other modifiers.

Squeeze

The modifier lets you create a squeezing [create bulge] effect on the objects [see Fig. 43]. The vertices closest to the object's pivot point move inward. The squeeze operation is applied around the **Squeeze** gizmo's local Z-axis.

STL Check

This modifier checks if the object is correct for exporting to an **STL** file format. **STL** [**stereolithography**] files are used by the specialized machines to create prototype models based on the supplied **STL** file. The **STL** file must have a complete and closed surface.

Stretch

The **Stretch Modifier** allows you to create traditional squash and stretch effects that are used in animations [see Fig. 44]. This modifier applies a scale effect along a specified axis and opposite scale along the two remaining minor axes.

Subdivide Modifier

See the **Subdivide Modifier (WSM)** modifier.

Substitute

This modifier allows you to replace one or more objects with other objects in a viewport or at the render time. The substitute object can be instanced in the current scene or can be referenced from an external file. This modifier is useful for designers who use 2D shapes in their AutoCAD drawings. When they link the AutoCAD drawing to 3ds Max, they want to see how the object will look like in their design. This modifier allows them to achieve that objective.

Surface

See the **Cross Section** modifier.

Surface Select

This modifier allows you to add a **NURBS** sub-object selection in the stack. Then, you can modify the selected sub-objects. It can select any kind of NURBS sub-objects except imports.

SurfDeform
See the **SurfDeform Modifier (WSM)** modifier.

Sweep
You can use this modifier to extrude a cross-section along an underlying spline or **NURBS** curve path. It provides several pre-made cross-sections such as angles, channels, wide flanges, and so on [see Fig. 45]. You can also use a custom spline or NURBS curve as custom sections.

Symmetry
See the **Mirror** modifier.

Taper
This modifier creates tapered contours by scaling both ends of an object's geometry [see Fig. 46]. It scales up to one end and scales down the other end. You can also limit the taper effect.

Tessellate
This modifier is used to subdivide the faces of a mesh [see Fig. 47]. It is useful in smoothing the curved surface and creating additional geometry for other modifiers to act on. The **Tension** parameter in the **Parameters** rollout allows you to add convexity or concavity to the subdivided surface.

Trim/Extend
This modifier is used to clean up the overlapping or open splines in a multi-spline shape. To trim, you need the intersecting splines. If the section intersects at both ends, the entire

section will be deleted by this modifier up to the two intersections. To extend, you need an open spline.

TurboSmooth
This modifier is like the **MeshSmooth** modifier with the following differences:

- **TurboSmooth** is faster and more memory efficient than the **MeshSmooth** modifier.
- **TurboSmooth** uses a single subdivision method, NURMS. It has no sub-object levels and outputs a triangle-mesh object.

Turn To Mesh Modifier/ Turn To Patch Modifier/ Turn To Poly Modifier
These modifiers allow you to apply the object conversions in the modifier stack. When you apply general-purpose modifiers, these modifiers give you the ability to explicitly control the output type of the object beforehand.

Twist
This modifier creates a twisting effect on the surface of an object [see Fig. 48]. You can control the angle of the twist as well as you can limit the effect of the **Twist** modifier. When you add this modifier to the stack, its gizmo is placed at the pivot point of the object, and the gizmo lines up with the local axis of the object.

48

UVW Mapping Modifiers
These modifiers are used to control the texture mapping. You can use them to manage UV coordinates and to apply materials to the objects.

UVW Map
Use this modifier to control how mapped and procedural materials appear on the surface of the object. The mapping coordinates define how bitmaps are projected onto an object.

UVW Mapping Add
This modifier is added to the object's modifier stack when you add a channel in the **Channel Info** utility.

UVW Mapping Clear
This modifier is added to the object's modifier stack when you clear a channel with the **Channel Info** utility.

UVW Mapping Paste

This modifier is added to the object's modifier stack when you paste a channel with the **Channel Info** utility.

UVW XForm

You can use this modifier to adjust the tiling and offset in existing UVW coordinates. If you have an object with complex UVW coordinates already applied, you can apply this modifier to adjust those coordinates farther.

Vertex Weld

This modifier works similarly to the **Weld** feature in an **Editable Poly** and similar objects. You can use this modifier to combine the vertices that lie within a specified distance from each other.

VertexPaint

This modifier allows you to paint vertex colors onto an object. The amount of color that 3ds Max applies to the vertex depends on the distance of the vertex from the position of the cursor on the face. You can also paint vertex alpha and illumination values.

Volume Select

This modifier lets you make a sub-object selection of vertices or faces. You can use a cylinder-shaped or a sphere-shaped gizmo, or an object in the scene to define the volume of the selection area to which you can then apply other modifiers.

Wave

This modifier creates a wave-like effect [see Fig. 49]. You can use the standard **Gizmo** and **Center** sub-objects to change the wave effect. This modifier is similar to the **Wave** space warp which is useful when you want to create a wave effect on a large number of objects.

XForm

This modifier is used to apply transformations to the objects. You can use it to animate the transformations of a sub-object selection. Also, you can transform an object at any point in the stack.

Chamfer Modifier

The **Chamfer** modifier is used to procedurally add edges to specific parts of an object. This modifier can be used to generate quadrilateral output. You can apply this modifier at all sub-objects levels and it is typically used to round off the edges.

Hands-on Exercises

Exercise 1: Creating a Microphone

In this exercise, you will create the model of a microphone [see Fig. E1]. Table E1 summarizes the exercise.

Table E1	
Skill level	Intermediate
Time to complete	40 Minutes
Topics	• Specifying the Units for the Exercise • Creating the Microphone
Resources folder	**modifiers**
Units	**Generic Units**
Final file	**microphone-finish.max**

Specifying the Units for the Exercise

Follow these steps:

1. From the **Customize** menu choose **Units Setup**. In the **Units Setup** dialog box that appears, select **Generic Units** from the **Units Setup** dialog box. Click **OK** to accept the changes made.

2. From the **File** menu, choose **Save** to open the **Save File As** dialog box. In the **File name** text box type **microphone-finish.max** and then click **Save** to save the file.

Creating the Microphone
Follow these steps:

1. In the **Create** panel, click **Geometry**, and then in the **Object Type** rollout, click **Plane**. In the **Perspective** viewport, create a plane. Switch to the **Modify** panel and then in the **Parameters** rollout, change **Length** to **50**, **Width** to **50**, **Length Segs** to **30**, and **Width Segs** to **30**. Place the plane at the origin.

2. **RMB** click on the plane and then choose **transform** quadrant > **Convert To:** > **Convert to Editable Poly**. In the **Modify** panel > **Selection** rollout, click **Edge** to activate the edge sub-object level.

3. Select the edge, as shown in Fig. E2 and then in the **Modify** panel > **Selection** rollout, click **Ring** followed by **Loop** to make the selection [see Fig. E3].

What next?
Now, you will create a shape from the selected edges. Next, you will use different modifiers to create a metal grid pattern for the mic.

4. In the **Edit Edges** rollout, click **Create Shape From Selection** to create the shape [see Fig. E4]. Click **OK** in the **Create Shape** dialog and then delete **Plane**.

5. Select splines and then in the **Modify** panel > **Selection** rollout, click **Vertex** to activate the vertex sub-object level. Now, select every alternative row of vertices in the **Left** viewport, as shown in Fig. E5. Move the selected vertices by **0.4** units in the **+Y** direction [see Fig. E6]. Invert the selection by pressing **Ctrl+I** and then move the vertices by **-0.4** unit in the **-Y** direction [see Fig. E7].

6. In the **Modify** panel > **Selection** rollout, click **Spline** to activate the spline sub-object level. Select alternate splines, as shown in Fig. E8. From the **Object-Space Modifiers** section of the **Modifier** list, select **Mirror**. In the **Parameters** layout, change **Mirror Axis** to **Z** [see Fig. E9]. Now, convert spline to **Editable Spline**.

7. In the **Object** level, create a copy of the shape using **Shift** and the **Rotate** tool by rotating it **90** degrees. Make sure the newly created spline is selected and then from the **Object-Space Modifiers** section of the **Modifier** list, select **Mirror**. In the **Parameters** layout, change **Mirror Axis** to **Z** [see Fig. E10]. Convert the shape to **Editable Spline**.

What next?
Now, we will create a sphere and then conform the splines to the sphere.

8. In the **Create** panel, click **Geometry**, and then in the **Object Type** rollout, click **Sphere**. In the **Perspective** viewport, create a sphere. Switch to the **Modify** panel and then in the **Parameters** rollout, change **Radius** to **12**, **Segments** to **60**, and **Hemisphere** to **0.5**. Also, select the **Squash** checkbox. Place the sphere at the origin.

9. Convert sphere to editable poly and delete the bottom faces [see Fig. E11]. From the **Object-Space Modifiers** section of the **Modifier** list, select **XForm**. Now, using the **Scale** tool, scale down the **Sphere** using the **XForm** gizmo [see Fig. E12]. Make sure you are at the **Object** level before scaling the sphere.

10. Attach the two spline objects using the **Attach** function and then select the new spline. From the **Object-Space Modifiers** section of the **Modifier** list, select **Skin Wrap**. In the **Parameters** rollout, click **Add** and then click on the **Sphere** the viewport. Now, select sphere and then turn off the **XForm** modifier.

11. Select spline and then select the **Skin Wrap** modifier in the **Modify** panel. In the **Parameters** rollout, make sure **Deformation Engine** is set to **Vertex Deformation**. Change **Fallloff** to **1.5**, **Distance Infl** to **6**, and **Face Limit** to **20**. Select the **Blend To Base Mesh** checkbox and then change **Bend Distance** to **30**. Also, select the **Weight All Points** checkbox [see Fig. E13].

12. From the **Object-Space Modifiers** section of the **Modifier** list, select **Renderable Spline**. In the **Parameters** rollout, select the **Enable In Renderer** and **Enable In Viewport** checkboxes, if not already selected. Change **Thickness** to **1**, **Sides** to **6**, and **Threshold** to **180** [see Fig. E14].

13. From the **Object-Space Modifiers** section of the **Modifier** list, select **Symmetry**. In the **Parameters** rollout, change **Mirror Axis** to **Z** [see Fig. E15].

14. In the **Create** panel, click **Geometry**, and then in the **Object Type** rollout, click **Tube**. Now, create a tube object. In the **Modify** panel > **Parameters** rollout, change **Radius 1** to **14.7**, **Radius** to **13.86**, **Height** to **1.208**, and **Sides** to **42**. Now, align the tube, as shown in Fig. E16. From the **Object-Space Modifiers** section of the **Modifier** list, select **Mirror**. In the **Modify** panel > **Parameters** rollout, change **Mirror Axis** to **Z**. In the **Options** group, select the **Copy** checkbox and then set **Offset** to **-0.31** [see Fig. E17].

15. From the **Object-Space Modifiers** section of the **Modifier** list, select **Chamfer**. In the **Parameters** rollout > **Chamfer Options** group, change **Amount** to **0.06** [see Fig. E18].

16. Select **Sphere** and then from the **Object-Space Modifiers** section of the **Modifier** list, select **Taper**. In the **Parameters** rollout, change **Amount** to **0.01** and **Curve** to **0.3**.

17. Using the **Line** tool, create a shape, as shown in Fig. E19. Now, smooth the vertices of the line using the **Fillet** function. From the **Object-Space Modifiers** section of the **Modifier** list, select **Lathe**. In the **Modify** panel > **Parameters** rollout > **Align** group, click **Min**. Now, select the **Weld Core** checkbox and change **Segments** to **32** [see Fig. E1].

Exercise 2: Creating a Model of a Building

In this exercise, you will create the model of a building using different modifiers [see Figs. E1 through E4]. Table E2 summarizes the exercise.

Table E2	
Skill level	Intermediate
Time to complete	45 Minutes
Topics	• Specifying the Units for the Exercise • Creating the Tower • Creating the Mullions • Creating the Outer Shell
Resources folder	**modifiers**
Units	**Metric - Meters**
Final file	**building-finish.max**

Specifying the Units for the Exercise
Follow these steps:

1. From the **Customize** menu choose **Units Setup**. In the **Units Setup** dialog box that appears, select the **Metric** option from the **Display Unit Scale** group. Next, select **Meters** from the drop-down list located below the **Metric** option, if already not selected. Click **OK** to accept the change.

2. From the **File** menu, choose **Save** to open the **Save File As** dialog box. In the **File name** text box type **building-finish.max** and then click **Save** to save the file.

Creating the Tower
Follow these steps:

1. In the **Create** panel, click **Geometry**, and then in the **Object Type** rollout, click **Box**. In the **Perspective** viewport, drag out a box of any size. Go to the **Modify** panel, and in the **Parameters** rollout, set **Length** to 80, **Width** to 80, and **Height** to 400. Also, set **Length Segs** to 8, **Width Segs** to 8, and **Height Segs** to 50 [see Fig. E5]. Place the box at the origin.

2. Change the name of the object to **Tower**. Now, you will apply various modifiers to create distinct building shapes. From the **Object-Space Modifiers** section of the **Modifier** list, select **Taper**. In the **Taper** group of the **Parameters** rollout, set **Amount** to **0.35**, and curve to **2.04**. The building bulges out [see Fig. E6].

3. From the **Object-Space Modifiers** section of the **Modifier** list, select **Bend**. In the **Bend** group of the **Parameters** rollout, set **Angle** to **27.5** and **Bend Axis** to **Y**. The building bends along the Y-axis [see Fig. E7]. From the **Object-Space Modifiers** section of the **Modifier** list, select **Twist**. In the **Twist** group of the **Parameters** rollout, set **Angle** to **45.5** and **Bias** to **93.5**. The building twists along the Z-axis [see Fig. E8].

Creating the Mullions

Follow these steps:

1. Select **Tower** in the **Scene Explorer** and then **RMB** click on it. From the **Quad** menu that appears, choose **Clone** to open the **Clone Options** dialog box. Select **Reference** from the **Object** group. Next, type **Mullions** in the **Name** text box and click **OK**.

2. In the **Scene Explorer**, click **Tower's** bulb icon to hide it. Select **Mullions** and then go to the **Modify** panel. From the **Object-Space Modifiers** section of the **Modifier** list, select **Edit Poly**. In the **Selection** rollout, click **Polygon** and then select the center polygons [see Fig. E9]. Click **Grow** thrice in the **Selection** rollout to select all top polygons of the building [see Fig. E10].

3. Delete the selected polygons by pressing **Delete**. Similarly, delete the bottom polygons. From the **Object-Space Modifiers** section of the **Modifier** list, select **Lattice**. In the **Geometry** group of the **Parameters** rollout, select **Struts Only from Edges** checkbox. In the **Struts** group, set **Radius** to **0.5**, and **Sides** to **5**. Also, select **Smooth**.

Creating the Outer Shell

Follow these steps:

1. In the **Scene Explorer**, click the **Mullions'** bulb icon to hide it. Select **Tower** and create a clone with the name **Shell**. Make sure to select **Reference** from the **Object group** in the **Clone Options** dialog box.

2. Make sure **Tower** and **Mullions** are not visible in the scene and **Shell** is visible in the scene. Select the top and bottom polygons of **Shell** and delete them as done earlier. Also, turn off the **Twist**, **Bend**, and **Taper** modifiers.

3. In the **Selection** rollout, make sure the **Ignore Backfacing** checkbox is clear. In the **Front** viewport, select polygons [see Fig. E11]. Press **Delete** to remove the selected polygons. Similarly, remove polygons from the other remaining two sides. Use a different pattern for these sides [see Fig. E12].

4. In the **Selection** rollout, click **Edge** and then select the four corner edges [see Fig. E13]. Now, click **Loop** to select the loops. In the **Edit Edges** rollout, click **Chamfer > Settings** to open the **Chamfer** caddy control. Set **Amount** to **1.636** and **Segments** to **5** [see Fig. E14]. Click **OK**.

5. From the **Object-Space Modifiers** section of the **Modifier** list, select **Shell**. In the **Parameters** rollout, set **Outer Amount** to **2.0** [see Fig. E15]. Now turn on the **Twist**, **Taper**, and **Bend** Modifiers.

6. Turn on the **Tower** and **Mullions** from the **Scene Explorer**. Assign colors of your choice to **Tower**, **Shell**, and **Mullions** [see Fig. E16].

7. Create a different version of the building by modifying the parameters of the modifiers [see Fig. E17].

Exercise 3: Creating a Model of a Paper Basket

In this exercise, you will model a waste paper basket using various modifiers [see Fig. E1]. Table E3 summarizes the exercise.

Table E3	
Skill level	Beginner
Time to complete	35 Minutes
Topics	• Specifying the Units for the Exercise • Creating the Basket
Resources folder	**modifiers**

Table E3	
Units	**Metric - Centimeters**
Final file	**basket-finish.max**

Specifying the Units for the Exercise
Follow these steps:

1. From the **Customize** menu choose **Units Setup**. In the **Units Setup** dialog box that appears, select the **Metric** option from the **Display Unit Scale** group. Next, select **Centimeters** from the drop-down list located below the **Metric** option, if already not selected. Click **OK** to accept the change.

2. From the **File** menu, choose **Save** to open the **Save File As** dialog box. In the **File name** text box type **basket-finish.max** and then click **Save** to save the file.

Creating the Basket
Follow these steps:

1. In the **Create** panel, click **Geometry**, and then in the **Object Type** rollout, click **Cylinder**. In the **Perspective** viewport, drag out a cylinder of any size. Go to the **Modify** panel, and on the **Parameters** rollout, set **Radius** to **14.5** and **Height** to **30**. Also, set **Height Segments** to **12** and **Sides** to **40** [see Fig. E2].

2. From the **Object-Space Modifiers** section of the **Modifier List**, select **Edit Poly**. In the **Selection** rollout, click **Vertex** and then select the top row of vertices of the cylinder in the **Front** viewport. **RMB** click on the **Select and Move** button on the **Main** toolbar.

3. In the **Offset: Screen** group of the **Move Transform Type-In** dialog box that appears, set **Y** to **5** and then press **Enter** to move the vertices by **5** units in the **Y** direction [see Fig. E3]. Select all the vertices except the bottom row and move them by **6** units in the **Y** direction [see Fig. E4].

4. In the **Selection** rollout, click **Polygon** and then select all the middle polygons [see Fig. E5]. In the **Edit Polygons** rollout, click **Inset > Settings**. In the **Inset** caddy control, select **By Polygon** for **Type**. Now, set amount to **0.3** and click **OK** to inset the selected polygons [see Fig. E6]. Delete the polygons.

5. Select the top cap polygon and delete it as well [see Fig. E7]. Switch to the **Object** mode and then from the **Object-Space Modifiers** section of the **Modifier** list, select **Shell**. In the **Parameters** rollout, set **Outer Amount** to **0.5**.

6. From the **Object-Space Modifiers** section of the **Modifier** list, select **Taper**. In the **Parameters** layout, set **Amount** to **0.44** and **Curve** to **-0.7**. From the **Object-Space Modifiers** section of the **Modifier List**, select **Twist**. In the **Parameters** layout, set **Angle** to **66.5**.

Exercise 4: Creating a Rope

In this exercise, we will create a rope [see Fig. E1]. Table E4 summarizes the exercise.

Table E4	
Skill level	Beginner
Time to complete	40 Minutes
Topics	• Specifying the Units for the Exercise • Creating the Rope
Resources folder	**modifiers**
Units	**Generic Units**
Final file	**rope-finish.max**

Specifying the Units for the Exercise

Follow these steps:

1. From **Customize** menu choose **Units Setup**. In the **Units Setup** dialog box that appears, select **Generic Units** from the **Units Setup** dialog box. Click **OK** to accept the changes made.

2. From the **File** menu, choose **Save** to open the **Save File As** dialog box. In the **File name** text box type **rope-finish.max** and then click **Save** to save the file.

Creating the Rope

Follow these steps:

1. In the **Create** panel, click **Shapes**, and then click **Freehand**. Using the **Freehand** tool, create a spline [see Fig. E2].

2. Make sure the spline is selected. From the **Object-Space Modifiers** section of the **Modifier List**, select **Spline Relax**. In the **Modify** panel > **Relax** rollout, change **Amount** to **1** and **Iterations** to **7** [see Fig. E3].

3. From the **Object-Space Modifiers** section of the **Modifier** list, select **Optimize Spline**. In the **Modify** panel > **Optimize Spline** rollout > **Reduce Knots** group, change **By %** to **10** [see Fig. E4].

4. From the **Object-Space Modifiers** section of the **Modifier** list, select **Renderable Spline**. In the **Modify** panel > **Parameters** rollout, select the **Enable in Renderer** and **Enable in Viewport** checkboxes, if not already selected. Now, change **Thickness** to **2** [see Fig. E5].

What next?
Notice in Fig. E5 the segments are going through each other instead of overlapping. Next, you will fix it.

5. From the **Object-Space Modifiers** section of the **Modifier List**, select **Spline Overlap**. In the **Modify** panel > **Overlap** rollout, change **Thickness** to **1.584** [see Fig. E6].

What next?
Notice in Fig. E6, the overlapping of segments is not clean because of the irregular distribution of the knots. Let's fix it.

6. Add the **Normalize Spline** modifier above the **Renderable Spline** in the stack [see Fig. E7]. In the **Modify** panel > **Parameters** rollout > **Normalize By** group, change **Seg Length** to **4.683** [see Fig. E8].

7. Select the **Renderable Spline** modifier in the stack and then in the **Parameters** rollout > **Capping Options** group, select the **Quad Cap** checkbox and then change **Segments** to **5** and **Sphere** to **1** [see Fig. E9]. Also, ensure that the **Twist Correction** checkbox is selected.

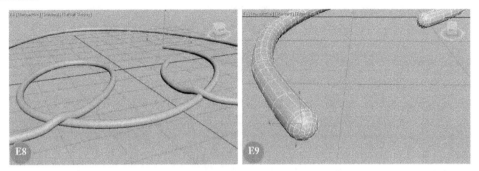

8. In the modifier stack, turn off the **Renderable Spline** modifier. From the **Object-Space Modifiers** section of the **Modifier** list, select **Noise**. In the **Modify** panel > **Parameters** rollout > **Noise** group, change **Scale** to **10**. In the **Strength** group, change **Z** to **50** [see Fig. E10].

 What just happened?
*Here, the **Noise** modifier modulating the position of the knots, and as you can see in Fig. E10, the **Noise** modifier is affecting the whole spline. If you want to affect a part of the spline, you need to use the influencers.*

9. In the **Create** panel, click **Helpers**, and then click **Influence**. Click-drag in the viewport to create the gizmo. In the **Modify** panel > **Parameters** rollout, change **Near** and **Far** to **31** and **42**, respectively [see Fig. E11].

10. Select the spline. From the **Object-Space Modifiers** section of the **Modifier** list, select **Spline Influence**. In the **Modify** panel > **Influence Parameters** rollout, click **Pick** and then click on the gizmo in the viewport. Also, change **Falloff Type** to **Smooth**.

11. Move the **Noise** modifier at the top of the stack. If you now move the influencer in the viewport, you will notice the knots are being affected only inside the area of the

influencer [see Fig. E12]. Turn on the **Renderable Spline** modifier in the stack display [see Fig. E13].

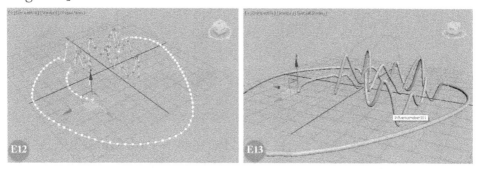

12. Turn off the **Renderable Spline** modifier in the stack display. In the **Create** panel, click **Geometry**, and then in the **Object Type** rollout, click **Cylinder**. In the **Perspective** viewport, create a cylinder. Switch to the **Modify** panel and on the **Parameters** rollout, change **Radius** to **2** and **Height** to **500**, and **Height Segments** to **35** [see Fig. E14]. Create two more copies of the cylinder and then align them as shown in Fig. E15.

13. Convert one of the cylinders to editable poly and then attach the remaining two cylinders using the **Attach** function.

14. From the **Object-Space Modifiers** section of the **Modifier** list, select **Path Deform**. In the **Modify** panel > **PathDeform** rollout, click **None** and then click the spline in the viewport. Change **Stretch** to **1.827** and then in the **Rotation** group, change **Twist** to **3000** [see Fig. E16]. Turn off **Noise** from the spline's modifier stack. Now, change the **Stretch** value according to the length spline.

15. Select the cylinder and then from the **Object-Space Modifiers** section of the **Modifier** list, select **TurboSmooth**. Place the **TurboSmooth** modifier below the **Path Deform** modifier. In the **TurboSmooth** rollout, change **Iterations** to **2** [see Fig. E17].

16. Select spline and then select the **Spline Overlap** modifier in the stack display. In the **Overlap** rollout, adjust the **Thickness** value as per your requirement [see Fig. E18].

17. Select the cylinder and then in the **Modify** panel > **Path Deform** modifier > **Path Deform** rollout > **Rotation** group, change **Twist** to **5569** [see Fig. E19].

Quiz

Evaluate your skills to see how many questions you can answer correctly.

Multiple Choice
Answer the following questions:

1. Which of the following keys is used to create an instance of a modifier?

   [A] Shift   [B] Alt
   [C] Ctrl   [D] Shift+Alt

2. Which of the following modifiers is used to add depth to a shape object?

   [A] Edit Spline   [B] Extrude
   [C] Chamfer   [D] All of the above

Fill in the Blanks

Fill in the blanks in each of the following statements:

1. OSM and WSM stand for _____ and _____.

2. The transformation values are stored in a matrix called _____.

3. The hair only renders in the _____ or _____ viewports.

True or False

State whether each of the following is true or false:

1. You can copy and paste modifiers between the object.

2. The **Fillet/Chamfer** modifier lets you fillet or chamfer corner vertices between linear segments of the shape objects.

Practice Activities

Create a spring: Crate the model of a spring using the **Helix** and **ChamferCyl** primitives, as shown in Fig. A1.

Hint:
*Use the **Renderable Spline** modifier with the spline.*

Create a ring: Create a ring, as shown in Fig. A2.

Hint:
*Use the **Donut** shape and the **Bevel** modifier.*

Create a ring: Create a ring, as shown in Fig. A3.

Hint:
*Extrude a donut shape using the **Bevel Profile** modifier. Use the **Improved** algorithm for the beveling. Also, use the **ThreeStep** option for the bevel profile. Use the **Symmetry** modifier to mirror the changes to the opposite axis.*

Create a molecular strand: Create a molecular strand, as shown in Fig. A4.

Hint:
*Create a **Plane** primitive and then apply the **Lattice** and **Twist** modifiers to create the shape.*

Summary
The unit covered the following topics:

- Using modifiers
- Stack display
- Object-Space modifiers vs World-Space modifiers
- How transform affects modifiers

Answer to Quiz
Multiple Choice
1. C, **2.** B

Fill in the Blanks
1. Object Space Modifier, World Space Modifier, **2.** Transformation Matrix,
3. Perspective, Camera

True/False
1. T, **2.** T

Unit 8: External Design Data

Autodesk 3ds Max is an extremely robust and powerful product, but it can't do everything you might need. However, it gives you the ability to share data and models with other applications such as Autodesk AutoCAD and AutoCAD Revit. For example, you can create a model of a house in Revit and then import it into 3ds Max for detailed rendering. In this unit, you'll look at ways that you can use the external data with 3ds Max in your design and visualization workflow.

Working with External Design Data

3ds Max offers a number of features that allow you to streamline your workflow. The **File Link Manager** allows you to create a live link to an AutoCAD drawing, a Revit architectural file, or an FBX file. Once linked, you can apply materials, maps, and animations in 3ds Max but still you can update your geometry if any changes are made to the original file.

Shared Views
You can use shared views to collaborate online with the people you're working with. Shared views allow you to create a visual representation of your model or design online. For example, you can use them to get approval of your design from the customer or to give access to your field sales team.

When you share a view, a link is generated. Anyone can use that link to view and comment on the design without needing to have an Autodesk product installed.

To create a shared view, you need to login to your Autodesk account. 3ds Max supports the following for the shared views:

- All bitmap types
- Rendering and uploading most procedural textures, including OSL maps
- Resizing textures on upload, reducing the size to 256 pixels wide or high
- The **Shell** material
- Autodesk materials
- Vray materials with textures
- Arbitrary UV channels limited to 1.

To share a view from 3ds Max, follow these steps:

1. Open the file you want to share.

2. Choose **File > Share View** from the menubar; the **Create a Shared View** dialog box appears [see Fig. 1].

3. Enter the name of the view in the **Name** field. Next, select the desired checkboxes in the **Options** group and then click **Share**. On doing so, the upload progress bar appears. On completion, two links appear in the **Share View** dialog box [see Fig. 2]. You can click **Copy link** to copy the link and share it with your desired audience.

4. Click on the **View in browser** link; the design appears in the **Autodesk Viewer** in your default browser. Fig. 3 shows the model I shared and Fig. 4 shows the same model in the **Autodesk Viewer**.

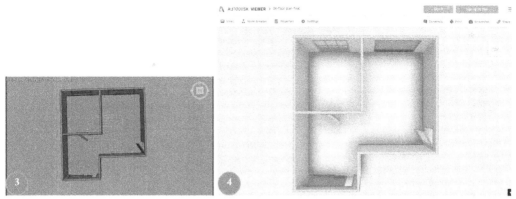

There are many tools available at the bottom area of the **Autodesk Viewer** that you can use to navigate the scene and comment on the design [see Fig. 5].

Importing Files

The **Import** command loads or merges the geometry files. To import, choose **File > Import > Import** from the menu bar to open the **Select File to Import** dialog box. Select the desired format from the **Files of type** drop-down list [see Fig. 6] and then select a file. Now, click **Open**; for some file types, a secondary dialog box appears with options specific to that file type. For example, if you import an AutoCAD **DWG** file, the **AutoCAD DWG/DXF Import Options** dialog box appears [see Fig. 7]. Choose the import options and click **OK** to complete the process.

All Formats
Autodesk (*.fbx)
3D Studio Mesh (*.3ds,*.prj)
Alembic (*.abc)
Adobe Illustrator (*.ai)
Catia V5 (*.catpart,*.catproduct,*.cgr)
Autodesk Collada (*.dae)
LandXML / DEM / DDF (*.dem,*.xml,*.ddf)
AutoCAD Drawing (*.dwg,*.dxf)
Legacy AutoCAD (*.dwg)
Flight Studio OpenFlight (*.flt)
Motion Analysis HTR File (*.htr)
IGES (*.ige,*.igs,*.iges)
Autodesk Inventor (*.ipt,.iam)
JT (*.jt)
Catia V4 (*.model,*.mdl,*.session,*.exp,*.dlv,*.dlv3,*.dlv4)
gw::OBJ-Importer (*.obj)
ProE (*.prt,*.prt.*,*.neu,*.g,*.asm)
UG-NX (*.prt)
Revit importer (*.rvt)
ACIS SAT (*.sat)
3D Studio Shape (*.shp)
SketchUp (*.skp)
SketchUp (2015 & older) (May be Removed) (*.skp)
SolidWorks (*.sldprt,*.sldasm)
StereoLitho (*.stl)
STEP (*.stp,*.step)
Motion Analysis TRC File (*.trc)
...esk Alias (*.wire)
...L (*.wrl,*.wrz)

Tip: Importing geometry by dragging and dropping
*You can import the geometry by dragging and dropping from the **File Browser** into a 3ds Max viewport.*

Caution: Orientation of the imported geometry
When you import a geometry by the dragging and dropping method, 3ds Max orients the imported geometry to the viewport into which you drop it. Therefore, choose the viewport carefully. For most file formats, after you release the mouse button in a viewport, you can move the mouse pointer to position the geometry. Then, click to set its position.

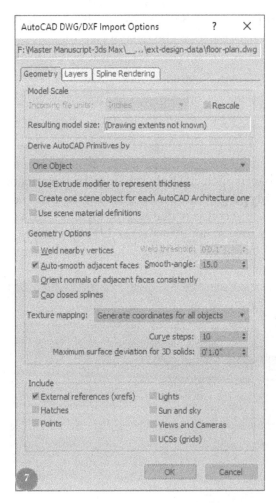

Exporting Files

You can use the **Export** command to export and convert a 3ds Max file into different geometry formats. To do so, choose **File > Export > Export** from the menubar to open the **Select File to Export** dialog box. Select the format from the **Save as type** drop-down list [see Fig. 8] and type the name in the **File name** field. Click **Save**; depending on the file type you chose, you might be presented with options available for the selected export choice. If a dialog box appears, choose the export options.

Note: Exporting selected objects
*To export selected objects to a file, select one or more objects and then choose **File >** **Export > Export Selected** from the menubar.*

Note: Sending geometry to other autodesk products
*3ds Max gives you the ability to send geometry to other Autodesk products. The **File** > **Send To** submenu provides interoperability options with other Autodesk products. You can send geometry to **Maya**, **Motion Builder**, and **Mudbox**.*

Importing AutoCAD Designs into 3ds Max

When you are using the same design data with two or more Autodesk products (for example using an AutoCAD **DWG** file to create a floor plan in 3ds Max), you should link to the files using the **File Link Manager.** It allows you to maintain a live link between the two connected files. You can launch the manager using one of the following ways:

- Choosing **File > Import > Link Revit**, **Link FBX**, or **Link AutoCAD** from the menubar.
- Choosing **File > Reference > Manage Links** from the menubar.
- **Command** panel > **Utilities** panel > click the **More** button > **Utilities** dialog > **File Link Manager**

The **File Link Manager** allows you to link these kinds of files:

- **DWG** and **DXF Files:** AutoCAD, AutoCAD Mechanical, and AutoCAD Architecture drawings.
- **FBX Files:** Format created by any Autodesk product: Revit, MotionBuilder, Maya, and Mudbox or any non-Autodesk product that supports the **FBX** file format such as Cinema 4D.
- **RVT Files:** Autodesk Revit Architecture files.

Keep the following in mind when linking files:

- Changes in AutoCAD, AutoCAD Mechanical, Autodesk Revit, and AutoCAD Architecture can change the data in 3ds Max but 3ds Max cannot change data in these applications.
- Changes you can make in AutoCAD, AutoCAD Mechanical, Autodesk Revit, and AutoCAD Architecture should be made in AutoCAD, AutoCAD Mechanical, Autodesk Revit, and AutoCAD Architecture.

Note: Project folder
*The name of the project folder for this chapter is **ext-design-data**.*

For this section, you will be importing an AutoCAD file and using it as a template to build wall, door, and windows. Follow these steps:

1. Start or reset 3ds Max.

2. From the **Customize** menu choose **Units Setup**. In the **Units Setup** dialog box that appears, select **US Standard** from the **Display Unit Scale** group. Next, choose **Feet w/ Decimal Inches** from the drop-down list located below **US Standard** and then click **OK** to accept the changes.

3. Choose **File > Import > Import** from the menubar to open the **Select File to Import** dialog box. Now, select the **floor-plan.dwg**

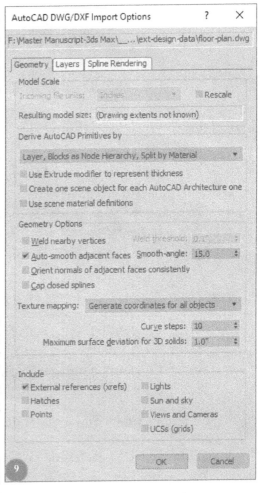

AutoCAD DWG/DXF Import Options   ?   ✕

F:\Master Manuscript-3ds Max___...\ext-design-data\floor-plan.dwg

| Geometry | Layers | Spline Rendering |

Model Scale
Incoming file units: Inches   ▼   ☐ Rescale
Resulting model size: (Drawing extents not known)

Derive AutoCAD Primitives by
Layer, Blocks as Node Hierarchy, Split by Material   ▼
☐ Use Extrude modifier to represent thickness
☐ Create one scene object for each AutoCAD Architecture one
☐ Use scene material definitions

Geometry Options
☐ Weld nearby vertices   Weld threshold: 0.1
☑ Auto-smooth adjacent faces   Smooth-angle: 15.0
☐ Orient normals of adjacent faces consistently
☐ Cap closed splines

Texture mapping: Generate coordinates for all objects   ▼

Curve steps: 10
Maximum surface deviation for 3D solids: 1.0"

Include
☑ External references (xrefs)   ☐ Lights
☐ Hatches   ☐ Sun and sky
☐ Points   ☐ Views and Cameras
    ☐ UCSs (grids)

9   OK   Cancel

file and click **Open**. This action invokes the **AutoCAD DWG/DXF Import Options** dialog box [see Fig. 9].

4. In the **AutoCAD DWG/DXF Import Options** dialog box, select **One Object** from the drop-down list available in the **Derive AutoCAD Primitives by** group. Next, click **OK**; a collection of 2D lines appears in the viewport [see Fig. 10].

5. Choose the **Select and Move** tool in the **Main** toolbar. Select the drawing and then in the **Status Bar** change the **X**, **Y**, **Z** values in the type-in boxes to **0** each. This action places the drawing at the center of the grid.

6. Maximize the **Top** viewport. Press and hold **LMB** on **Snap Toggle** in the **Main** toolbar and then choose the **2D Snaps Toggle** button from the flyout.

7. **RMB**-click on any snap toggle button in the **Main** toolbar. In the **Grid and Snap Settings** dialog box that opens, clear the **Grid Points** checkbox and select the **Vertex** checkbox. Now, close the dialog box.

What just happened?
*Here, you have enabled the 2D snapping. This will make it possible for the AEC tools (**Walls**, **Doors**, and **Windows**) to snap with the vertices of the AutoCAD drawing.*

Next, you will create the walls.

8. Go to the **Command** panel > **Create** panel and from the **Create** panel drop-down list, select **AEC Extended**. Next, click the **Wall** button. In the **Parameters** rollout, make

sure **Width** is set to **0'5.0"** and **Height** to **8'0.0"**. Now, set **Justification** to **Right** in the **Justification** group.

9. In the **Top** viewport, snap the mouse pointer to the left-bottom outside vertex of the drawing [see Fig. 11] and move in the counter-clockwise direction to create the wall [see Figs. 12 and 13]. If you make any mistake, press **Backspace** to undo the last click. When you have made it around the room, click on the corner where you started; the **Weld Ponint?** message box appears. Click **Yes** to close the spline and then **RMB**-click to release the **Wall** tool.

10. Change justification to **Left** and then create the interior walls [see Figs. 14 and 15].

11. Save the file as **my-imported-drawing-walls.max**.

12. Make sure the interior walls are selected and then go to the **Modify** panel. In the **Edit Object** rollout, click **Attach** and then click the exterior wall in the viewport to combine both the walls to a single wall object. Rename the new object as **walls-mesh**.

If you want to modify the walls, you can do so by using the wall's sub-object levels. Go to the **Modify** panel and then expand the wall object in the modifier stack. The wall object has three components: **Vertex**, **Segment**, and **Profile**. When you select a sub-object level, the corresponding options appear in the rollouts.

You can edit a wall primitive in a way that's similar to how you edit splines. Each wall segment has two vertices; one in each bottom corner. In wireframe views, vertices appear as + symbols. When you move a wall vertex, the associated wall segment scales up. However, you cannot rotate or scale wall vertices.

Each wall segment is defined by two wall vertices. Moving a segment is the same as moving its two vertices in tandem. When you select the **Segment** level, the **Width**, **Height**, and **Bottom Offset** parameters appear [see Fig. 16] in the **Parameters** group of the **Edit Segment** rollout that you can use to modify the shape of the wall. However, you cannot rotate a segment.

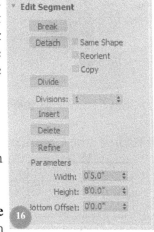

Next, you will create doors and windows.

13. Select the **walls-mesh** object if not already selected and then make sure that 2**D Snap** toggle is still active.

14. Go to the **Command** panel > **Create** panel and from the **Create** panel drop-down list, select **Doors**. Next, click the **Pivot** button in the **Object Type** rollout.

15. Refer to Fig. 17, with the **Pivot** tool active, in the **Top** viewport, click-hold-snap on **A**. Don't release the mouse button and then drag the pointer to snap to **B**. Release the mouse button to set the **Width** of the door. Now, drag the pointer (without holding any button) to **C** and then click to set the **Depth** of the door. Next, move the pointer toward the top of the viewport to create the door **Height** and then click to finish the

process. Don't try to get the exact height because it is difficult yo set exact height in the **Top** viewport, you can modify it anytime.

16. Go to the **Modify** panel and then in the **Parameters** rollout, change **Height** to **6'5.0"** [see Fig. 18]. Change **Open** to **40**; notice that an opening automatically appears because you used snapping to precisely place the door on the wall. Also, you will notice that the swing direction of the door is not as per the AutoCAD drawing [see Fig. 19]. To fix it, select the **Flip Swing** checkbox in the **Parameters** rollout.

17. Similarly, create another **Pivot** door [see Fig. 20]. Next, create a sliding glass door using the **Sliding** door tool [see Fig. 21]. The height of all doors should be **6'5.0"**.

18. Save the file as **my-imported-drawing-doors.max**.

19. Go to the **Command** panel > **Create** panel and from the **Create** panel drop-down list, select **Windows**. Next, click the **Fixed** button. Create a fixed window at the center of the wall, see Fig. 22. You need to set the **Height** of the window in the **Modify** panel to **6'0.0"**.

20. Similarly, create a **Sliding** window [see Fig. 22].

21. Save the file as **my-imported-drawing-windows.max**.

Next, you will add a floor and ceiling.

22. In the **Create** panel, click **Shapes**, and then on the **Object Type** rollout, click **Line**. Make sure 2D snapping is still active. In the **Top** viewport, click on one of the outside corners and then click the other corners around the room in a clockwise direction, and then click again on the corner where you started. Click **Yes** to close the spline.

23. Go to the **Modify** panel and then from the **Object-Space Modifiers** section of the **Modifier** List, select **Extrude**. In the **Parameters** rollout, change **Amount** to **0'1.0"**. Rename the new object as **floor-mesh**. Switch to the **Front** view and then align the floor, as shown in Fig. 23.

24. Now, to create the ceiling, make a copy of **floor-mesh**. Rename the new object as **ceiling-mesh** and then align it [see Fig. 24]. Hide the **ceiling-mesh** object for the time being.

25. Save the file as **my-imported-drawing-floor-ceiling.max**.

Next, you will create the baseboard for the floor. Baseboards are used to cover the gap between the wall and the floor. Also, they add a sense of style to the room. You will use the **Sweep** modifier to create the baseboard. To achieve this, you need a baseboard profile and a path for the profile. You already have a spline in the scene that you used for creating the **floor-mesh**. Let's modify the spline and use it as a path for our baseboard profile.

26. Select the **floor-mesh** object and then choose **Edit > Clone** from the menubar to open the **Clone Options** dialog box. Select **Copy** and change **Name** to **baseboard-path**. Click **OK**.

27. Delete the **Extrude** modifier connected to **baseboard-path**. Press **Alt+Q** to isolate the path. Select the **Spline** sub-object in the modifier stack and then enter **-6"** in the **Geometry** rollout > **Outline** spinner [see Fig. 25]. Use **Delete** to delete the original spline.

? *What just happened?*
*The original spline was created using outside vertices of the wall object. You need the baseboard inside the room, therefore, you offset the spline using the **Outline** feature.*

28. Choose **File > Import > Merge** from the menubar to open the **Merge File** dialog box. Select **baseboard-profile.max** and click **Open**. In the **Merge** dialog box that appears, select **baseboard-profile** and click **OK**.

29. Select the **baseboard-path** spline and then go to the **Modify** panel. Next, from the **Object-Space Modifiers** section of the **Modifier List**, select **Sweep**.

30. In the **Selection Type** rollout, select the **Use Custom Section** radio button and then click **Pick**. Click the **baseboard-profile** spline in the viewport [see Fig. 26]. You can make any baseboard profile of your choice using the spline editing tools.

31. If the baseboard is not facing in the correct direction, in the **Sweep Parameters** rollout, select the **Mirror on XZ Plane** to fix the issue [see Fig. 27]. Next, you will fix it. Press **Alt+Q** to exit the isolation mode. If there is any gap between the wall and baseboard, or the baseboard is not aligned properly, fix it using the **X Offset** option [see Fig. 28].

Notice in Fig. 28, the baseboard molding is going straight through the doors. The molding should only run along the wall not doors. Next, you will fix it.

32. Select the **floor-plan** and **baseboard-path** splines. Next, isolate them by pressing **Alt+Q.**

33. Select the **baseboard-path** spline and turn off the **Sweep** modifier. Activate the **Vertex** mode for the **Line** and then in the **Geometry** rollout, click **Refine**. Click on the spline on both sides of the door to create new vertices [see Fig. 29]. **RMB**-click to exit the **Refine** mode.

34. Switch to the **Segment** mode. Next, select the segment that is in between the two newly created vertices and then press **Delete** to remove the segment [see Fig. 30].

35. Repeat the process for the sliding door. Turn on the **Sweep** modifier and exit the isolation mode [see Fig. 31].

36. Save the file as **my-imported-drawing-baseboard-01.max**.

37. To create baseboard for the internal walls, first, create the path splines using the **Line** tool, and then create molding using the **Sweep** modifier as discussed above [see Fig. 32].

38. Save the file as **my-imported-drawing-baseboard-02.max**.

39. Now, properly align the baseboards with the walls so that there is no gap between the walls and baseboards. To do so, you need to activate the **Vertex** mode for the lines and then align vertices with the corners of the walls. Fig. 33 shows the final floor plan.

40. Save the file as **my-imported-drawing-final.max**.

Using the Substitute Modifier with Linked Geometry

Typically, designers use two-dimensional shapes to represent objects such as furniture in their AutoCAD space-planning designs. You can substitute a complex model created in 3ds Max for a simple outline drawn in AutoCAD using the **Substitute** modifier. This modifier allows you to quickly replace one or more objects with another in the viewport or at the render time. The substitute object can be instanced from the current scene or you can reference it from an external file.

1. Start or reset 3ds Max.

2. From the **Customize** menu choose **Units Setup**. In the **Units Setup** dialog box that appears, select **US Standard** from the **Display Unit Scale** group. Next, choose **Decimal Inches** from the drop-down list located below **US Standard** and then click **OK** to accept the changes.

3. Choose **File > Import > Link AutoCAD** from the menubar to open the **Open** dialog box. Select the **blocks.dwg** file and then click **Open**; the **Manage Links** dialog box appears.

4. In this dialog box, choose the **Presets** tab and then select the **DWG File Saved from AutoCAD** option from the **Named Presets** list box. Click the **Modify** button; the **File Link Settings: DWG Files** dialog box appears.

5. In the **Advanced** tab, select **Layer, Blocks as Node Hierarchy** option from the **Derive AutoCAD Primitives** by drop-down list, and then click the **Save** button. Switch to the **Attach** tab and then click the **Attache this file** button to make a connection with the drawing [see Fig. 34]. Close the **Manage Links** dialog box.

What just happened?
Here, you have made a connection between the drawing file and 3ds Max. If you now make changes in the drawing, the changes will automatically affect the 3D models in the scene.

6. Select the chair symbol in the viewport [see Fig. 35] and then switch to the **Modify** panel. Notice in the modifier stack that the symbol appears as linked geometry.

7. Go to **Modifier List**, and select **Substitute** from the **Object Space Modifiers** section. In the **Parameters** rollout > **Substitute Assignment** group, click **Select XRef Object**; the **Open File** dialog box appears.

8. In this dialog box, select **chair.max** and click **Open**; the **XRef Merge** dialog box appears. Select **chair** in this dialog box and then click **OK**; the **Substitution Question** message box displayed promoting you to assign the substitute object's material to the selected object. Click **Yes**; the 3D model of the chair appears in the viewport substituting the chair polylines that were there previously [see Fig. 36].

9. Similarly, replace the rectangular splines with the **coffee-table.max** file [see Fig. 37]. Select any chair model and reduce it's scale; notice that all other chair models are scaled simultaneously [see Fig. 38].

10. Save the file as **blocks.max**.

You have seen now how easy it is to link a space-planning drawing into 3ds Max and substitute 2D space holders with the complex 3ds Max models. After seeing the realistic depiction of the scene in 3ds Max, you may want to revise the space plan in AutoCAD. When the revised plan is reloaded into 3ds Max, changes will automatically affect 3D models in the scene.

Importing a Truss

Tubular steel roof trusses are used for large span constructions such as factories, industry worksheds, shopping malls, huge exhibition centers, multiplexes, and so on. The following steps will show you how the tubular truss drawings can be turned into a 3D model in 3ds Max:

1. Start or reset 3ds Max.

2. From the **Customize** menu choose **Units Setup**. In the **Units Setup** dialog box that appears, select **US Standard** from the **Display Unit Scale** group. Next, choose **Decimal Inches** from the drop-down list located below **US Standard** and then click **OK** to accept the changes.

3. Choose **File > Import > Import** from the menubar to open the **Select File to Import** dialog box. Now, select the **truss.dwg** file and click **Open**. The **AutoCAD DWG/DXF Import Options** dialog box appears.

4. In the **Geometry** tab > **Model Scale** group, select the **Rescale** checkbox. Select **Layer, Blocks as Node Hierarchy** from the drop-down list available in the **Derive AutoCAD Primitives by** group.

5. In the **Geometry Options** group, select the **Weld nearby vertices** checkbox and then click **OK**; the truss displays in the viewport [see Fig. 39].

6. Press **H**; the **Select from Scene** dialog box displays. In this dialog box, double-click on **Layer: Truss-Brace** to select it. Click the **Modify** tab in the **Command** panel.

7. In the **Rendering** Rollout, select both the **Enable in Renderer** and **Enable In Viewport** checkboxes. Now, change **Thickness** to **4"** [see Fig. 40].

8. Press **H**; the **Select from Scene** dialog box displays. In this dialog box, double-click on **Layer: Main-Frame** to select it. Click the **Modify** tab in the **Command** panel.

9. In the **Rendering** Rollout, select both the **Enable in Renderer** and **Enable In Viewport** checkboxes. Now, change **Thickness** to **6"** [see Fig. 41].

10. Save the file as **my-imported-truss.max**.

Creating Topography using Contour Line Data

You can use the contour line data to create a terrain. You can import an AutoCAD drawing to use as contour data. Follow these steps:

1. Start and reset 3ds Max.

2. Choose **Customize > Units Setup** from the menubar. In the **Units Setup** dialog box that appears, select **US Standard** from the **Display Unit Scale** group. Next, select **Feet w/Decimal Inches** from the drop-down list located below **US Standard**. Then, click **OK** to accept the changes.

3. Choose **File > Reference > Manage Links** from the menubar; the **Manage Links** dialog box appears. Next, in the **Attach** tab, click **File** to open the **Open** dialog box. In this dialog box, select **contour-data.dwg** and then click **Open**.

4. Choose the **Presets** tab and then select the **DWG File Saved from AutoCAD** option from the **Named Presets** list box. Next, click the **Modify** button; the **File Link Settings: DWG Files** dialog box appears.

5. In the **Basic** tab of the dialog box, make sure the **Weld nearby vertices** checkbox is selected. In the **Advanced** tab of the dialog box, select **Layer, Blocks as Node Hierarchy** option from the **Derive AutoCAD Primitives by** drop-down list, and then choose the **Save** button.

6. Switch to the **Attach** tab and then click the **Attache this file** button to make a connection with the drawing [see Fig. 42]. Now, close the **Manage Links** dialog box.

> ⚠️ *What just happened?*
> *Here, you have used the **Manage Links** dialog box to link to an AutoCAD drawing. When you do so, you keep the imported geometry linked with the original AutoCAD file. Whenever any changes occur in the AutoCAD file, it would affect the geometry in the 3ds Max scene. Notice in Fig. 42, an axis arrow appears at the center of the origin of the scene. It identifies the coordinate system origin point of the linked file. If you select the axis arrow and switch to **Modify** panel, you will notice that the origin point is associated with **Link Origin Pt Helper** [see Fig. 43].*

7. Press **H**; the **Select From Scene** dialog box appears. Expand the **contour-data.dwg** entry and then select both **Layer:contour01** and **Layer: Layer:contour02**. Next, click **OK**.

8. In the **Create** panel, click **Geometry**, and then select **Compound Objects** from the drop-down list. Next, in the **Object Type** rollout, click **Terrain**. A surface appears in the viewports [see Fig. 44].

9. In the **Create** panel, scroll down to **Color by Elevation** rollout and open it. Next, click **Create Defaults** [see Fig. 45].

 What just happened?
*Here, you have defined the color bands for the terrain using the elevation data. It helps in improving the visibility of the shape of the terrain. You can change colors by first selecting the elevation from the list box located below **Create Defaults** and then changing color using the **Color Zone** group > **Base Color** parameter. You can also change the vertical location of the color by changing the **Base Elev** parameter in the **Color Zone** group.*

10. Save the file as **my-contour-terrain.max**.

Importing Revit Files

Autodesk Revit is a building design product suite for specifying architectural design, structural engineering, and construction. In addition to linking to a Revit file using **File Link Manager**, you can import the **.rvt** files in 3ds Max. Follow these steps:

1. Navigate to the following link and then download the Revit model:
https://grabcad.com/library/house-plan-23

2. Rename the model as **house.rvt**.

3. Open or reset 3ds Max.

4. Choose **Customize** > **Units Setup** from the menubar. In the **Units Setup** dialog box that appears, select **US Standard** from the **Display Unit Scale** group. Next, select **Fractional Feet** from the drop-down list located below **US Standard**. Then, click **OK** to accept the changes.

5. Choose **File** > **Import** > **Link Revit** from the menubar to open the **Open** dialog box. In this dialog box, select **Autodesk Revit (*.rvt;*.fbx)** from the **File of type** drop-down list.

6. Select **house.rvt** and then click **Open** to open the **Manage Links** dialog box. In the **Presets** tab of the dialog box, select **Autodesk Revit - Do Not Combine Entities** option from the **Named Presets** drop-down list and then click **Copy**.

7. The **New Settings Preset** dialog box appears. Set **New Name** as **my-revit-preset** and click **OK**. Select **my-revit-preset** in the **Named Presets** list box and then click **Modify**; the **File Link Settings: Revit Files** dialog box appears. At the bottom, in the **Materials** group, select both the **Keep 3ds Max scene materials parameters on reload** and **Keep 3ds Max scene materials assignments on reload** checkboxes. Then, click **Save**.

What just happened?
Here, you have created a new preset for the Revit import. You can create a copy of the presets and then modify them, if you want to leave those presets to default settings that ships with 3ds Max.

8. Switch to the **Attach** tab and then select **my-revit-preset** in the **Preset** drop-down list. Now, click **Attach this file**. 3ds Max processes the file and the house appears in the viewports [see Fig. 46]. Close the **Manage Links** dialog box.

9. Now, you can modify and apply materials to meshes, add lighting to the scene, and render the scene as would any other scene in 3ds Max. Save the file as **my-imported-revit-model.max**.

Importing Inventor Files

Autodesk Inventor is a 3D mechanical solid modeling design software. It is used for 3D mechanical design, tooling creation, and product simulation. Both the IPT (parts) and IAM (assemblies) are the native Inventor file formats. You can import both file formats in 3ds Max. You can import Inventor files as **Body Objects**. They are an object class that natively supports the **ACIS** solid models imported from Autodesk Inventor. They remain in the **ACIS** format in 3ds Max.

When you import Inventor models, 3ds Max retains their object naming as assigned in the Inventor. Once imported to 3ds Max, you can edit the Inventor model as you would any other type of object. You can apply materials and modifiers, add lights and cameras, and so on. Constraint and Joint Drive animation applied to the Inventor model imports to 3ds Max as baked keyframes.

There are some limitations that you need to keep in mind:

- The camera animation paths created in Inventor are not converted to 3ds Max cameras. Any animation that you setup in Inventor will be lost on import.
- You have to relight the scene once the import is complete.
- If you drag and drop an inventor file to 3ds Max, it uses the settings that you last set on the **Inventor File Import** dialog box except for **Mesh Resolution**, which always resets to **0**.
- Materials and material assignments are imported as **Architectural** materials and are retained during import. If a single object has several materials applied to it, they are imported as **Multi/Sub-Object** material.

Follow these steps:

1. Start or reset 3ds Max.

2. From the **Customize** menu choose **Units Setup**. In the **Units Setup** dialog box that appears, select **US Standard** from the **Display Unit Scale** group. Next, choose **Decimal Inches** from the drop-down list located below **US Standard** and then click **OK** to accept the changes.

3. Choose **File > Import > Import** from the menubar to open the **Select File to Import**

dialog box. In this dialog box, navigate to **\ext-design-data\assembly** and then select **Toggle Push Clamp.iam**. Then, click **Open**.

4. The **Autodesk Inventor File Import** dialog box appears [refer to Fig. 47].

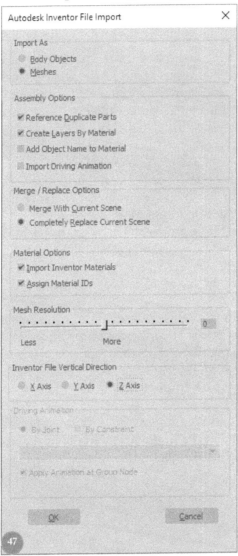

5. In this dialog box, select **Meshes** in the **Import As** group and then select the **Z- Axis** radio button from the **Inventor File Vertical Direction** group. Next, click **OK**; 3ds Max will process the data, and you will see a model in the viewports [see Fig. 48].

6. With the model selected, if you switch to the **Modify** panel, you would notice that there is nothing selected there. This is because the Inventor assembly is imported as a group.

7. Choose **Group > Open** from the menubar to open the group. Press **H** to open the **Select from Scene** dialog box. Expand the **Toggle Push Clamp.iam** group to see different parts of the assembly [see Fig. 49]. Click **OK**.

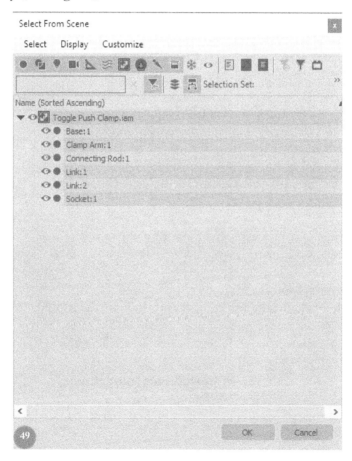

8. Save the file as **my-inventor-imported-model.max**.

Importing STP/STEP Files

STEP stands for **Standard for the Exchange of Product Data**. It is an **ISO** standard exchange format used for transferring graphics data between CAD/CAM systems. You can import both the **STEP** and **STP** files into 3ds Max. Follow these steps:

1. Start or reset 3ds Max.

2. From the **Customize** menu choose **Units Setup**. In the **Units Setup** dialog box that appears, select **US Standard** from the **Display Unit Scale** group. Next, choose **Decimal Inches** from the drop-down list located below **US Standard** and then click **OK** to accept the changes.

3. Choose **File > Import > Import** from the menubar to open the **Select File to Import** dialog box. Select **STEP (*.stp, *.step)** from the **Files of type** drop-down list and then select **ring-adapter.step**. Now, click **Open**; the **Import Settings** dialog box appears [see Fig. 50].

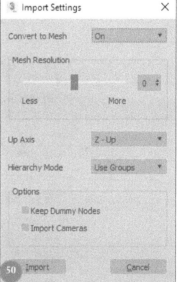

4. Make sure **On** is set for the **Convert to Mesh** drop-down list. If you set it to **Off**, imported geometry converts to the **Body Objects** formats.

Different applications use different axes for the up-axis. Select the appropriate axis from the **Up Axis** drop-down list.

5. Click **Import**; 3ds Max processes the data for a while and the model is displayed in the viewports [see Fig. 51].

With the model selected if you switch to the **Modify** panel, you would notice that there is nothing selected. This is because the model is imported as a group.

6. Choose **Group > Open** from the menubar to open the group.

7. Save the file with the name **my-imported-step-model.max**.

Importing Adobe Illustrator Files

If you are in the broadcast or motion graphics industry, there is a very high chance that you will get the Illustrator files from the graphic artist, customer, or design department. Adobe Illustrator is a robust vector-based graphics application. 3ds Max gives you the ability to import and export Adobe Illustrator files. Let's see how it works:

1. Open or reset 3ds Max.

2. From the **Customize** menu choose **Units Setup**. In the **Units Setup** dialog box that appears, select **US Standard** from the **Display Unit Scale** group. Next, choose **Decimal Inches** from the drop-down list located below **US Standard** and then click **OK** to accept the changes.

3. Choose **File > Import > Import** from the menu bar; the **Select File to Import** dialog box appears. Next, select **Adobe Illustrator (*.ai)** option from the **File of type** drop-down list. Then, select the **3dsmax-rocks.ai** file and click **Open**; you are presented with the **AI Import** dialog box [see Fig. 52].

If you are bringing a logo or an element into an existing scene, you should select the **Merge objects with current scene** option. If you are making a standalone art, you should select the **Completely replace current scene** option.

4. Leave the default **Merge objects with current scene** option selected and click **OK**; the **Shape Import** dialog box appears.

When you import Illustrator files, 3ds Max converts polygons to shape objects. When the **Single Object** option is selected, all polygons in the imported **.ai** file are converted to bezier splines and placed inside a single composite shape object. On selecting the **Multiple Objects** option, each polygon in the **.ai** file is converted to a bezier spline and placed inside an independent shape object.

5. Leave the default **Single Object** option selected and click **OK**; the Illustrator artwork appears in the viewport [see Fig. 53].

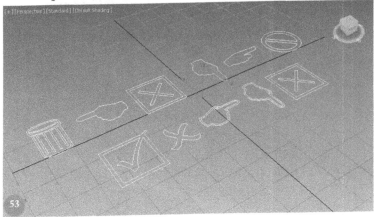

6. Click the **Modify** tab of the **Command** panel. Notice in the **Modifier** stack, the artwork is an **Editable Spline** object. Rename the spline as **row-1**.

7. In the **Selection** rollout, click the **Spline** sub-object level button. Next, select the bottom row [see Fig. 54]. Scroll down to the **Geometry** rollout and then click **Detach**.

8. In the **Detach** dialog box that appears, type **row-2** in the **Detach as** field and click **OK**.

9. Select **row-2**, go to **Modifier List**, and select **Bevel** from the **Object Space Modifiers** section.

10. In the **Bevel Values** rollout, set **Start Outline** to **-0.05**, **Level 1 > Height** to **1.75**, and **Outline** to **0.1**.

11. Select the checkbox in front of **Level 2** and then set **Height** to **3** and **Outline** to **0.5**.

12. Select the checkbox in front of **Level 3** and then set **Height** to **8** and **Outline** to **-0.38** [see Fig. 55].

13. Select **row-1** and make sure you are the object level. Next, go to **Modifier List**, and select **Extrude** from the **Object Space Modifiers** section.

14. In the **Parameters** rollout, set **Amount** to **5** [see Fig. 56].

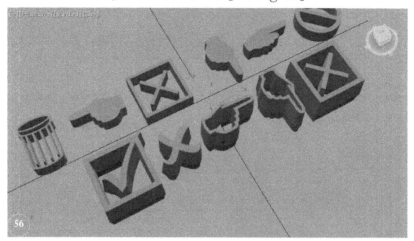

15. Save the file with the name **my-imported-ai-data.max**.

Importing FBX Files

The FBX file format is originally native to Autodesk MotionBuilder. This format provides interoperability between most 3D software regardless of the software vendor and platform. It can also be used in building design workflows using software such as Revit.

 Tip: Game Exporter
*If you work in the gaming projects, you can use the **Game Exporter** utility to easily export models and animation clips in the FBX format to your game engine.*

In the next exercise, you will import a FBX file, exported from Cinema 4D. Follow these steps:

1. Start or reset 3ds Max. Choose **Customize** > **Units Setup** from the menubar. In the **Units Setup** dialog box that appears, select **Generic Units**. Then, click **OK** to accept the changes.

2. Choose **File > Import > Import** from the menubar to open the **Select File to Import** dialog box. Select **Autodesk (*.fbx)** from the **Files of type** drop-down list and then select **ball-bounce.fbx**. Then, click **Open**; the **FBX Import** dialog box appears.

> ✎ *Note: The ball-bounce.fbx file*
> *This file contains a simple bouncing ball animation created in Cinema 4D.*

3. Make sure the **Autodesk Media & Entertainment** is set for the **Current Preset** drop-down list and then click **OK** at the bottom of the dialog box; the model appears in the viewports [see Fig. 57].

Notice that there is a camera icon in the viewport that was imported from Cinema 4D.

4. Press **C** to enable the camera view [see Fig. 58] and then press **/** to play the animation.

5. Save the file as **my-fbx-imported-file.max**.

As you can see, 3ds Max allows you to efficiently share data and models with other applications using different file formats. You have already learned about some of them. Here's a quick list of other formats that you can import in 3ds Max:

*   You can import Alias formats such as **WIRE** and **OBJ** to 3ds Max. However, you can not export the wire format.
*   The Alembic (**ABC**) files are used by VFX and animation professionals to convert complex animations into a non-procedural, application-independent set of baked geometric results. This file format is very useful in liquid simulations.
*   You can import CATIA V4 models into 3ds Max. CATIA is a design software developed by Dassault Systèmes. You can import the **MODEL, DLV4, DLV3, EXP, SESSION**, and **MDL** formats in 3ds Max.
*   CATIA V5 formats such as **CATPART** and **CATPRODUCT**. However, you cannot export the CATIA V5 format. CATIA R6 to V5-6R2016 versions are supported in 3ds Max.
*   3ds Max also supports the AutoCAD Interchange (**DXF**) files. These files are used to export modeling data to and from CAD programs that have support for **DXF**

but not **DWG** files.

- You can import and export **IGES** (Initial Graphics Exchange Specification) files with 3ds Max. This format is used to exchange data between dissimilar CAD/CAM systems.
- The land development data format **LanXML** (**XML, DEM**) can be imported into 3ds Max. This data comes from civil engineering projects.
- You can import the Motion Analysis Files (**HTR/HTR2, TRC**) in 3ds Max. This format is used by the motion capture data.
- 3ds Max also supports **OpenFlight** format (**FLT**) that is used in visual-simulation systems.
- You can import **SAT** files in 3ds Max. These files are used to import and export precise geometric boundary representation (**BREP**) data, also known as **ACIS** solids, for trimmed surfaces, solids models, and assemblies as 3ds Max **Body Objects**.
- 3ds Max can import SolidWorks Part (**SLDPRT**) and Assembly files (**SLDASM**).
- 3ds Max supports **STL** format which imports data in a format used for stereo-lithography.

Quiz

Evaluate your skills to see how many questions you can answer correctly.

Multiple Choice
Answer the following questions:

1. Which the following feature is not supported when you create a shared view?

   [A] All bitmap types   [B] The Shellac material
   [C] Autodesk materials   [D] Texture resizing

2. Which of the following formats are supported by 3ds Max for importing the geometry?

   [A] .3ds   [B] .ai
   [C] .rvt   [D] All of these

Fill in the Blanks
Fill in the blanks in each of the following statements:

1. The _____ allows you to create a live link to an AutoCAD drawing, a Revit architectural file, or an FBX file.

2. You can use _____ to collaborate online with the people you're working with.

3. To export selected objects to a file, select one or more objects, and then choose _____ from the menubar.

4. The options in the _____ submenu provide interoperability options with other Autodesk products.

5. You can use the _____ data to create a terrain.

6. _____ are an object class that natively supports the _____ solid models imported from Autodesk Inventor.

7. Constraint and Joint Drive animation applied to the Inventor model imports to 3ds Max as _____ keyframes.

8. If you drag and drop an inventor file to 3ds Max, it uses the settings that you last set on the **Inventor File Import** dialog box except for **Mesh Resolution**, which always resets to _____.

9. STEP stands for _____.

10. When you import Illustrator files, 3ds Max converts polygons to _____ objects.

True or False
State whether each of the following is true or false:

1. The **Autodesk Viewer** allows you to share a model with your team or customer without needing to have an Autodesk product installed.

2. You cannot import the geometry by dragging and dropping from the **File Browser** into a 3ds Max viewport.

3. When you import a geometry by dragging and dropping method, 3ds Max doesn't orient the imported geometry to the viewport into which you drop it.

4. The **Substitute Mesh** modifier allows you to quickly replace one or more objects with another in the viewport or at the render time.

5. If you make changes in a linked drawing, the changes will automatically affect the 3D models in the 3ds Max scene.

6. You can also change the vertical location of the color of a **Terrain** object by changing the **Base Elev** parameter in the **Color Zone** group.

7. When you import Inventor models, 3ds Max retains their object naming as assigned in the Inventor.

8. You can use the **Game Exporter** utility to easily export models and animation clips in the FBX format to your game engine.

9. 3ds Max supports the **WIRE** format for exporting geometry.

10. The **DXF** files are used to export modeling data to and from CAD programs that have support for DXF but not **DWG** files.

Practice Activities

Create an AutoCAD Drawing file link preset: Create a new file-link preset with the name **My AutoCAD Preset** for linking AutoCAD designs so that you can repetitively use the same settings when you link a drawing file into the 3ds Max scene.

Import AutoCAD plans into 3ds Max: Use the **Import** dialog box to link the **\practice-activities\room-layout.dwg** drawing into 3ds Max [see Fig. A1]. Create walls, windows, doors, floor, and ceiling for the room. Use some of the other AEC primitives; add a different type of window or door. Using the spline modeling tools, try creating a different profile for the molding. Add some picture frames in the room using the **Sweep** modifier.

Link Autodesk Revit files into 3ds Max: Try importing different Revit architectural files into 3ds Max. You can find free Revit files on many websites.

Import Autodesk Inventor assembly files into 3ds Max: Using the **Import** dialog box, bring the **\practice-activities\flage-coupling-assembly\Flange Coupling.iam** file into 3ds Max. Import the assembly as **Meshes** and then ungroup the imported geometry [see Fig. A2]. Ensure that you choose the correct up-axis during the import process.

Link FBX files into 3ds Max: Use the FBX import workflow to bring **\practice-activities\wave.fbx** file into 3ds Max. This file contains a wavy animation created using the **MoGraph** module of Cinema 4D [see Fig. A3]. Make the imported camera active and then play the animation.

Import Adobe Illustrator artwork into 3ds Max: Using the **Import** workflow, import the **\practice-activities\illus-artwork.ai** file into 3ds Max [see Fig. A4] and then apply the **Bevel** modifier to the artwork to create geometry.

Summary
The unit covered the following topics:

- Shared Views
- Importing AutoCAD Designs
- Importing Revit Files
- Importing Inventor Files
- Importing STP/STEP Files
- Importing Adobe Illustrator Files
- Importing FBX Files

Answer to Quiz
Multiple Choice
1. B, **2.** D

Fill in the Blanks
1. File Link Manager, **2.** shared views, **3.** File > Export > Export Selected, **4.** File > Send To, **5.** contour line, **6.** Body Objects, ACIS, **7.** baked, **8.** 0, **9.** Standard for the Exchange of Product Data, **10.** shape

True/False
1. T, **2.** F, **3.** F, **4.** F, **5.** T, **6.** T, **7.** T, **8.** T, **9.** F, **10.** T

Unit 9: Bonus Hands-on Exercises [Modeling]

Exercises - Modeling

Exercise 1: Creating a Serving Bowl

In this exercise, you will create the model of a bowl [see Fig. E1]. Table E1 summarizes the exercise.

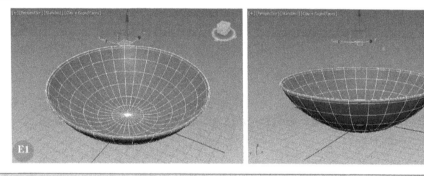

Table E1	
Skill level	Beginner
Time to complete	20 Minutes
Topics	• Specifying the Units for the Exercise • Creating the Bowl
Resources folder	**bonus-hoes**
Units	**Metric - Centimeters**
Final file	**bowl-finish.max**

Specifying the Units for the Exercise
Follow these steps:

1. From the **Customize** menu choose **Units Setup**. In the **Units Setup** dialog box that appears, select **Metric** from the **Display Unit Scale** group. Next, choose **Centimeters** from the drop-down list located below **Metric**. Click **System Unit Setup** to open the **System Unit Setup** dialog box and then make sure **1 Unit** is equal to the **1 Centimeters** [see Fig. E2]. Click **OK** and then click **OK** in the **Units Setup** dialog box.

2. From the **File** menu, choose **Save** to open the **Save File As** dialog box. In the **File name** text box type **bowl-finish.max** and then click **Save** to save the file.

Creating the Bowl
Follow these steps:

1. In the **Create** panel, click **Geometry**, and then in the **Object Type** rollout, click **Sphere**. In the **Perspective** viewport, create a sphere. Switch to **Modify** panel and on the **Parameters** rollout, change **Radius** to **26**.

2. **RMB** click on the sphere and then choose **transform** quadrant > **Convert To:** > **Convert to Editable Poly**. In the **Modify** panel > **Selection** rollout, click **Polygon** to activate the polygon sub-object level.

3. In the **Front** viewport, select the polygons, as shown in Fig. E3 and then press **Delete** to delete the selected polygons [see Fig. E4]. In the **Modify** panel > **Selection** rollout, click **Vertex** to activate the vertex sub-object level and then select the vertices, as shown in Fig. E5.

4. In the **Modify** panel > **Edit Geometry** rollout, click the **Z** button corresponding to the **Make Planer** parameter to make the selected vertices coplanar [see Fig. E6]. Press **Ctrl+A** to select all vertices and then slightly scale them down along the negative **Y**-axis using the **Scale** tool [see Fig. E7]. Switch to the **Object** mode and then place the bowl at the origin. Fig. E8 shows the bowl at the origin.

 What next?
*If you look at Fig. E8, the surface of the bowl is paper-thin. To give it some volume, you will use the **Shell** modifier.*

5. From the **Object-Space Modifiers** section of the **Modifier** list, select **Shell**. In the **Parameters** layout, change **Outer Amount** to **0.7** and **Segments** to **2** [see Fig. E9]. From the **Object-Space Modifiers** section of the **Modifier** list, select **Edit Poly**.

6. In the **Modify** panel > **Selection** rollout, click **Edge** to activate the edge sub-object level and then select the newly added segment [see Fig. E10]. Move it slightly up using the **Move** tool.

411

7. Select the outer edge loops, as shown in Fig. E11. In the **Modify** panel > **Edit Edges** rollout, click **Chamfer** > **Settings** to open the **Chamfer** caddy control. In the caddy control, change **Amount** to **0.13** and then click **OK** [see Fig. E12].

8. From the **Object-Space Modifiers** section of the **Modifier** list, select **MeshSmooth** [see Fig. E13].

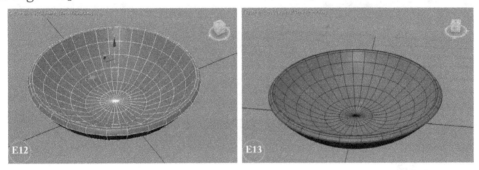

Exercise 2: Creating a Plate

In this exercise, you will create the model of a plate [see Fig. E1]. Table E2 summarizes the exercise.

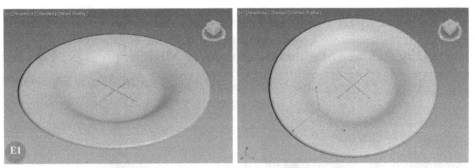

Table E2	
Skill level	Beginner
Time to complete	20 Minutes
Topics	• Specifying the Units for the Exercise • Creating the Plate

Table E2	
Resources folder	**bonus-hoes**
Units	**Generic Units**
Final file	**plate-finish.max**

Specifying the Units for the Exercise

Follow these steps:

1. From the **Customize** menu choose **Units Setup**. In the **Units Setup** dialog box that appears, select **Generic Units** from the **Units Setup** dialog box. Click **OK** to accept the changes made.

2. From the **File** menu, choose **Save** to open the **Save File As** dialog box. In the **File name** text box type **plate-finish.max** and then click **Save** to save the file.

Creating the Plate

Follow these steps:

1. Enable 2D snapping from the **Main** toolbar. In the **Create** panel, click **Shapes,** and then click **Line**. In the **Front** viewport, create a shape [see Fig. E2].

2. From the **Object-Space Modifiers** section of the **Modifier** list, select **Lathe**. In the **Modify** panel > **Parameters** rollout > **Align** group, click **Min** [see Fig. E3]. Now, select the **Weld Core** checkbox and change **Segments** to **32** [see Fig. E4].

3. From the **Object-Space Modifiers** section of the **Modifier** list, select **Shell**. In the **Parameters** layout, change the **Outer Amount** to **2**. From the **Object-Space Modifiers** section of the **Modifier List**, select **Edit Poly**.

4. In the **Modify** panel > **Selection** rollout, click **Edge** to activate the edge sub-object level. Now, select the edge loop, as shown in Fig. E5. Also, select the opposite loop at the bottom of the plate. In the **Modify** panel > **Edit Edges** rollout, click **Chamfer** >

Settings to open the **Chamfer** caddy control. In the caddy control, change **Amount** to **4.5** and **Segments** to **0**. Then, click **OK** [see Fig. E6].

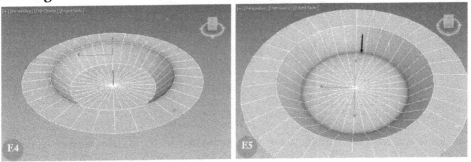

5. Switch to the **Object** level. From the **Object-Space Modifiers** section of the **Modifier** list, select **MeshSmooth** [see Fig. E7].

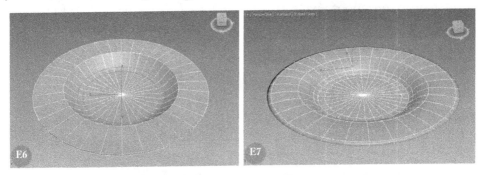

Exercise 3: Creating a Braided Cable

In this exercise, you will create a braided cable [see Fig. E1]. Table E3 summarizes the exercise.

Table E3	
Skill level	Intermediate
Time to complete	40 Minutes
Topics	• Specifying the Units for the Exercise • Creating the Cable

Table E3	
Resources folder	**bonus-hoes**
Units	**Generic Units**
Final file	**braided-cable-finish.max**

Specifying the Units for the Exercise
Follow these steps:

1. From the **Customize** menu choose **Units Setup**. In the **Units Setup** dialog box that appears, select **Generic Units** from the **Units Setup** dialog box. Click **OK** to accept the changes made.

2. From the **File** menu, choose **Save** to open the **Save File As** dialog box. In the **File name** text box type **braided-cable-finish.max** and then click **Save** to save the file.

Creating the Cable
Follow these steps:

1. In the **Create** panel, click **Shapes**, and then click **Rectangle**. In the **Front** viewport, create a rectangle and then place it at the origin. In the **Modify** panel > **Parameters** rollout, change **Length** to **30** and **Width** to **30**. Now, align the rectangle, as shown in Fig. E2.

2. **RMB** click on the rectangle and then choose **transform** quadrant > **Convert To:** > **Convert to Editable Spline**. Create a copy of the rectangle using **Shift** and snap the end vertices [see Fig. E3].

3. Select one of the rectangles and then in the **Modify** panel > **Geometry** rollout, click **Attach** and then click on the other rectangle to attach the rectangles. In the **Modify** panel > **Selection** rollout, click **Segment** to activate the segment sub-object level. Now, select and delete segments, refer to Fig. E4.

4. Select the segments, refer to Fig. E5 and then in the **Modify** panel > **Geometry** rollout, click **Detach** to open the **Detach** dialog box. In this dialog box, type **RightShape** in the **Detach as** text box and then click **OK**. Now, rename the remaining shape as **LeftShape**.

5. Select **LeftShape**, in the **Modify** panel > **Selection** rollout, click **Vertex** to activate the vertex sub-object level. Select the center vertices and then in the **Modify** panel > **Geometry** rollout, click **Weld** to weld the vertices. Repeat the process for **RightShape**. Place the shape at the origin [see Fig. E6].

6. In the **Perspective** viewport, move the spline by **63** units along the **+Y** axis and then select **Use Transform Coordinate Center** from the **Use Center** flyout [see Fig. E7]. Choose **Array** from the **Tools** menu to open the **Array** dialog box. Set the values as shown in Fig. E8, Fig. E9 shows the result.

7. Select **LeftShape** and then in the **Modify** panel > **Geometry** rollout, click **Attach Mult** to open the **Attach Multiple** dialog box. Select all left shapes and then click **Attach**. Similarly, repeat the process for the right shapes.

8. Select **LeftShape** and then in the **Modify** panel > **Selection** rollout, click **Vertex** to activate the vertex sub-object level. Select **Use Transform Coordinate Center** from the **Use Center** flyout. Select the center vertices [see Fig. E9] and then scale them by **94%** [see Fig. E10]. Now, press **Ctrl+I** to invert the selection and then scale them by **104%**.

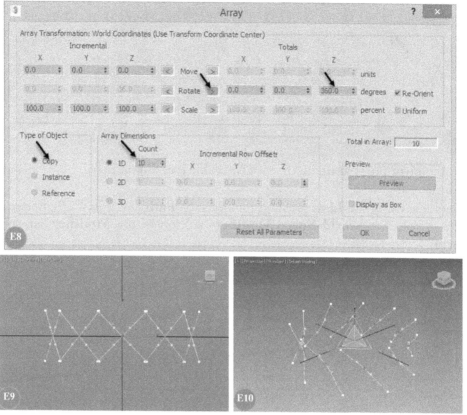

9. Select **RightShape**. Scale the center vertices by **104%** and the rest of the vertices by **94%** [see Fig. E11]. Now, attach **LeftShape** and **RightShape** as done earlier. Now, weld the top and bottom vertices [see Fig. E12].

10. In the **Front** viewport create **30** copies of the spline using **Shift** and then attach them [see Fig. E13].

11. From the **Object-Space Modifiers** section of the **Modifier** list, select **Sweep**. In the **Modify** panel > **Selection Type** rollout, change **Built-In Section** to **Pipe**. In the **Parameters** group, change **Radius** to **5.229** and **Thickness** to **0.21** [see Fig. E14].

12. Move the pivot point at the bottom of the cable [see Fig. E15].

13. Create a line using the **Line** tool and rename it as **Path** [see Fig. E16]. Select the cable and then from the **World-Space Modifiers** section of the **Modifier** list, select **Path Deform**.

14. In the **Modify** panel > **Parameters** rollout, click **Pick Path** and then click **Path** in the viewport. Now, in the **Path Deform Axis** group, change the axis to **Y**. In the **Path Deform** group, change **Percent** to **38.5** [see Fig. E17].

Exercise 4: Creating a Chair

In this exercise, you will create the model of a chair, as shown in Fig. E1.

E1

Table E4.1 summarizes the exercise.

Table E4.1	
Skill level	Intermediate
Time to complete	40 Minutes
Topics	• Getting Started • Creating the Frame of the Chair • Creating the Seat of the Chair
Resources folder	**bonus-hoes**
Units	**Decimal Inches**
Final file	**chair-finish.max**

Getting Ready
Start a new scene in 3ds Max and set units to **Decimal Inches**.

Creating the Frame of the Chair
Follow these steps:

1. Go to the **Create** panel, click **Shapes**, and then click **Line**. Expand the **Keyboard Entry** rollout and then set **X**, **Y**, and **Z** to **9.886**, **-10.75**, and **0.086**, respectively. Click **Add Point** to create the 1st point. Similarly, create other points using the values given in Table E4.2. After entering the values shown in the table, click **Finish**; the line appears in the viewports [see Fig. E2]. If you want to skip this step, open the **chair-curve.max** file.

Table E4.2 - Coordinates for creating points			
Point	X	Y	Z
1st	9.886"	-10.75"	0.086"
2nd	-9.836"	-10.75"	0.086"
3rd	-9.836"	-10.75"	14.834"
4th	6.285"	-10.75"	14.834"
5th	9.886"	-10.75"	27.011"

2. In the **Modify** panel > **Rendering** rollout, select the **Enable In Renderer** and **Enable In Viewport** checkboxes. Now, set **Thickness** to **0.9** and **Sides** to **14**. Make sure **Line001** is selected and then create a copy of the line by **Shift** dragging it about **21** units along the **Y**-axis [see Fig. E3].

3. Select **Line001** and then in the **Modify** panel > **Geometry** rollout, click **Attach**. Now, click **Line002** in the viewport to attach the two lines. Turn on **Vertex** snapping from the **Main** toolbar. Activate the **Vertex** sub-object level and then click **Create Line** from the **Geometry** rollout.

4. Drag from one vertex to another to create a line [see Fig. E4]. Click **Yes** when prompted to weld the vertices. Click on **Create Line** to deactivate it. Disable snapping. Select all vertices and then **RMB** click. Choose **Bezier Corner** from the **tool1** quadrant of the **Quad** menu.

5. Select the vertices [see Fig. E5] and then click **Weld** from the **Geometry** rollout to weld the vertices. Now, select the vertices shown in Fig. E6. In the **Geometry** rollout, type **1.5** in the field located next to **Fillet** parameter and then press **Enter** to fillet the vertices [see Fig. E7].

6. In the **Create** panel, click **Geometry** and then in the **Object Type** rollout, click **Tube**. Create a tube in the viewport. Go to the **Modify** panel and then in the **Parameters** rollout, set **Radius 1** to **0.641**, **Radius 2** to **0.429**, and **Height** to **2.133**. Also, set **Sides** to **32**. Align the tube with the frame [see Fig. E8]. Create a copy of the tube and then align it with the other side of the frame.

Creating Seat of the Chair
Follow these steps:

1. In the **Create** panel, click **Geometry** and then in the **Object Type** rollout, click **Box**. Create a box in the **Top** viewport. Go to the **Modify** panel and then in the **Parameters** rollout, set **Length** to **24.283**, **Width** to **14.152**, and **Height** to **2.988**. Set **Length Segs**, **Width Segs**, and **Height Segs** to **4**, **4**, and **3**, respectively. Align the box, as shown in Fig. E9. From the **Modifier List > Object-Space Modifiers** section, choose **TurboSmooth**. In the **Parameters** rollout, set **Iterations** to **2**.

2. Now, you'll create piping for the seat. Convert the object to editable poly. Activate the **Edge** mode and select the edge loops [see Fig. E10]. In the **Modify** panel > **Edit Edges** rollout, click **Create Shape From Selection** to open the **Create Shape** dialog box. Click **OK** to close the dialog box and create the shape.

3. Select **Shape001** and then in **Modify** panel > **Rendering** rollout, set **Thickness** to **0.2** [see Fig. E11]. Select **Box001** and then in **Modify** panel > **Edit Geometry** rollout, click **Attach**. Click on **Shape001** to combine the two objects.

4. From the **Modifier** list > **Object-Space Modifiers** section, choose **FFD 3x3x3**. Activate the **Control Points** sub-object level and select the middle control points. Move the points downwards to create a bend in the seat [see Fig. E12]. Convert the stack to the editable poly. Now, create a copy of the seat and then rotate/scale to create the back support [see Fig. E13].

Tip: Aligning back seat
*To easily align [rotate] the back support with the frame, move the pivot point at the bottom of the back support. Also, use the **Local** coordinate system.*

Exercise 5: Creating a Lamp

In this exercise, you will create the model of a lamp [see Fig. E1]. Table E5 summarizes the exercise.

Table E5	
Skill level	Intermediate
Time to complete	40 Minutes

Table E5	
Topics	• Getting Started • Creating the Lamp
Resources folder	**bonus-hoes**
Units	**Generic Units**
Final file	**lamp-finish.max**

Getting Ready
Start a new scene in 3ds Max and set units to **Generic Units**.

Creating the Lamp
Follow these steps:

1. In the **Create** panel, click **Geometry**, and then in the **Extended Primitives** > **Object Type** rollout, click **Hedra**. Create a hydra in the viewport. Go to the **Modify** panel and then on the **Parameters** rollout > **Family** group, select **Dodec/Icos**. In the **Family Parameters** group, set **P** and **Q** to **0.32** and **0.35**, respectively. Set **Radius** to **40** [see Fig. E2]. Convert hedra to editable poly. Activate the **Polygon** mode and select the polygon shown in Fig. E3.

2. In the **Ribbon** > **Modeling** tab > **Modify Selection** panel, click **Similar** [see Fig. E4] to select the polygon similar to the selected polygon [see Fig. E5]. Press **Delete** to delete the selected polygons. Press **Ctrl+A** to select all polygons.

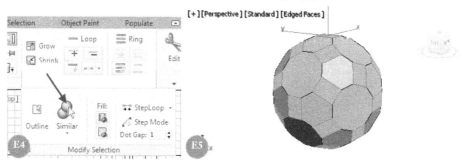

3. Click **Settings** on the right of **Extrude** in the **Modify** panel > **Edit Polygons** rollout. In the **Extrude Polygon** caddy control, set extrude **Type** to **Local Normal** and **Height** to **10** and click **Apply and Continue**. Now, click **OK** [see Fig. E6]. In the **Modify** panel > **Selection** rollout, click **Grow**. Press **Ctrl+I** to invert the selection and then press **Delete** to delete the polygons. Select all polygons and then in the **Modify** panel > **Polygon: Smoothing Groups** rollout, click **Auto Smooth** to smooth the polygon [see Fig. E7].

4. Activate the **Edge** mode and then select the edges, as shown in Fig. E8. In the **Ribbon** > **Modeling** tab > **Modify Selection** panel, click **Similar**. Click **Settings** on the right of **Chamfer** in the **Modify** panel > **Edit Edges** rollout. In the **Chamfer's** caddy, set **Mitering** to **Quad**, **Edge Chamfer Amount** to **0.294**, and **Connect Edge Segments** to **1**. Click **OK**.

5. Select the **Element** mode and click on the hedra in the viewport. In the **Ribbon** > **Modeling** tab > **Subdivision** panel, click **Tessellate** [see Fig. E9]. Activate the **Edge** mode and then select the edges shown in Fig. E10. In the **Ribbon** > **Modeling** tab > **Modify Selection** panel, click **Similar**. In the **Modify** panel > **Edit Edges** rollout, click **Create Shape From Selection** to open the **Create Shape** dialog box. Click **OK** to create the shape [see Fig. E11].

6. Select **Shape001**. In the **Modify** panel > **Rendering** rollout, select the **Enable In Renderer** and **Enable In Viewport** checkboxes. Now, set **Thickness** to **0.9** and **Sides** to **14**. Select **Hedra001** and then in the **Modifier List > Object-Space Modifiers** section, choose **TurboSmooth**. In the **Parameters** rollout, set **Iterations** to **2** [see Fig. E12]. Select **Shape001** and **Hedra001**. Group them with the name **Lamp**.

E12

7. Now, create the stand for the lamp and align it with the stand.

Exercise 6: Creating a Waste Bin

In this exercise, you will create the model of a waste bin [see Fig. E1]. Table E6 summarizes the exercise.

E1

Table E6	
Skill level	Intermediate
Time to complete	50 Minutes
Topics	• Getting Started • Creating the Waste Bin
Resources folder	**bonus-hoes**
Units	**Decimal Inches**
Final file	**bin-finish.max**

Getting Ready

Start a new scene in 3ds Max and set units to **Decimal Inches**.

Creating the Waste Bin
Follow these steps:

1. In the **Create** panel, click **Geometry**, and then in the **Object Type** rollout, click **Cylinder**. Create a cylinder in the **Top** viewport. Go to the **Modify** panel and then in the **Parameters** rollout, set **Radius** to **15**, **Height** to **45**, **Sides** to **50**, and **Height Segments** to **30**. Convert cylinder to editable poly. Activate the **Polygon** mode, select the top polygon, and then delete it [see Fig. E2].

2. Select the top and bottom polygon loops [see Fig. E3] and then click **Settings** on the right of **Extrude** in the **Modify** panel > **Edit Polygons** rollout. In the **Extrude Polygons** caddy control, set **Type** to **Local Normal** and **Height** to **1.2** and click **OK**.

3. Ensure the newly created polygons are still selected and then click **Settings** on the right of **Bevel** in the **Modify** panel > **Edit Polygons** rollout. In the **Bevel** caddy control, set **Type** to **Local Normal**, **Height** to **0.6**, **Outline** to **-0.9333**. Click **OK** [see Fig. E4].

4. Select every alternate column of polygons using **Shift**, see Fig. E5. Now, using the **Alt** key, remove polygons from the selection [see Fig. E6]. Click **Settings** on the right of **Extrude** in the **Modify** panel > **Edit Polygons** rollout. In the **Extrude Polygons** caddy control, set **Type** to **Local Normal** and **Height** to **-0.5** and click **OK**.

5. From the **Modifier** list > **Object-Space Modifiers** section, choose **Shell**. In the **Modify** panel > **Parameters** rollout, set **Outer Amount** to **0.15** [see Fig. E7]. Now, apply a **TurboSmooth** modifier to the cylinder. Now, we'll create a lid for the waste bin.

6. In the **Create** panel, click **Geometry**, and then in the **Object Type** rollout, click **Cylinder**. Create a cylinder in the **Top** viewport. Go to the **Modify** panel and then in the **Parameters** rollout, set **Radius** to **17**, **Height** to **2**, **Sides** to **50**, and **Height Segments** to **1**.

7. Convert the cylinder to the editable poly object. Activate the **Polygon** mode and select the bottom polygon [see Fig. E8], and then click **Settings** on the right of **Inset** in the **Modify** panel > **Edit Polygons** rollout. In the **Inset Polygons** caddy control, set **Amount** to **1**, and click **OK** [see Fig. E9].

8. Click **Settings** on the right of **Extrude** in the **Modify** panel > **Edit Polygons** rollout. In the **Extrude Polygons** caddy control, set **Type** to **Local Normal** and **Height** to **-1** and click **OK** [see Fig. E10]. Now, align the lid with the bin.

9. Select the outer edges [refer to Fig. E11] of the lid and then chamfer them. Refer to Fig. E12 for chamfer settings. Select the top polygon of the lid and then click **Settings** on the right of **Inset** in the **Modify** panel > **Edit Polygons** rollout. In the **Inset** caddy control, set **Amount** to **9** and click **OK**. Make sure the polygon is still selected and then move it slightly upwards [see Fig. E13]. Let's now create a handle for the lid.

10. In the **Create** panel, click **Geometry**, and then in the **Object Type** rollout, click **Torus**. Create a torus in the **Top** viewport. Go to the **Modify** panel and then on the **Parameters** rollout, set **Radius 1** to **4.64**, **Radius 2** to **0.84**, **Segments** to **50**, and **Sides** to **18**. Also, select the **Slice On** checkbox and then set **Slice From** and **Slice To** to **90**, and **270**, respectively. Now, align the torus at the center of the lid [see Fig. E14].

Exercise 7: Creating a Bottle

In this exercise, you will create a bottle using the **Loft** compound object [see Fig. E1]. Table E7 summarizes the exercise.

Table E7	
Skill level	Intermediate
Time to complete	45 Minutes
Topics	• Getting Started • Creating the Bottle
Resources folder	**bonus-hoes**
Units	**Generic Units**
Final file	**bottle-finish.max**

Getting Ready

Follow these steps:

1. Switch to the **Create** panel, click **Geometry**, then click **Plane**. In the **Front** viewport, create a plane. In the **Modify** panel > **Parameters** rollout, change **Length** to **180** and **Width** to **150**.

2. Invoke the **Move** tool from the **Main** toolbar. Set the **Transform Type-In** boxes to **0** in the **Status Bar** to place the box at the origin. Also, clear the **Real-World Map Size** checkbox in **Plane > Modify** panel > **Parameters** rollout, if not already clear. In the **Front** viewport, change the display mode to **Default Shading**.

3. Click **Material Editor** in the **Main** toolbar; the **Slate Material Editor** appears. Drag the **Physical Material** from the **Slate Material Editor** > **Material/Map Browser** > **Materials** rollout > **General** rollout to **View1** tab and then apply it to the plane.

4. Use the **whiskey.jpg** for the **Base Color** map using the **Bitmap** node and then set **Transparency** weight to **0.8** for the material.

5. **RMB** click on the material node and then select **Show Shaded Material in the Viewport** option (if not already selected) to display the image on the plane in the viewport.

6. Select the **Bitmap** node and then in the **Parameter Editor** > **Coordinates** rollout, make sure **Use Real-World Scale** is off and **U Tiling** and **V Tiling** are set to **1** each.

7. **RMB** click on the plane and then choose **Object Properties** from the **Quad** menu. Select the **Freeze** checkbox from the **Interactivity** area and clear the **Show Frozen in Gray** checkbox from the **Display Properties** area. Click **OK**. Press G to turn off the grid [see Fig. E2].

Creating the Bottle

Follow these steps:

1. Go to the **Create** panel, click **Shapes**, and then click **Line**. In the **Front** viewport, create a shape [see Fig. E3] that is aligned with the vertical center of the bottle [create the first point at the bottom of the bottle]. You can create the line anywhere in the scene but placing it at the center of the bottle will help you in the modeling process.

2. Go to the **Create** panel, click **Splines**, and then click **Rectangle**. Create a rectangle in the **Top** viewport. In the **Modify** panel > **Parameters** rollout, set **Length** to **40**, **Width** to **40**, and **Corner Radius** to **8**. Go to the **Create** panel, click **Splines**, and then click

Circle. Create a circle in the **Top** viewport. In the **Modify** panel > **Parameters** rollout, set **Radius** to **7.5** [see Fig. E4].

3. Ensure the line is selected in and then click **Loft** on **Create** panel > **Geometry** > **Compound Objects** > **Object Type** rollout. Click **Get Shape** on the **Creation Method** rollout and then click the rectangle in the viewport to create the lofted object. In the **Path Parameters** rollout, set **Path** to **100**. Click **Get Shape** on the **Creation Method** rollout and then click the circle in the viewport to create the basic shape of the bottle [see Fig. E5].

4. **RMB** click on the lofted objects and choose **Object Properties** from the **Quad** menu to open the **Object Properties** dialog box. In the **Display Properties** group of the dialog box, select the **See-Through** checkbox. Click **OK** to close the dialog box.

> **(?)** *What just happened?*
> *Notice in Fig. E5, the image is obscured by the lofted object. Here, I have enabled the x-ray mode for the object so that we can see through it.*

5. Enable the **Shape** sub-object level of the **Loft** object from the **Modify** panel and then select the rectangle shape on the loft object. Create a copy of the shape using **Shift**-drag operation. Now, uniformly scale the copied rectangle so that it fits in the profile of the bottle [see Fig. E6]. Repeat the process until you get a rough shape using the copies of the rectangle and circle objects [see Fig. E7].

6. Now, hide the plane geometry and turn off the x-ray mode [see Fig. E8] from the **Object Properties** dialog box. Make sure the bottle is selected and then in **Modify** panel > **Skin Parameters** rollout, clear the **Cap End** checkbox. From the **Modifier** list > **Object-Space**

Modifiers section, choose **Shell**. In the **Parameters** rollout, set **Outer Amount** to **0** and **Inner Amount** to **1**. If you render the geometry, you would see that facets are appearing on the bottle. Let's fix it.

7. From the **Modifier** list > **Object-Space Modifiers** section, choose **Smooth**. In the **Parameters** rollout, select the **Auto Smooth** checkbox to smooth the geometry.

What just happened?
*Here, I've applied the **Smooth** modifier to eliminate facets on the geometry by grouping faces into smoothing groups. Faces in the same smoothing group appear as a smooth surface when you render the geometry.*

Exercise 8: Creating a Chair

In this exercise, you will create a chair using the spline and polygon modeling techniques [see Fig. E1]. Table E8 summarizes the exercise.

Table E8	
Skill level	Intermediate
Time to complete	45 Minutes
Topics	• Getting Started • Creating the Chair
Resources folder	**bonus-hoes**
Units	**Decimal Inches**
Final file	**chair1-finish.max**

Getting Ready

We'll first create a box that will work like a template that will help us in the modeling process. Follow these steps:

1. In the **Create** panel, click **Geometry** and then in the **Object Type** rollout, click **Box**. Create a box in the **Top** viewport.

2. Go to the **Modify** panel and then in the **Parameters** rollout, set **Length** to **20**, **Width** to **20**, and **Height** to **30**. Set **Length Segs**, **Width Segs**, and **Height Segs** to **1**, **4**, and **2**, respectively. Set the **Transform Type-In** boxes in the **Status Bar** to **0** to place the box at the origin [see Fig. E2].

Creating the Chair

Follow these steps:

1. Activate the **Front** viewport and enable snapping [**Vertex**] by pressing **S**. Go to the **Create** panel, click **Shapes**, and then click **Rectangle**. In the **Front** viewport, create a shape [see Fig. E3]. Convert rectangle to editable spline. Activate the **Vertex** level and then press **Ctrl+A** to select all vertices. **RMB** click and then choose **Corner** from **Quad** menu > **tool1** quadrant. Now, move the top vertices as shown in Fig. E4.

2. Press **Ctrl+A** to select all vertices and then on the **Modify** panel > **Geometry** rollout, enter **2** [type 2 and then press **Enter**] in the **Fillet** field to fillet all the vertices [see

Fig. E5]. In the **Modify** panel > **Rendering** rollout, select the **Enable In Renderer** and **Enable In Viewport** checkboxes. Now, set **Thickness** to **1.5**. Turn off snapping.

3. In the **Create** panel, click **Geometry**, and then in the **Extended Primitives** > **Object Type** rollout, click **ChamferBox**. Create a box in the **Top** viewport. Go to the **Modify** panel and then on the **Parameters** rollout, set **Length** to **1.9**, **Width** to **4.02**, **Height** to **1.9**, and **Fillet** to **0.045**. Set **Length Segs**, **Width Segs**, **Height Segs**, and **Fillet Segs** to **1**, **1**, **1**, and **3**, respectively. Align it with the base of the chair [see Fig. E6]. Create a copy of the box and then align, as shown in Fig. E7.

4. Select the line and the two chamfer boxes. Click **Mirror** in the **Main** toolbar. In the **Mirror** dialog box that appears, set the values shown in Fig. E8 and click **OK** to accept the value and create a copy of the selected geometry [see Fig. E9]. Hide **Box001**.

5. In the **Create** panel, click **Geometry**, and then in the **Object Type** rollout, click **Plane**. Create a plane in the **Top** viewport. In the **Modify** panel > **Parameters** rollout, set **Length**, **Width**, **Length Segs**, and **Width Segs** to **23**, **20**, **1**, and **1**, respectively. Align it with the base [see Fig. E10]. Convert the plane to editable poly.

6. Active the **Edge** mode and select the back edge [refer to Fig. E11]. Now, extrude the edge upward by **15** units [see Fig. E12] using **Shift**+drag. Similarly, extrude the front edge [see Fig. E13]. Now, select the middle edge. Click **Settings** on the right of **Chamfer** in the **Modify** panel > **Edit Edges** rollout.

7. In the **Chamfer** caddy control, set **Mitering** to **Uniform**, **Edge Chamfer Amount** to **1.5**, and **Connect Edge Segments** to **4**. Click **OK** [see Fig. E14]. Now, create edges as shown in Fig. E15 using the **Swift Loop** tool.

8. From the **Modifier** list > **Object-Space Modifiers** section, choose **Shell**. In the **Modify** panel > **Parameters** group, set **Outer Amount** to **0.53**. From the **Modifier** list > **Object-Space Modifiers** section, choose **TurboSmooth**. In the **Modify** panel > **Parameters** group, set **Iterations** to **2**.

Exercise 9: Creating an Exterior Scene

In this exercise, you will model an exterior scene using various modeling techniques [see Fig. E1]. Table E9 summarizes the exercise.

Table E9	
Skill level	Intermediate
Time to complete	60 Minutes
Topics	• Getting Started • Creating the Scene
Resources folder	**bonus-hoes**
Units	**Meters**
Final file	**ext-finish.max**

Getting Ready

Start a new scene in 3ds Max and set units to **Meters**.

Creating the Scene

Follow these steps:

1. In the **Create** panel, click **Geometry** and then in the **Object Type** rollout, click **Box**. Create a box in the **Top** viewport. Go to the **Modify** panel and then in the **Parameters** rollout, set **Length** to **20**, **Width** to **60**, and **Height** to **8**. Create another box and then set its **Length** to **14**, **Width** to **52**, and **Height** to **8**. Also, set **Length Segs**, **Width Segs**, and **Height Segs** to **4**, **14**, and **1**, respectively. Now, align the boxes [see Fig. E2].

2. Select the **Box001** in a viewport and then convert it to **Editable Poly**. Activate the **Edge** mode and then connect the edges [see Fig. E3]. Activate the **Polygon** mode and then inset the front two faces [see Fig. E4]. Now, extrude the faces by **-5** units [see Fig. E5].

3. Create a box and then set its **Length** to **4.61**, **Width** to **0.602**, and **Height** to **6.827**. Also, set **Length Segs**, **Width Segs**, and **Height Segs** to **1** each. Now, align the box [see Fig. E6]. You might need to adjust the height of the cube as per the inset amount you have specified. Create instances of the box using **Shift** dragging [see Fig. E7].

4. Select **Box002** and convert it to **Editable Poly**. Select the polygon shown in Fig. E8. Now, inset the polygons by **0.22** units [see Fig. E9]. Now, extrude the polygons by **-0.25** units. Make sure the polygons are still selected and then enter **glassSelection** in the **Named Selection Sets** field in the **Main** toolbar.

5. Create a **Plane** primitive and then set its **Length** and **Width** to **600**, and **800**, respectively. Align the plane as shown in Fig. E10. Create a box with **Length** to **36**, **Width** to **71**, and

Height to **0.2**. Also, set **Length Segs**, **Width Segs**, and **Height Segs** to **1** each. Align it as shown in Fig. E11. Also, align the plane below it.

6. Create a **Rectangle** spline in the viewport and then set its **Length**, **Width**, and **Corner Radius** to **12**, **48**, and **4**, respectively. Apply the **Extrude** modifier to it and then set **Amount** to **0.4**. Align the rectangle, as shown in Fig. E12.

7. Now, create a light pole using the spline and polygon modeling techniques. Create an instance of the pole and align [see Fig. E13]. Create doors for the building [see Fig. E14]. Now, create a logo using the **TextPlus** primitive [see Fig. E15].

Index

Other Publications by
PADEXI ACADEMY

Visit *www.padexi.academy* to know more about the books, eBooks, and video courses published by PADEXI ACADEMY.

Cinema 4D

- MAXON Cinema 4D R20: Modeling Essentials
- MAXON Cinema 4D R20: A Detailed Guide to Modeling, Texturing, Lighting, Rendering, and Animation
- MAXON Cinema 4D R20: A Detailed Guide to XPresso
- Exploring 3D Modeling with Cinema 4D R19
- Exploring MoGraph with Cinema 4D R19
- Exploring XPresso With Cinema 4D R19

3ds Max

- Autodesk 3ds Max 2020: Modeling Essentials
- Autodesk 3ds Max 2020: A Detailed Guide to Modeling, Texturing, Lighting, and Rendering
- Autodesk 3ds Max 2019: A Detailed Guide to Arnold Renderer
- Autodesk 3ds Max 2019: A Detailed Guide to Modeling, Texturing, Lighting, and Rendering
- Autodesk 3ds Max 2019: Arnold Essentials
- Exploring 3D Modeling with 3ds Max 2019
- MAXON Cinema 4D R20 and Autodesk 3ds Max 2019: Modeling Essentials

Photoshop

- Exploring Filters With Photoshop CC 2017

Coming Soon:

- Autodesk 3ds Max 2021: A Detailed Guide to Modeling, Texturing, Lighting, and Rendering
- MAXON Cinema 4D R21: Modeling Essentials
- MAXON Cinema 4D R21: A Detailed Guide to Modeling, Texturing, Lighting, Rendering, and Animation